# GRAND
# ILLUSION

ALSO BY JOHN B. JUDIS

*William F. Buckley, Jr.: Patron Saint of the Conservatives*

# GRAND ILLUSION

*Critics and Champions
of the American Century*

## JOHN B. JUDIS

*Farrar, Straus & Giroux*

NEW YORK

*Copyright © 1992 by John B. Judis*

ALL RIGHTS RESERVED

Printed in the United States of America

Published simultaneously in Canada by HarperCollins*CanadaLtd*

*Designed by Tere LoPrete*

FIRST EDITION, 1992

Library of Congress Cataloging-in-Publication Data
Judis, John B.
Grand illusion : critics and champions of the twentieth century /
John B. Judis. — 1st ed.
p. cm.
Includes index.
1. United States—Civilization—20th century.   2. United States—
Foreign relations—20th century.   I. Title.
E169.1.J75     1992     973.9—dc20     91-14940     CIP

*For Ruth Judis and the memory of Hilliard Judis*

# Contents

# GRAND
# ILLUSION

# *Prologue*

## America After the American Century

At the end of an hour we saw a faraway town sleeping in a
valley by a winding river; and beyond it on a hill, a vast gray
fortress, with towers and turrets, the first I had ever seen out of
a picture.
"Bridgeport?" said I, pointing.
"Camelot," said he.

—MARK TWAIN, *A Connecticut Yankee in King Arthur's Court*

The F-117 "stealth" fighter sped silently through the summer
skies, looking like the tip of an arrow. Behind it followed the
drone of the Apache helicopters, suspended above the parade
route like giant grasshoppers. Then along the parched pave-
ment rumbled the Abrams M1A1 tanks, the Bradley fighting
vehicles, the Patriot missile batteries, the MLRS multiple-
launch rocket systems, and the Tomahawk cruise missiles. Lin-
ing the street, almost a million Americans cheered lustily—
"Way to go!" "Hooray America!"—as the weapons and 30,000
troops, clad in desert fatigues, made their way toward the White
House reviewing stand, where they passed in front of President
George Bush, his Vice President and Cabinet.

In the wake of the six-week war against Iraq in the winter
of 1991, federal, state, and city governments staged victory
rallies that dwarfed those after World Wars I and II. Celebra-
tions went on twice as long as the war itself. More than 300
parades were held. In Washington, on June 8, 1991, the fes-
tivities began in the morning and ended late at night with a
fireworks display of a sixty-by-forty-foot American flag. Two

days later, in New York's downtown, dubbed its "Canyon of Heroes," almost five million people witnessed the largest ticker-tape parade ever, dropping five tons of confetti on 24,000 troops.

Bush, surveying America's success in Iraq, invoked *Time* founder Henry Luce's concept of an American Century—a century in which American values and goods ruled the globe. Speaking to Congress, he boasted of a "next American century" and declared that the nation's "best days" were ahead of it. At the Air Force Academy graduation, Bush told the cadets that the war showed that the United States "still possessed the strength and the will to bear the burden of world leadership. . . . Through strength of example and commitment we lead . . . Our examples reshape the world." Six months later, on Veterans Day, Bush was still waxing poetic over America's role. The war, Bush declared, demonstrated that "America holds a special place in history. As we preserved and strengthened our own democracy, we've sought to extend the blessings of liberty throughout the world."

As Bush extolled America's leadership, the nation had already plunged into a recession. In the first quarter of the year, America's economy had declined by an annual rate of three percent. At the same time, the United States had continued to lose ground to other nations' economies, even becoming dependent on Japanese semiconductor technology and flat panel displays for its military prowess. Yet Bush brushed aside fears of American economic decline. Speaking at the California Institute of Technology graduation of June 14, Bush explained how through the power of the free market American technological know-how was laying the basis for "the next American century."

If we face this future foursquare, if we accept the call to unleash our imaginations, we will transform this nation, and I have no doubt America will transform the world.

We begin with the free market, the powerhouse of ingenuity. Free markets and free people breathe life into the American dream.

During those months after the war, Bush, who disdained what he called the "vision thing," came as close as he ever would to articulating a vision of the American future. Bush's America occupied a "special place in history." It had a responsibility to "reshape the world" through the spread of its products, the example of its values, and the power of its military. And the key to American success lay in the free market's "powerhouse of ingenuity."

Bush's vision was by no means new. His view of American superiority and of America's mission in the world had been invoked by the first Puritan settlers in New England and updated by Luce in his February 1941 *Life* magazine essay on the American Century. "It now becomes our time," Luce wrote, "to be the powerhouse from which the ideals spread throughout the world and do their mysterious work of lifting the life of mankind from the level of beasts to what the Psalmist called a little lower than the angels." Bush's view of the free market was first articulated by American revolutionaries of the 1770s and in the twentieth century had become a staple of business conservatives, from Calvin Coolidge to Ronald Reagan.

But while such a vision was firmly rooted in the American past, it was by no means relevant to the circumstances in which America found itself at the end of the twentieth century. The vision of America as evangel fit the country's mission at the beginning of World War II, but did it really explain the country's objectives at the end of the Cold War and of the American Century? Equally, optimism about the market's potency may have been appropriate in the 1820s and even the 1950s, but was it relevant to an America threatened by international economic competition and by deteriorating schools and cities?

As the memories of the Gulf War faded, Americans increasingly met Bush's exhortations with indifference rather than enthusiasm. What they saw as they peered into the future was not the beginning of a new American Century but only the end of the old one. And the question recurred: How should Americans come to terms with their new situation? How should the country define its purposes?

In this book, I chronicle the attempts by American politicians, businessmen, and intellectuals to come to terms with the dawn and then sunset of the American Century. The story pivots on a continuing debate over how Americans should understand their place in the world and the relation of their government to the free market: it pits an evangelical against a realistic view of America's mission and a conservative against a progressive view of the government's purpose. In this introduction, I want to sketch briefly how these alternatives originated and how an American leader, in the closing decade of the twentieth century, came to champion views that dated from the country's founding.

When George Bush stated that America "holds a special place in history," he was reflecting a view of America that dates from the early seventeenth century, when the nation was born as a utopian religious community. Beginning with the Puritans, Americans have seen themselves as a "chosen people" and America as a "new Israel" or "new Eden." And they have sought to transform the world after their own image—initially through example, but later through active intervention in the world's affairs.

This evangelical view was carried to America on the first ships from England. The Americans who settled New England attempted to build communities that would set an example both to the brethren they had left behind and to unregenerate Catholic Europe. In 1630, John Winthrop, the leader of the Massachusetts Bay Company, reminded his fellow passengers on the *Arbella* that they had not sailed across the Atlantic to find wealth, but to build a "city on a hill" so that in the future "men shall say of succeeding plantations: the lord make it like that of New England."

As it developed from New England, Americans' evangelical understanding was based on a contrast between the New World and the Old. America and the New World were uniquely virtuous (or later powerful and rich), while the Old World was feudal, Catholic, and corrupt (and later imperialist, Fascist, or Communist). Americans were determined to convert the Old World to America's prevailing faith and values—seen initially as Christian Congregationalist and later as free-market capitalist and democratic.

From the early seventeenth century through the Civil War, Americans concentrated on transforming the world through example—expanding their own utopian community over the continent while steering clear of Old World corruption. George Washington voiced this perspective in his famous farewell address of 1796. America's role, Washington said, was to give "mankind the magnanimous and too novel example of a people always guided by an exalted justice and benevolence." At the same time, he warned Americans not to "implicate" themselves "by artificial ties in the ordinary vicissitudes of [European] politics, or the ordinary combinations and collisions of her friendships or enmities."

In 1801, Jefferson warned his countrymen in his first inaugural address to avoid "entangling alliances" and thanked Providence for separating the United States "by nature and wide ocean from the exterminating havoc of one quarter of the globe." In 1823, President James Monroe announced the Monroe Doctrine, barring further European colonization of the Western Hemisphere in order to insulate the Americas from

Old World feudalism. In the 1840s, Americans justified westward expansion as America's Manifest Destiny—as an attempt
to bring the benefits of American civilization to the continent.
It is, Democratic editor John L. O'Sullivan wrote in 1845, "the
right of our manifest destiny to overspread and to possess
the whole of the continent which Providence has given us for
the development of the great experiment of liberty and fed-
erative government entrusted to us."

At the century's end, however, Americans were forced to
abandon their splendid isolation. With European powers carv-
ing the world up into commercially exclusive colonies, leading
American intellectuals such as Brooks Adams and Theodore
Roosevelt came to believe that if the United States didn't intervene, Americans would lack markets for their burgeoning
industries and farms and would be plunged into another
depression as deep as that of the 1890s. The United States had
to compete for world supremacy or it would be devoured,
Adams warned in 1900, by "that gangrene which attacks every
stagnant society."

After the United States defeated Spain in Cuba and the
Philippines in 1898, a great debate took place over American
objectives, with an imperialist faction, led by Roosevelt
and Senators Albert Beveridge (R-IN) and Henry Cabot Lodge
(R-MA), arguing for annexation of the Philippines, and an anti-
imperialist faction, led by William Jennings Bryan and former
President Grover Cleveland, bitterly opposed to American overseas colonization. Both factions argued their position on evangelical grounds. The imperialists contended, in Beveridge's
words, that God "has marked the American people as His chosen nation to finally lead in the redemption of the world."
Bryan, representing the earlier evangelism, claimed that by
trying to incorporate what he saw as an alien and inferior
race—the Filipinos—Americans would be "endangering our
civilization."

The debate was resolved when the United States adopted in

1901 the approach implicit in Secretary of State John Hay's Open Door Notes, which declared American opposition to the partition of China and support for open markets. Hay's initiative committed America to opposing Old World imperialism —the division of China by European powers and Japan into "spheres of influence." But Hay's initiative also sought to impose on China the protections of the Monroe Doctrine. Hay committed America to seeking to transform the world through the export of its goods and values rather than through creating a formal empire.

Over the next five decades, evangelical aims provided the public rationale for America's decision to enter World Wars I and II and to prosecute the Cold War. In April 1917, calling for a declaration of war against Germany, President Woodrow Wilson told Congress that America's aim would be "to vindicate the principles of peace and justice in the life of the world as against selfish and aristocratic power and to set up amongst the really free and self-governed peoples of the world such a concert of purpose and of action as will henceforth ensure the observance of those principles." After the war, Wilson sought to make the League of Nations an instrument to purge the globe of Old World imperialism. The League, with the power to enforce its will over member states, would be the basis of a new "community of power" that would transcend the old balance of power among nations. The nations of the world would be united just as the original thirteen American colonies were.

Franklin Roosevelt portrayed World War II as an attempt to secure the "four freedoms" (freedom of speech and worship and freedom from want and fear), while his Vice President, Henry Wallace, waxed poetic about a global New Deal and the "century of the common man," calling the war a "people's revolution" and warning that "the devil and all his angels cannot prevail against it. They cannot prevail, for on the side of the people is the Lord."

After World War II, the Truman administration justified a

succession of measures, from the Marshall Plan to loyalty checks, on the grounds of preserving American values against the threat of alien Soviet-led Communism, endowing Soviet Communism with the same evil that Americans had earlier attributed to Catholic Europe or Imperial and Nazi Germany. When the United States intervened in Korea in 1950 and in Vietnam in the 1960s, it claimed that it was defending freedom against Communism. And when George Bush forced Iraq out of Kuwait, he described the war against Iraq as an expression of America's special responsibility "to extend the blessings of liberty throughout the world."

But America's failure to secure a lasting peace caused politicians and intellectuals to look critically at America's foreign policy. After World War I, Walter Lippmann and others developed what came to be called a realistic critique of foreign policy. Lippmann spelled out this view in a series of articles in the 1930s and then in his 1943 classic, *Foreign Policy: Shield of the Republic*. After World War II, other policy experts also rejected evangelism for realism. These included Senator William Fulbright, diplomat George Kennan, theologian Reinhold Niebuhr, and a young Harvard professor, Henry Kissinger.

According to the realists' view, America was not a "new Israel," but one nation among others; and its peace and security were guaranteed by the balance of power rather than by superior virtue. Its primary objective in foreign policy was not to proselytize for Christianity or democracy, but to ensure the prosperity and security of its citizens by maintaining open markets for American goods and preventing commercial rivals from threatening America militarily.

Realism did not provide a foolproof alternative to the follies of evangelism. If evangelism's sin was to ignore the balance of power among nations and to substitute virtue for power and to clothe America with a historical hubris, realism's potential source of error lay in disregarding any idealistic concerns, including a commitment to encouraging the spread of democracy—whether American or European style. Some realists, such as James Burnham and Kissinger, were quick to condone American intervention against sovereign nations and foreign despotism in the name of the balance of power and to ignore that democratic reform in nations could itself contribute to international stability. Others, like arms-control expert Paul Nitze, came to measure the balance of power in terms of nuclear throw weight, ignoring all other factors. But realism was nevertheless an important and needed corrective to the evangelical tradition.

Lippmann and other realists acknowledged that most major American foreign policy decisions had a realistic component but said that it was hidden from public view or subordinated to evangelical aims. From America's founding through World War II, the realistic approach was based on America's commercial and military ties to Britain—until 1917, the possessor of the most powerful navy and the center of world finance, and after that, America's principal ally. American Presidents, from James Monroe through Franklin Roosevelt, recognized that America's ability to sail the seas unhindered and to sell its surplus depended on this alliance.

Monroe presented his doctrine as a unilateral expression of America's virtue, but it was based on British agreement to back up the feeble American navy. Protected by Britain's "stout walls," Secretary of State John Quincy Adams wrote privately, the United States could blow a "Republican blast" at Europe. When America went to war a century later, Woodrow Wilson publicly framed American objectives in evangelical terms, but Wilson asked for a declaration of war only after Germany threatened Anglo-American supremacy on the seas and America's access to European markets. In 1940, when Hitler attacked

Britain, the United States took the first steps toward intervening against the Nazis. Roosevelt acted because of the threat to British-American control of the seas and American access to markets, not because of the character of Hitler's regime. "The Nazi regime was as evil from January 1933 to May 1940 as it was afterwards," Lippmann wrote in *U.S. War Aims.*

After World War II, American administrations recognized that the United States would have to take prime responsibility for the stability of world capitalism. During the Cold War, the Truman administration presented the Marshall Plan as an attempt to stave off a Soviet takeover of Western Europe. But administration policymakers were not as worried about a Soviet invasion of France as they were concerned about the ability of Western Europe to buy American goods. They feared the recurrence of trading blocs and another depression. Without immediate, massive economic aid, State Department official Will Clayton warned in a private memo in May 1947, "the immediate effects on our economy would be disastrous: markets for our surplus production gone, unemployment, depression, a heavily unbalanced budget on the background of a mountainous war debt."

Unlike later left-wing critics, the realists did not attack American foreign policy for being based on economic considerations. On the contrary, they thought economics should be a central factor in foreign policy. What concerned them was that at key junctures evangelical considerations took precedence over concerns about prosperity and security—with disastrous results. After World War I, they argued, Wilson had been so eager to create a League of Nations that he ignored the balance of power in Europe and laid the basis for World War II. Convinced that he could transcend the balance of power, Wilson caved in to Britain and France's atavistic demands on Germany in exchange for their nominal agreement to his League of Nations. The reparations exacted from Germany then fueled the rise of Nazism.

After World War II, realists pointed out that the Truman

administration's use of evangelical arguments for realistic initiatives—inspired by Senator Arthur Vandenberg's advice to President Harry Truman to "scare hell out of" the American people—had unintended consequences. By promoting the myth of a monolithic world Communist conspiracy, American policymakers blinded themselves as well as the public to rifts within the Communist world and justified policy moves that only aggravated U.S.-Soviet relations. Cold War evangelism poisoned American politics by lending credence to Senator Joseph McCarthy's witch hunt and to the apocalyptic anti-Communism of the new conservatives of the 1950s.

During the Vietnam War, Lippmann, Kennan, and Fulbright argued that in accepting an evangelical definition of the Cold War the United States had fatally overextended itself—becoming embroiled in a civil war in Southeast Asia that was tearing apart American society and bankrupting the economy. They called on the United States to abandon the Cold War and to recast American foreign policy in realistic terms. Their arguments found unexpected support from the arch anti-Communist Richard Nixon, who became President in 1968, and from Henry Kissinger, his National Security Adviser and later Secretary of State. Nixon and Kissinger began to transform the structure of post-World War II economic and military relations with the Soviet Union, China, Europe, and Japan. But they were not willing to take what should have been the first step, extricating America quickly from Vietnam. The failure to do so undermined Nixon's presidency, contributing eventually to the Watergate scandal and to his resignation. Kissinger outlasted Nixon, but was unable to withstand his enemies on the right and left.

Ronald Reagan's election in 1980 dealt a definitive defeat to realism and marked the revival of Cold War evangelism. For Reagan, the United States was an "island of freedom" created by "Divine Providence" and the Soviet Union the "focus of evil in the modern world." Reagan's Cold War church militancy sustained a trillion-dollar military buildup that undermined the

American economy. It also contributed to years of high tension between the United States and the Soviet Union—cut short finally by the emergence in 1985 of Soviet Premier Mikhail Gorbachev and a new reform leadership in the Soviet Union dedicated to reducing that nation's military budget and to re-structuring its economy.

Even after the Cold War ended, George Bush continued the evangelical approach. While Bush attempted in practice to mimic Kissinger's realism, he justified his actions publicly in evangelical terms. He portrayed the war against Iraq, not as an attempt to restore stability in an economically vital region, but as a crusade for freedom and liberty, even though America's immediate political objective was to return the Emir of Kuwait to his throne. Bush compared Saddam Hussein to Hitler and the war itself to World War II. The effect of such an argument was to strand American policy in the distant past and to make impossible a fresh understanding of what America's place in the world is and what America's aim should now be.

Americans' view of their domestic promise has been equally rooted in the past. When George Bush invoked the magic of the market and inveighed against government interference in business, he was echoing a business conservatism that could claim such incongruous forebears as Thomas Paine and Thomas Jefferson. It, too, was challenged, and even soundly refuted, by intellectuals and politicians describing themselves as pro-gressives and liberals, but like its evangelical cousin, it has returned with a vengeance in the last decade.

This business conservatism was a product of the transition from an agricultural to an industrial America. Americans' faith in the market and antipathy toward central government dates from the revolution and from the classical liberalism of Thomas

Paine, Thomas Jefferson, and Andrew Jackson. The generation that led the revolution of 1776 against British rule conceived of government as an alien force imposed upon their own self-regulating society. "Society in every state is a blessing, but government, even in its best state, is but a necessary evil," Paine wrote in *Common Sense*.

This vision of government endured through most of the nineteenth century. Jefferson saw government as the instrument for preserving an "artificial aristocracy." Jackson saw it as protecting "monopolies and exclusive privileges." The "true strength" of government, Jackson declared in his 1832 veto of the charter of the Bank of the United States, "consists in leaving individuals and States as much as possible to themselves."

Complementing this distrust of government was an ideal of society based on the promise of westward expansion. Jefferson and other founding fathers based their hopes for American democracy on the widespread availability of cheap land. "Here everyone may have land to labor for himself, if he chooses," Jefferson wrote John Adams in 1813. "Everyone, by his property, or by his satisfactory situation, is interested in the support of law and order." In Europe, by contrast, democracy was made impossible by the existence of titled aristocrats and the urban mob.

The Jeffersonian opposition to government and the vision of a society of equal property owners complemented each other. It was Jefferson and Jackson's assumption that, in the absence of government restraints—which were inherited from feudal Europe—American society would naturally evolve into a kind of free-market paradise of equal small farmers and artisans.

In the first half of the nineteenth century, Americans had grounds for believing that this Arcadia would come into existence. In 1830, four out of five free Americans who worked owned property, and three out of four Americans worked on farms. But the North's victory in the Civil War set in motion those forces that would doom forever the dream of free-market liberty and equality. Industrialization created the urban class society—characterized by sharp divisions between owner-managers and workers and between rich and poor—that the Jeffersonians had feared; at the same time, the mechanization of agriculture raised output while radically reducing the number of Americans working on farms. According to the 1900 census, 80 percent of Americans had become engaged in non-farm commercial or industrial jobs.

From the 1890s through World War I, Americans tried to come to terms with this new urban industrial reality. The first major reaction came from Populists in the South and Midwest. Calling for government regulation of the new trusts or monopolies, the Populists challenged the new order in the name of the old, seeking to use the power of government to restore Jefferson's Arcadia of small farmers. When the Populist movement disintegrated, some Populists joined the Democrats, while others gravitated to Eugene Debs's Socialist Party. Unlike the Populists, the Socialists accepted the inevitability of industrialization and of the rise of giant corporations, but sought to realize the Jeffersonian dream by having the working class own and control the corporations themselves.

Businessmen found solace in the face of these attacks in the new doctrine of Social Darwinism propounded by sociologist William Graham Sumner, who became a professor at Yale in 1872, but whose most influential writings dated from the first decade of the twentieth century. Sumner argued that the class divisions of industrial society were the inevitable result of competition. He termed the new corporate elite a "natural" rather than an artificial aristocracy, and warned that reinjecting government into the market could bring back Old World feudalism. "Let it be understood that we cannot go outside of this alternative: liberty, inequality, survival of the fittest; not—liberty, equality, survival of the unfittest," Sumner wrote. "The former carries society forward and favors all its best members; the latter carries society downwards and favors all its worst members."

Populists preached a reactionary faith, and their socialist cousins a utopian one; Sumner was content to abandon Jefferson's dream of equality in the name of preserving his opposition to governmental tyranny—to use liberalism in the service of business conservatism. In this way, classical liberalism was transformed into business conservatism.

Theodore Roosevelt and progressive intellectuals such as Herbert Croly and Lippmann rejected both the socialism of the left and the business conservatism of the right and sought to create a genuinely new synthesis. Like the socialists and social Darwinists, the progressives accepted that industrialization was inevitable, but unlike the business conservatives and Social Darwinists, they believed that through what Roosevelt called a "corresponding increase in governmental power over big business," the growth of industry could be shaped to serve egalitarian ends. "Our basic problem in the twentieth century," Roosevelt said in 1910, "is to see that the marvelously augmented powers of production bequeathed to us by the nineteenth century be made to administer to the needs of the many rather than be exploited for the profit of the few." The progressives did not accept as inevitable the maldistribution of wealth, the spread of poverty, and the increase in class tensions that industrialization had brought in its wake. Using the power of government and scientific expertise, they sought to readapt the Jeffersonian dream of liberty and equality to the industrial era.

The clearest and most radical expression of progressivism was Herbert Croly's book *The Promise of American Life*, from which Roosevelt adopted his platform for the Progressive Party of 1912 and his slogan: the "new nationalism." Croly argued that Americans' continued adherence to Jeffersonian individualism and to the unfettered market had caused the glaring inequality from which America had come to suffer. The Jeffersonian faith "in individual freedom has resulted in a morally and socially undesirable distribution of wealth," Croly wrote.

To keep the promise of American life, "the national government must step in and discriminate; not on behalf of liberty
and the special individual, but on behalf of equality and the
average man."

Roosevelt, Croly, Lippmann, and Woodrow Wilson accepted
the existence of classes, but insisted that government use its
power of taxation and regulation to ensure greater equality. To
replace the Jeffersonian dream of liberty and equality through
small property ownership, many progressives also favored what
came to be called "industrial democracy." They wanted business to recognize unions as management's partner in running
industry. For workers, labor unions provided the equivalent of
property ownership, giving them a stake in society and a power
to exercise it. "It is labor organized that alone can stand between America and the creation of a servile class," Walter
Lippmann wrote in *Drift and Mastery*. "Without unions industrial democracy is unthinkable."

In the 1920s, business conservatives staged a comeback. Presidents Warren Harding and Calvin Coolidge promoted the view
of America in which the success of large corporations would
redound to all American wage earners. They opposed any
initiatives—from progressive taxation to labor unions—that
might impede corporate profits. They redefined the progressive
concept of industrial democracy to mean workers' freedom to
consume through increased wages. According to Coolidge,
what was of "real importance to wage-earners was not how
they might conduct a quarrel with their employers but how
the business of the country might be so organized as to ensure
steady employment at a fair rate of pay." But the Great
Depression—coming on the heels of a decade of laissez-faire
policy—destroyed the credibility of business conservatives for
five decades.

Franklin Roosevelt's victory in 1932 meant the revival of
progressivism. Roosevelt promised to put the "organized power
of government" to the service of promoting equality of op-

portunity and combating "the abuse of the concentration of economic power." As Roosevelt's Secretary of Agriculture, Henry Wallace introduced national planning to curb the ruinous deflation that was bankrupting farmers; as Roosevelt's Vice President, Wallace became the main proponent of a national economic planning that would regulate the free market in the interests of equity and efficiency.

Writing in 1937, Wallace maintained that government must become responsible "for peaceful, dependable security in the economic world as well as in the social world." He wanted the federal government to use its tax and spending power "more consciously to promote economic stability, conservation of natural resources, and conservation of human resources." And he called for government to cooperate with business in long-range planning to prevent new depressions and to ensure that "the various economic groups must have equality of bargaining power."

Like realism, its counterpart in foreign policy, progressivism was not without its flaws. As Lippmann warned in *The Good Society*, progressivism, if taken to extremes, could encourage a stifling statism that threatened democracy and individual initiative. But like realism, progressivism was a significant corrective to the views that it replaced. Just as the Jeffersonian view was rooted in agricultural America, the progressive view reflected the needs of an urban, industrial nation that had learned during the depression of the 1890s and then the Great Depression of the 1930s that private enterprise, if left entirely to its own devices, would eventually create poverty and unemployment. To make capitalism work, government had to intervene.

Yet in 1980, America returned to the business conservatism of the 1880s and 1920s. Ronald Reagan won election on a promise to remove government from the private sector. "Government is the problem, not the solution," Reagan declared in his inaugural address in January 1981. "It is time to check and reverse the growth of government which shows signs of having grown beyond the consent of the governed." In words that echoed those of Coolidge's Secretary of the Treasury, Andrew Mellon, Reagan predicted that by cutting taxes and regulations, Americans would "reawaken this industrial giant." All Americans would benefit. "All must share in the productive work of this 'new beginning,' and all must share in the bounty of a revived economy."

Reagan's argument ran directly contrary to that of the progressives. Reagan was arguing that government had caused poverty and recession and that by removing government, and letting the market operate independently, the industrial giant would awaken and create prosperity for all Americans. Like the conservatives of the 1920s, Reagan and Bush reduced the taxes of the wealthy and corporations and eliminated regulations on corporations, while at the same time subsidizing business and tilting government on the side of management against labor.

The results were exactly as the populists, socialists, and progressives had earlier warned. Acting in the name of Jefferson, Reagan and Bush moved society in the direction that Jefferson feared: toward greater maldistribution of wealth, toward the creation of intractable poverty and crime within cities, toward corruption and greed among the business classes. Indeed, Reagan's implementation of business conservatism created a level of corruption in Washington that had not been seen since the Gilded Age.

Under the impact of Reagan and Bush's Jeffersonianism, Americans grew apart—rich from poor, white from black, and suburb from city. As the fires of Cold War evangelism dimmed, and as the hopes for a next American Century faded, what remained was a callous and often cynical individualism. The lessons of the past lay forgotten—from the failure of Wilson's evangelism to the breakdown of America under Coolidge and Hoover's business conservatism. The words and deeds of the progressives—the two Roosevelts, Herbert Croly, Henry Wallace—and the realists—Lippmann, Kennan, and Fulbright—became dim memories.

The purpose of this book is to revive those memories so that Americans will be better able to face the great questions about America's promise and place in the world that now loom before us.

# 1

# *Herbert Croly and the New Nationalism*

A man who is a sturdy sinner all the week hardly improves his moral standing by attending church on Sunday and professing a noble Christian theory of life. There must surely be some better way of excusing our sins than by raising aloft a noble theory of which these sins are a glaring violation.

—HERBERT CROLY, *The Promise of American Life*, 1909

In April 1910, Senator Henry Cabot Lodge sent his friend former President Theodore Roosevelt a book by "Herbert Croly, of whom I have never heard before," adding, "There are plenty of things in the book with which you will disagree as I do but you will not say of any of them that the writer has not thought hard about it." Roosevelt, who was just completing an eleven-month safari in Africa, wrote Lodge that he had ordered Croly's book from Macmillan of London. Roosevelt landed in the United States in June and a month later, after reading *The Promise of American Life*, wrote Herbert Croly, "I do not know when I have read a book which I felt profited me as much as your book on American life . . . All I wish is that I were better able to get my advice to my fellow countrymen in practical shape according to the principles you set forth."

Croly was ecstatic. "Whatever gratification I may feel as an author," he wrote his friend Learned Hand, "is entirely swallowed by my sentiment of personal loyalty to the man in his position who could lend me so firm & cordial a hand." That summer, the two men—the buoyant, boisterous, exuberant former Rough Rider and the shy, retiring former editor of an architectural journal—had lunch at Roosevelt's Oyster Bay home. Croly agreed to assist Roosevelt in his speeches, and in August he helped draft the former President's speech at Osawatomie—perhaps the most famous that he ever gave. In that speech, Roosevelt laid out the principles of Croly's "new nationalism," calling for the energetic use of government to place national interest above that of private corporations and to "prevent the political domination of money in any parts of our affairs." It was the high point of American progressivism.

For Croly, the denouement came nine years later—on May 7, 1919—as he paced his living room in New York while his wife read to him from the New York *Evening Post* the terms of the Treaty of Versailles ending World War I. In 1914, Croly had founded *The New Republic*, and had become its editor. Once closely linked to Roosevelt, Croly and the magazine had established even firmer ties to the Wilson administration, cheering its reforms and applauding its deliberate entry into World War I. Croly saw American participation in the war as an opportunity to make good on the new nationalism at home while creating the conditions for a new international order overseas.

But as Louise Croly read him the treaty, the *New Republic* editor realized that it laid the groundwork for future war rather than for peace. For three days, Croly remained in seclusion, pacing the floor, but on the fourth, he directed the editorial meeting at which the magazine's editors decided unanimously to come out fighting against Wilson and the treaty. Describing the decision, Croly wrote Supreme Court Justice Louis Brandeis that it was "practically a confession of failure, so far as our work during the last few years is concerned."

Between these two events lies Herbert Croly's earnest and still unsurpassed attempt to adapt America's democratic ideals—what he called the "promise of American life"—to the conditions of twentieth-century America. More than any other American philosopher or politician, Croly understood the extent to which industrialization and America's emergence as a great power had undermined the principles that had guided Americans since the nation's founding. In *The Promise of American Life* and in the pages of *The New Republic*, Croly sought to create a politics appropriate to an America of great corporations and global competitors. But in the end, he did not succeed.

Croly was a slight man with a broad forehead, a large, flat nose, and small green eyes that looked painfully upon the world from behind rimless glasses. He was the antithesis of the modern media personality. He was highly private, agonizingly shy, reluctant to speak before audiences. In his memoir of Croly, former *New Republic* literary editor Edmund Wilson wrote:

> It was never easy for him to deal with people, and if the visitor himself were at all diffident, he would be likely to find the conversation subsiding into a discontinuous series of remarks more and more haltingly delivered by himself, to which Croly would mutter responses more and more fragmentary and more and more imperfectly audible.

He was also the opposite of the modern political insider. In both his professional relations and his writing, Croly strove for what he called "disinterestedness." He was passionate in his convictions, but he wanted nevertheless to avoid the passions of the moment: to be beyond factions or fashions or special interests. He wanted to bring a larger philosophical outlook to bear upon the most mundane details of politics.

Unlike other prominent progressives, Croly was the offspring of self-made immigrants, and he looked on America from a peculiar European vantage. Croly's mother, Jane Cunningham Croly, emigrated from England when she was a child and become a well-known writer on women's fashion and habits. His father, David Goodman Croly, came from Ireland and became an editor and journalist and one of the foremost American disciples of French philosopher Auguste Comte. Herbert Croly, Edmund Wilson later remarked, was the first child christened in Comte's "religion of humanity," and Comte's influence, as transmitted through his father, provided the unique window through which he viewed the America of the early twentieth century.

Comte was a strange genius, a combination of seer and kook, French *philosophe* and Hegelian idealist. He saw history passing through three stages: from the theological to the metaphysical to the positivist. In the theological stage, human beings attributed motive power to gods; in the metaphysical stage to underlying natural causes; and in the positivist stage to observable and verifiable laws. Comte associated the theological stage with the Middle Ages; the metaphysical with the French Revolution; and the positivist with the millennium that he believed was imminent. While Comte praised the French Revolution for freeing humanity from the crush of church and lord, he condemned it for introducing the new dogmas of natural rights and abstract equality.

For Comte, what would usher in the positivist stage of history was industrialization. It would elevate empirical above metaphysical knowledge and create a class of experts that would manage society scientifically through a centralized state. Industrialization would also supplant the egoism and individualism of the metaphysical stage of history with a new altruism; through the web of goods and machines, citizens would recognize that their own welfare was bound up with each other. Comte's experts would run society in accordance with what he called the "religion of humanity." Its slogan was "live for others." In his last, deranged years, Comte even devised a set of prayers, rituals, and saints' days for his religion.

Herbert Croly's father sought to adapt Comte to America. He polemicized against the prevailing laissez-faire individualism, which assumed that the society would achieve the greatest good simply through individuals' pursuing their own self-interest. He championed industrialization, including the growing consolidation of capital, but insisted that it must be regulated from above. He conceived of society itself as a giant industrial corporation in which businesses would be subsidiaries. "All corporations must be subordinated to the greater corporation which sits in its place of power at Washington," he wrote in *The Real Estate Record and Builders' Guide*, a trade newspaper that the elder Croly edited and occasionally filled with what must have seemed like irrelevant editorials. He called for a political party that "would espouse economic justice under a federal government of far greater powers."

David Croly tutored his sickly son, born in 1869, in Comte's philosophy, and when Herbert went off to Harvard in 1886, kept careful track of his son's philosophical studies. Two years later, Herbert returned home to help his terminally ill father edit *The Real Estate Record and Builders' Guide*. David Croly died in 1889, and in 1892 Herbert returned to Harvard, where he continued to study philosophy under Josiah Royce, George Santayana, and William James. Croly withdrew again in 1893 because of a nervous breakdown. In 1895, he returned to Harvard again, only to drop out in 1899. In 1910, after the publication of *The Promise of American Life*, Harvard belatedly awarded him a bachelor's degree.

Of all Croly's teachers, Royce, a Christian idealist, seems to have had the greatest impact on him. Royce, like Comte, was heavily influenced by Kant and Hegel. Like Comte, he envisaged individuals and facts, not as separate components that made up a whole, but as being defined by their membership in a totality. The nation defines the citizens rather than vice versa. Like Comte, Royce also stressed a higher morality (loyalty in his case rather than altruism) as the supreme form of human conduct. But unlike Comte, Royce was a devout Christian who believed that Christianity defined that morality. Royce converted Croly from Comte's religion of humanity to Christianity.

Croly abandoned the unconventional religion of his father for the more conventional, but still passionate, belief of Royce. Some of Croly's friends later speculated that his breakdown in 1893 was due to the clash between his father's and Royce's beliefs. According to fellow *New Republic* editor Alvin Johnson, Croly underwent "a profound spiritual crisis . . . in revolt against Auguste Comte, the God of his father." Croly's Christianity would remain merely an undercurrent in his earlier political writings—providing metaphor rather than argument—but after Croly's disillusionment with politics in 1919, he would become a straightforward advocate of Christian renewal.

In 1899, after leaving Harvard, Croly took a job as the editor of the *Architectural Record,* a publication owned by his father's former employer on *The Real Estate Record.* Croly had had no training as an architect, but over the six years he edited the magazine he developed considerable skill as a critic. What came to interest him was whether American architects could produce work that reflected American rather than European experience. He disdained Henry Richardson's revival of Romanesque style, but praised the work of Midwesterner Louis Sullivan and "a very able architect, who issues from Mr. Sullivan's office, Mr. Frank Wright."

Croly also dwelled on the looming conflict between popular taste and the architect's own aesthetic standards. Could architects produce distinguished works for a public that preferred debased imitations? Croly doubted "that the plastic arts in a modern democratic community can ever be both genuinely popular and thoroughly self-respecting." Croly's architectural criticism anticipated Van Wyck Brooks's plea for an American literature that synthesized the "lowbrow" and the "highbrow," but for Croly, the real import of the conflict over popular taste lay in the analogy between the architect and the progressive intellectual. The question that consumed Croly over the last twenty-five years of his life was how the disinterested progressive intellectual who was attempting to "mold social life in the light of the best available knowledge and in the interests of a humane ideal" could influence a public and a corporate elite committed to the quest for individual gain.

In 1905, Croly, who became independently wealthy through his marriage, stepped down from full-time editorship of the *Architectural Record* and began to work on *The Promise of American Life*. Published in 1909, it was the ultimate contribution of the progressive era to American political thought; it was also a work that transcended the profound limitations of much contemporary progressive thought.

Croly wrote at a particular crossroads in American history. In the eighteenth and nineteenth centuries, Americans believed that their society held a unique promise of liberty and equality. Through economic liberty, Thomas Jefferson and his successors had maintained, Americans would be able to achieve widespread and roughly equal ownership of property and a modicum of prosperity. On this foundation, the democracy of a virtuous, independent citizenry could thrive. Moreover, because of America's island isolation, Americans would not be corrupted by Europe's mores or swept into its wars.

But Jefferson and Jackson's vision of an American Arcadia was predicated on the availability of cheap, fertile land and an economy limited to small-scale agriculture and manufacturing. The closing of the frontier and the onset of industrialization intruded upon this bucolic dream. By 1909, the small farm and business—once the basis of the American economy—had become subsidiaries of the larger corporate system.

Industrialization had a dramatic effect on America's fluid class structure. Immigrants, lured by the promise of factory jobs, were pitted against descendants of the *Mayflower* settlers, farmers against merchants, country against city. In the last decades of the nineteenth century and the first decade of the twentieth century, the nation was rocked by bitter and bloody strikes. In

January 1902, for instance, 180 union workers were killed in labor violence, 1,651 were injured, and over 5,000 were arrested. As immigrants crowded into cities like New York, Philadelphia, Chicago, and St. Louis, public life became dominated by corrupt politicians like "Bath Tub" John Coughlin and Boss Tweed.

At the same time, America was inexorably drawn into the growing imperial rivalries among Great Britain, Germany, France, Russia, and Japan. German bankers and warships suddenly intruded upon the Caribbean, and the European powers and the Japanese threatened to carve up China, closing this potentially lucrative market to American merchants. If Americans wanted to sell their goods overseas, they could no longer afford to ignore these conflicts. They had to become a world power, ending the nation's historic isolation.

By the time Croly wrote *The Promise of American Life*, most reformers recognized that America had sharply diverged from the nation's ideals. But for Croly that wasn't enough. "A man who is a sturdy sinner all the week hardly improves his moral standing by attending church on Sunday and professing a noble Christian theory of life," he wrote. "There must surely be some better way of excusing our sins than by raising aloft a noble theory of which these sins are a glaring violation." In *The Promise of American Life*, Croly undertook a reexamination of the ideals themselves, seeking to modify them to the new world of the twentieth century.

Croly condemned the growing division between rich and poor that industrialization had wrought. He contended that "gross inequalities in wealth, wholly divorced from economic efficiency on the part of the rich," were threatening the "social bond" upon which democracy rests. But Croly believed that Americans were being prevented from taking effective action against those conditions by their own ideals—by the political and social philosophy that they had inherited from the Jeffersonians and Jacksonians who had dominated American politics in the nineteenth century.

Progressive era historians like Vernon Parrington and Charles Beard had cast the conflict between Thomas Jefferson and Alexander Hamilton in the 1790s as the fulcrum of American political thought, but while Beard and Parrington took Jefferson's side, Croly took Hamilton's. Hamilton erred, Croly argued, in envisioning government as a bulwark against popular democracy, but Jefferson erred more gravely by equating democracy with "extreme individualism." "Jefferson sought an essentially equalitarian and even socialistic result by means of an essentially individualistic machinery," he wrote.

Jefferson's vision led to hypocrisy and contradiction. Once in power, the Jeffersonians made ample use of the state machinery to encourage economic growth; but insofar as they allowed the economy to grow without constraint, they laid the groundwork for the inequality of industrial society. Jeffersonian liberty bequeathed inequality. "The traditional American confidence in individual freedom has resulted in a morally and socially undesirable distribution of wealth," Croly wrote.

The Jeffersonians also destroyed the integrity of government by infecting it with a fatal hypocrisy. "They accepted the national organization as a fact and as a condition of national safety; they rejected it as a lesson in political wisdom, and as an implicit principle of political action. By so doing, they began that career of intellectual lethargy, superficiality, and insincerity which ever since has been characteristic of official American political thought."

The Jacksonian Democrats imbued Jefferson's utopian vision of political and economic equality with a vision of social equality, rooted in the experience of the American frontier. The Jacksonians championed the "average man" and sought to "suppress men with special vocations." They glorified men "successful in popular and remunerative occupations." The result was that Americans devalued the disinterested pursuit of excellence that had characterized the lives of the best of Americans—foremost among them Abraham Lincoln. "Of the individuality which may reside in the gallant and exclusive devotion to some disinterested, and perhaps unpopular, moral, intellectual, or technical purpose, they have not the remotest conception; and yet it is this kind of individuality which is indispensable to the fullness and intensity of American national life."

Croly saw the populists and progressive trustbusters as latter-day Jeffersonians and Jacksonians who wanted to re-create the conditions that had given rise to the problems they sought to solve. In trying to break up the industrial trusts, for instance, they were simply trying to re-create the fierce competition between smaller firms that had given rise to the monopolies. In contrast, Croly believed that "the new organization of American industry has created an economic mechanism which is capable of being wonderfully and indefinitely serviceable to the American people." What was needed was not to dismantle that mechanism but—by means of a strong state—to direct its benefits toward the entire nation. "The public has nothing to gain," Croly wrote, "from the mutilation or destruction of these nationalized economic institutions. It should seek, on the contrary, to preserve them, just insofar as they continue to remain efficient; but it should at the same time seek the better distribution of the fruits of this efficiency."

Croly saw echoes of the Jacksonian disdain for excellence and expertise in both the populist agitation for direct popular rule through initiatives and referenda and the socialist program for working-class control of government. Following Comte, Croly believed that industrialization had created managers, engineers, and other experts who were uniquely qualified to run society, albeit on behalf of a populace that elected them. He had nothing but contempt for the socialists who believed that the working class could actually run society. "Professional socialists may cherish the notion that their battle is won as soon as they can secure a permanent popular majority in favor of a socialistic policy; but . . . the action of a majority composed of the ordinary type of convinced socialists could and would in a few years do more to make socialism impossible than could be accomplished by the best and most prolonged efforts of a majority of malignant anti-socialists."

As Comte had argued, Croly held that society should be ruled by a managerial elite who would emerge from the new professional classes. Croly insisted on a pure meritocracy rather than the rigid class system made possible by the inheritance of wealth. "A democracy, not less than a monarchy or an aristocracy, must recognize political, economic, and social distinctions," Croly wrote, "but it must also withdraw its consent whenever these discriminations show any tendency to excessive endurance. The essential wholeness of the community depends absolutely on the ceaseless creation of a political, economic, and social aristocracy and their equally incessant replacement."

In *The Promise of American Life*, Croly presented himself as a new species: a democratic Hamiltonian. He believed that a good society—one that exhibited brotherhood, justice, happiness, and virtue—could be created only by concerted social and government action toward those ends. Democracy should not be dedicated, Croly wrote, "either to liberty or to equality in their abstract expressions, but to liberty and equality insofar as they make for human brotherhood." Economic liberty had to be restricted to prevent widespread inequality. And while unearned power and wealth should be suppressed in the name of equality, distinctions based on superior talent and dedication should not be.

Croly's program for changing America was subtly different from that of many of his contemporaries. Unlike those progressives who believed that political consciousness simply reflected economic "interests," Croly believed that Americans' understanding of their place in society was mediated by their underlying philosophies. (In Croly's view, Beard's theory of economic interests shaping the Constitution was itself a reflection of Jeffersonian individualism.) Thus, unless Americans changed how they understood themselves, they would succeed in changing laws but not in reforming society. Changing society meant abandoning not only the Jeffersonian view of democracy through self-interest but also the Jacksonian exaltation of the average man. Americans had to understand, Croly wrote, "that in a democratic system the intelligence has a discipline, an interest and a will of its own, and that this special discipline and interest call for a new conception both of individual and of national development."

Croly also rejected the facile progressive view that what Americans needed was simply more education. As long as Americans believed that the goal of education was merely to become more successful "in popular and remunerative occupations," then further individual education was irrelevant to America's adjustment to the new industrial era. What was needed was what Croly called "national education." "Just insofar as a people is sincerely seeking the fulfillment of its national promise," Croly wrote, "individuals of all kinds will find their most edifying individual opportunities in serving their own country."

But how could such a national education take place? Here Croly's solution rang of both Comte and John Dewey. National education could be achieved by legislators and politicians who were able to win support for and then undertake programs— such as those that Roosevelt had advocated—that would advance broader national goals. Politics could be its own education. Croly summed up his case in this way: "The good American usually wishes to accomplish by education a result which must be partly accomplished by national education," he wrote. "The nation, like the individual, must go to school; and the national school is not a lecture hall or library. Its schooling consists chiefly in experimental collective action aimed at the realization of the collective purpose."

In *The Promise of American Life* and in his next book, *Progressive Democracy*, Croly always framed his programmatic proposals in pragmatic terms as "experimental" or "transitional" measures whose effectiveness would have to be tested in practice. He advocated national labor legislation and corporate recognition of unions. He called for a sharply graduated inheritance tax. And he advocated government regulation of corporations. His program for corporate regulation closely resembled that of German evolutionary socialist Eduard Bernstein and of the British Fabians. He distrusted mixed forms of ownership in which the government and private managers jockeyed for control. He preferred either indirect means of regulation through taxation or outright appropriation—in the cases where a corporation became a genuine monopoly. If regulated corporations "survived from some generations and increased in efficiency and strength," Croly wrote, "a policy must be adopted of converting them into express economic agents of the whole community and of gradually appropriating for the benefit of the community the substantial economic advantages which these corporations had succeeded in acquiring."

In *The Promise of American Life*, Croly failed, however, to explain how Americans would come to accept his program. On one level, Croly's reasoning was circular: he was arguing that Americans would become politically educated by undertaking a collective national experiment in reforming the society. But how could the American people first become sufficiently educated to support the enactment of such a reform program?

Insofar as Croly's reasoning was not merely circular, he relied on agents and circumstances of change that were highly du-

bious and would lead later to his disillusionment and withdrawal from politics. Croly, lacking any confidence in the
general populace, placed his hopes for political change on businessmen and on bankers such as J. P. Morgan & Co. partners
Willard Straight and George Perkins, who had backed civic
reform and Theodore Roosevelt's candidacy for President in
1904 and then again in 1912. In *The Promise of American Life*,
Croly was continually trying to convince businessmen that they
would be better off trusting their fate to national government
than to "irresponsible radicals" who might win control of state
governments. Like his father, Croly seemed to conceive of society itself as a corporation for which enlightened business
leaders could serve as the board of directors. But, as he later
acknowledged, Croly wildly overestimated the foresight of
American business leaders. While they were willing to back
good-government candidates against Tammany Hall and
cheered arguments against trustbusters and populists, they
were not only unenthusiastic about recognizing unions or even
abolishing child labor but irate about having their assets
nationalized.

Croly also placed hope for change in a political hero who
could single-handedly reform American politics. Lincoln had
been such a politician, and Croly held out similar hope for
Theodore Roosevelt, who had just left the presidency after two
terms when *The Promise of American Life* appeared. When Roosevelt, dissatisfied with his successor, William Howard Taft,
bolted the Republican Party in 1912 to form the Progressive
Party, Croly enthusiastically followed him. While the party's
positions on such issues as workers' compensation and child
labor reflected broad agreement among progressives, Croly
could take singular credit for Roosevelt's support for regulating
rather than busting up the trusts. But Roosevelt was narrowly
defeated by Wilson, and in December 1914, just after *The New
Republic* began publishing, Roosevelt broke off relations with
Croly over an editorial taking him to task for his harsh rejection

of Wilson's foreign policy. By this time, Croly recognized that Roosevelt had had his day in the sun.

But most important, Croly rested his hopes for a national political transformation on the creation of circumstances that would force Americans to think in national terms. Unlike Roosevelt, Croly had little of the jingoist about him. When he called for a national approach to politics, he meant national as opposed to individual and sectional. But like Roosevelt and Brooks Adams, he understood that America's days as an isolated power were drawing to a close. "Hitherto, the American preference and desire for peace has constituted the chief justification for its isolation," Croly wrote. "At some future time the same purpose, just in as far as it is sincere and rational, may demand intervention."

Croly also maintained that the creation of a new global policy might force the United States to reconsider its domestic policy. "In truth, the work of international reconstruction and amelioration, so far from being opposed to that of the vigorous assertion of a valid foreign policy, is really correlative and supplementary thereto," Croly wrote in *The Promise of American Life*. "And it is entirely possible that hereafter the United States will be forced into the adoption of a really national domestic policy because of the dangers and duties incurred through her relations with foreign countries." Not only the danger of war but that of economic competition would spur America to adopt domestic reform. "Under modern conditions, a country which takes its responsibilities lightly, and will not submit to the discipline necessary to political efficiency . . . goes down with a crash, as France did in 1870, or as Russia has just done."

Croly was correct, of course, in believing that the United States was about to break with its isolated past and fear of "foreign entanglements" and that doing so would transform domestic politics. He was mistaken, however, about the kind of transformation that America's new foreign commitments would bring.

Croly got a chance to put his program and his hopes to the test in 1914. Willard Straight and his wife, Dorothy, who had admired *The Promise of American Life*, offered to finance a new political magazine to counter the growing support for Woodrow Wilson (and opposition to Theodore Roosevelt's Progressive Party) among the opinion journals. Straight associated Wilson with laissez-faire policy and Roosevelt with opposition to trustbusting and support for an aggressive foreign economic policy. Croly recruited fellow progressives Walter Lippmann and Walter Weyl, who also shared Croly's conception of a new national politics and his disdain for Jeffersonian individualism. The first issue of the magazine, called *The New Republic*, came out on November 7, 1914. It quickly became a publishing success, with its circulation climbing from 2,500 to 45,000 in four years. But it eventually foundered on the same assumptions about political change that had weakened Croly's case in *The Promise of American Life*.

*The New Republic* began publishing four months after World War I broke out in Europe. Croly hoped that the threat of American involvement would impart a new urgency to national politics and lay the groundwork for the kind of reforms he had earlier proposed. Croly regarded American preparation for, and involvement in, the Great War—to be the bloodiest ever—as a means to domestic ends. He wrote his friend Learned Hand in August 1914 that the war might "prove in the end an actual help to *The New Republic*. It will tend to dislocate conventional ways of looking at things and stimulate public thinking." In the magazine's first editorial, Croly wrote that the crisis created by the war "should bring with it a political and economic organization better able to redeem its obligations at home."

As the war deepened, he continued to hold high hopes for

its effect on American politics. He heartily endorsed Wilson's proposals for military preparedness. "The advocates of military preparedness are, I think, justified in anticipating that any army and a navy large enough to be dangerous may introduce into American domestic life a useful ferment—one which may prove hostile to the prevalent spirit of complacent irresponsibility," Croly wrote in June 1916.

He shared Wilson's optimism about the "new world order" that would emerge from the war. While Croly was pro-British, believing that German militarism was primarily, but not solely, to blame for the war, he hoped that the war could produce a settlement to make future wars unlikely and to promote liberal democracy abroad. With the Wilson administration, he pressed for a diplomatic policy aimed at "peace without victory"—a phrase that Wilson borrowed from a *New Republic* editorial. "The special problem of the Western Powers is the immensely difficult and dubious one of making a world war contribute to permanent pacification," he wrote.

Croly explained how his own nationalism squared with Wilson's looming internationalism. As early as May 1915, Wilson had proposed that after World War I the belligerents should create a League to Enforce the Peace that would make future conflicts less likely. Croly endorsed Wilson's plan. In the nineteenth century, Croly reasoned, Britain's unchallenged supremacy had prevented the outbreak of a major European war; now the rise of Germany had upset the continental balance of power. Croly thought that Wilson's League could serve the same purpose as unchallenged British supremacy: it would promote "the better aspect of the balance of power as it existed in the nineteenth century and discourage its worse aspects."

By the 1916 election, Croly and the *New Republic* editors had become exuberant backers of Wilson's administration. When Congress declared war on Germany in April 1917, Croly waxed eloquent in a letter to Willard Straight: "But what a rare opportunity is now opened up, my dear Willard. During the next few years, under the stimulus of the war and its circumstances, there will be a chance to focus the thought and will of the country on high and fruitful purposes such as occurs only once in many hundred years."

As the Wilson administration, under the pressure of war, introduced precisely those measures of industrial planning advocated in *The Promise of American Life*, Croly began to cast Wilson himself in the role he had reserved for Lincoln and Roosevelt. When Wilson quoted the magazine's phrase "peace without victory," Croly told Wilson's chief adviser, Colonel Edward House, that it was "the greatest event" of his life. Croly told House that he wanted him to examine *The New Republic*'s copy carefully to see whether it faithfully reported the President's viewpoint. "We merely want to back him up on his work and be the faithful and helpful interpreter of what seems to us to be one of the greatest enterprises ever undertaken by an American President," Croly wrote him. An equally buoyant Lippmann joined the administration as a presidential adviser and was responsible, under House's aegis, for drafting the "Fourteen Points" that Wilson used to win an armistice.

Croly's support for Wilson's more cautious and limited intervention and for Wilson's League proposal set him at odds with Theodore Roosevelt and with his own prior conception of progressive nationalism. Roosevelt had insisted early on American entry into the war and had rejected talk of international organization, referring derisively to plans for a "world league of righteousness." Roosevelt was committed to the assertion of American power overseas and to an international order based squarely on balanced military power, but Croly was drawn to a more Wilsonian conception in which the goal of American intervention overseas was to eliminate the need for American military preparedness—to create an international order in which American economic power could assert itself and domestic reform could take place.

But Croly's view of the international organization and the new League also subtly differed from Wilson's, although the differences would not appear significant until 1919. Croly still thought that a balance of power was necessary among nations, but that the League could help to maintain and enforce it; Wilson believed that an international organization could replace the balance of power as the instrument of regulating the relations among nations. "There must be, not a balance of power, but a community of power; not organized rivalries, but an organized common peace," Wilson told Congress in January 1917. Thus Wilson was willing to agree to an inequitable settlement on the Continent in the vain hope that the League would later be able to amend and even to transcend it.

The war's end did not bring the world Croly or Wilson envisaged; instead, their vision was shattered. Croly had already begun to wince at the administration's heavy-handed repression of wartime dissent, but his discomfort was little compared to his reaction to the Versailles settlement. After his wife read him its draconian terms, putting Germany's economy in thrall to Britain and France and making a mockery of Wilson's concept of self-determination, Croly went into seclusion for three days. He emerged to denounce Wilson, the war, and the vindictive peace. "Wilson for lack of courage and knowledge and administrative capacity has yielded to a settlement which means a Europe of wars and revolution and agony," a bitter Croly wrote in *The New Republic* in June 1919. He even rejected the League of Nations. The treaty, he wrote, "would convert the League into the instrument of competitive imperialist nationalism whose more disinterested members would labor in vain to mold it into a cooperative society."

Ironically, in the last months of his presidency, before he was crippled by a final stroke, Wilson eloquently defended his own conception of how a new international order would contribute to a better society at home. Roosevelt, Brooks Adams, and the Croly of *The Promise of American Life* had argued that military preparedness was a means toward domestic reform, but now Wilson, with the bitter experience of war behind him, reversed the equation. Constant military preparedness would destroy any possibility of social reform. "You know how impossible it is to effect social reform if everybody must be under orders from the government. You know how impossible it is, in short, to have a free nation if it is a military nation and under military orders," Wilson declared in St. Louis in September 1919. But as Croly understood, Wilson's League and the Treaty of Versailles only made future wars more likely.

As the Wilson administration began to dismantle the economic reforms it had introduced during the war and as Attorney General A. Mitchell Palmer fomented a "Red Scare," deporting so-called alien radicals and raiding union halls in search of Bolsheviks, Croly grew even more disillusioned. In 1920, facing an election between a Republican reactionary, Warren Harding, and a Democratic conservative, Croly voted for the doomed Farmer-Labor Party candidate, Parley P. Christensen, plunging *The New Republic* into left-wing opposition— a stance from which it would not waver for the next forty years.

Overcome by despair, Croly abandoned the tattered remains of his old theory of change. He rejected military nationalism and jingoism as a means to domestic reform. He had not understood, he admitted, "what the psychology of the American people would be under the strain of fighting a world war." Croly also repudiated the quest both for a new Lincoln (Wilson, Croly wrote, had "shattered what was left of American progressivism as a coherent body of conviction") and for enlightened business leadership. In an October 1920 article in *The New Republic*, "The Eclipse of Progressivism," the once hopeful Croly depicted a business class that "exploits the organization and shibboleths of democracy in order to disqualify any attack on its autocratic authority in industry as anti-social agitation." What was needed, he wrote, was to strengthen "the wage-earners to resist capitalist domination" in order "to restore a wholesome balance of economic and social power in the American commonwealth."

Departing from his previous model of government by experts, and from his model of society as a corporation with a board of directors, Croly called for "the participation of the workers in the management of the industry as an essential part of a democratic industrial policy and of democratic education for citizenship."

Croly's new program was partly the result of his having exchanged one utopian fantasy for another. He didn't explain how a predominantly immigrant, still largely unorganized working class was to master running an industrial enterprise. But Croly's approach also showed his determination to seek within corporate America the fulfillment of the original promise of liberty and equality. Most progressives would either abandon the promise itself—opting for a diluted liberalism—or project onto Bolshevism their hopes for a new Soviet America. Indeed, after Croly's death *The New Republic* would first embrace the Soviet experiment—and then thirty years later resign itself to Kennedy liberalism.

Croly's change of heart and mind consigned him and *The New Republic* to the margins of politics and publishing in the 1920s. The journal's circulation dropped below 15,000 by 1923. Weyl died in 1919, and Lippmann departed in 1921 to far greater renown as a newspaper editor and columnist (see Chapter 3). Croly, with the help of Edmund Wilson and other talented recruits, kept alive the flickering flame of progressivism. From the war's end through the 1929 stock market crash, the magazine published some of its most important articles, from the first serialized version of John Maynard Keynes's *Economic Consequences of the Peace* to John Dewey's *Individualism Old and New*. Its literary section regularly featured such young upstart critics as Edmund Wilson and Malcolm Cowley.

Returning to the preoccupations of his college days, Croly turned increasingly to pondering the role of religion in healing what he called "the sickness of civilization." He even dabbled in mysticism and the obscure teachings of Georges Gurdjieff in an effort to discover a method to reawaken America. If his writings in the previous decades had been earnest, his writings of the 1920s verged on the solemn. ("Crolier than thou" became a quip among writers and editors.) Turning Comte on his head, Croly argued that the West was suffering from a split between religion and knowledge that dated from the Protestant Reformation. "Owing to the divorce between knowledge and religion," Croly wrote, "the engineers of the new knowledge transmuted it into irresponsible rather than responsible power. The present awful predicament of civilization is born of this transmutation." What he was mourning was the birth of the modern world.

Croly wrote increasingly less about politics than he had in the previous decade (according to Edmund Wilson, "he despaired of politics and never quite took them seriously again"). His writings amounted to a telling indictment of the greed and complacency of the Republican decade—a period when "Americanism itself became popularly confused with a combination of optimism, fatalism, and conservatism."

Croly especially disdained the business leaders of the 1920s—the men upon whom his hopes for enlightened national leadership had rested. "The processes whereby wealth is produced, distributed, and protected tend in many respects to breed extravagant, shiftless, torpid, intolerant, unenlightened, self-satisfied and undeveloped American citizens," he wrote.

Croly also directed his criticism at what remained of the progressive movement that he had helped to create. In July 1928, at the moment of Herbert Hoover's nomination by the Republican convention, Croly explained in the last article published under his byline why the party of Theodore Roosevelt had failed to endure. "A national party," Croly wrote, "cannot be forged out of the personal followers of one political leader, supplemented chiefly by propagandists, no matter how ardent for a body of liberal ideas." Parties, he argued, must combine specific "class interests."

In 1920 and 1924, Croly had endorsed the Farmer-Labor Party candidate, but in 1928, faced with the alternatives of Herbert Hoover and Al Smith, Croly recommended a "suspension of judgment." Instead of creating third parties, he argued, progressives should remain "free and flexible," portentously suggesting that "four years from now the disintegration of one or both of the two major parties under the impact of class or sectional conflicts may provide the raw material for the formation of a consciously progressive party."

Croly died in 1930, a year after the Great Depression had commenced. He had little inkling that in two years the Depression would usher into power a new Democratic administration committed to many of the ideas that he had championed in *The Promise of American Life* and "The Eclipse of Progressivism." If Franklin Roosevelt was the proper successor to Wilson and to Theodore Roosevelt, such administration intellectuals as Henry Wallace and Rexford Tugwell were the successors to Croly and to the pre-World War I progressive intellectuals.

But Croly's legacy remained incomplete. He had begun by making explicit what was implicit in Theodore Roosevelt's presidency and Brooks Adams's writings—the connection between America's imperial destiny and the imperatives of domestic reform. He had seen these connections sundered in World War I and in its Republican aftermath. But while he had revised his conception of domestic reform, he, like many Americans of the 1920s, had not come to terms with the country's new place in the world.

# 2

# *Henry Wallace and the Century of the Common Man*

Now at last the nations of the world have a second chance to erect a lasting structure of peace—a peace such as that which Woodrow Wilson sought to build but which crumbled away because the world was not yet ready,

—HENRY WALLACE, 1942

On September 12, 1946, more than 20,000 New Yorkers, supporters of the left-wing American Labor Party, jammed Madison Square Garden to hear Secretary of Commerce Henry Wallace issue a clarion call for "real peace" between the United States and the Soviet Union. A tall man, with a long angular face and striking blue eyes that appeared to be fixed on a distant horizon, Wallace became impassioned as he contrasted the prospects of peace with the specter of another world war. "Under peaceful competition, the Russian world and the American world will gradually become more alike," Wallace predicted.

Wallace's speech put him directly at odds with the Truman administration's increasingly contentious posture toward the Soviet Union. A week later, amid the furor caused by the speech, Truman fired him. Wallace did not go quietly. He became the administration's most outspoken critic. Running on the Progressive Party ticket, he challenged Truman for the presidency in 1948. But as members of the American Communist Party took over his campaign, Wallace's candidacy was doomed. He failed to win a single state, and afterward retired from politics, never to serve in government or run for office again.

This is the Henry Wallace that both his supporters and his detractors remember. His supporters have hailed him as a prophet and a Cold War martyr who understood the perils of American intransigence toward the Soviet Union; his detractors have dismissed him as a dupe of Stalinism. But Wallace's political career began more than two decades before he took the stage at Madison Square Garden. Of all the officials in the Roosevelt administration, he perhaps best embodied the spirit of Croly and *The New Republic*'s progressivism. And his convictions on foreign policy—however distorted—reflected the legacy of Woodrow Wilson rather than Joseph Stalin.

As Franklin Roosevelt's Secretary of Agriculture, Wallace introduced social planning to the chaotic farm economy, getting farmers to meet together to decide how much to produce. Wallace's program set a precedent for successful government action. On the same day that Truman fired Wallace for foreign policy disagreements, he admitted in a letter to his mother and sister in Missouri that Wallace "was the best secretary of agriculture this country ever had." Truman was not alone in this assessment. Columnist Walter Lippmann called Wallace's plan for managing the agricultural surplus "the most daring economic experiment ever seriously proposed in the United States."

Before he became a Cold War critic, Wallace was one of the main intellectual voices of the New Deal. In a constant stream of books, articles, and pamphlets, he articulated the most advanced aspirations of Franklin Roosevelt's administration, from its break with the Republicans' ruinous protectionism to its support for full-employment planning. Roosevelt explained in July 1940 to Labor Secretary Frances Perkins that he wanted Wallace as his Vice President not only because he had "a following among liberal thinkers" but also because he would be of great value in helping the "people with their political thinking."

In the first years of World War II, serving as Vice President and the head of the Board of Economic Warfare, Wallace became the chief critic of Henry Luce's conception of an American Century and the foremost proponent of an international New Deal that would eradicate poverty and colonialism while providing new markets for American goods. But at the same time, Wallace began to nourish the same wartime illusions about social planning and world organization that had doomed Croly, Wilson, and the progressives. Just as Wilson and Croly's hopes for a new world order were dashed upon the rocks of Versailles, Wallace's were destroyed by the onset of the Cold War.

Wallace's political outlook was formed when he was growing up in Iowa. The man that Washington grande dame Alice Longworth disparagingly referred to as "Farmer Wallace" was the third generation of the country's preeminent family of agrarian intellectuals. His grandfather, widely known as "Uncle Henry," was a minister turned farmer who became a newspaper columnist and editor. Uncle Henry founded *Wallaces' Farmer*—"a weekly journal for thinking farmers"—and became a leading expert on farm problems. Unwilling to move to Washington, he turned down William McKinley's offer to become Secretary of Agriculture. His son and Henry's father, Henry C. Wallace, was a farmer and professor of agriculture at Iowa State. He served as Secretary of Agriculture under Harding and Coolidge from 1921 to 1924, when he died suddenly.

Henry A. Wallace, born in 1888, was raised on the Iowa State campus, where one of his boyhood friends was his father's graduate student George Washington Carver. Young Henry was more studious and introverted than his father and grandfather. Author Paul de Kruif, who visited the Wallaces, described him as "a thin boy whose face was too earnest for his age." By his twenties, Wallace had become a respected plant geneticist. He developed the first commercially viable hybrid corn, which he called "copper cross," and successfully marketed it through his own company, the Hi-Bred Corn Co. Wallace was also an outstanding agricultural economist, the author of the first book to chart the cyclical nature of corn prices.

Wallace took over *Wallaces' Farmer* after his father became Secretary of Agriculture. In the newspaper, whose motto was "Good Farming Clear Thinking Right Living," Henry Wallace ventured opinions on subjects ranging from Soviet Bolshevism to Irish poetry, and he offered advice on the most mundane farm problems. To one reader, he wrote, "If I had hogs weighing 200 pounds, I think I would feed them out to weight of 235 pounds before I let them go. There is a chance that there will be a pickup of 50 or 75 cents a hundred in hog prices during February." As Secretary of Agriculture, he was sometimes suspected of preferring plants to people. One of his 1930s radio talks was enthusiastically titled "The Strength and Quietness of Grass."

As a farm editor, Wallace witnessed the onset of the Great Depression well before 1929, and he was able to understand the Depression's causes far earlier than other editorialists and economists. Wallace saw that laissez-faire capitalism, as practiced on America's farms, had not created prosperity, but rather plummeting prices and massive unemployment. Wallace also understood the pitfalls of the Republican isolationism that followed Wilson's downfall. He saw that America's high tariffs, combined with American insistence that Europe repay its huge war debts, were making it impossible for Europeans to buy American imports and would eventually trigger a world economic collapse.

From the farm experience, Wallace realized that within an unregulated capitalism, technological improvement was a mixed blessing. On farms, the introduction of the combine had destroyed jobs and driven down prices. As long as an expanding manufacturing industry could absorb displaced farm workers, and a growing world market would support a greater volume of farm products, farmers prospered. However, as improved technology in manufacturing led employers to lay off workers, and as the world market began to shrink under the impact of high tariffs, first farms and then American manufacturing sank into a deep depression. As Wallace wrote in a 1930 pamphlet on the causes of worldwide depression, "The beautiful rose of technological improvement has in it a worm eating at its heart."

Like Uncle Henry, Wallace cast a farm editor's jaundiced eye on the trusts and giant corporations that were changing the American economic landscape. He argued that when these firms maximized their profits, Americans did not necessarily maximize their own happiness and prosperity. On the contrary, Wallace believed that the corporations had a tendency to "hold back too much of their profits for their owners and to distribute too little of the increased efficiency in lower prices or higher pay."

Wallace's solution to economic depression was a regulated national capitalism and an open world economy. The government, Wallace wrote in *Whose Constitution?*, must provide "a democratic mechanism which can direct action in behalf of the general welfare." Government, Wallace wrote in *New Frontiers*, had to make corporations act "fairly and in the public interest." The United States also had to lower, if not eliminate, its high tariff barriers. Creditor countries like the United States and Great Britain, Wallace argued, were better off with low tariffs that allowed other countries to sell them their goods so that they had the income to buy American and British goods and pay their debts. Eventually, other liberals and progressives would espouse this combination of government regulation and free trade, but in 1930 Wallace, expressing these views in *Wallaces' Farmer*, was almost alone. On the basis of his experience in Iowa, he was formulating a political economy whose virtues wouldn't become widely accepted until after World War II— and then only by Democratic intellectuals.

Like Croly, Wallace had a vision of society that diverged from nineteenth-century individualism and twentieth-century socialism. He was heavily influenced by Thorstein Veblen, a Norwegian-American who had grown up on a small farm in Minnesota and who expressed a farmer's disdain for the profit-driven and profligate modern capitalist. Veblen stood for the triumph of the engineer over the financier, industry over business, and social efficiency over profit. Veblen was not necessarily anticapitalist, but he aspired to a society that embodied the values of husbandry and craftsmanship. Wallace had this same view.

Veblen's vision was evident from Wallace's first book, *Agricultural Prices*, published in 1920. Wallace called for replacing "most business men with production engineers and statistical economists." "Most men," Wallace wrote, "desire to do their work well, and this desire will find more complete expression, to the benefit of the bulk of the people, under the guidance of men whose supreme motive is not profit but technical understanding and love of the work to be done."

When Henry Wallace was growing up, his principal political influence was his grandfather rather than his father. Uncle Henry shared the populists' anger at the trusts, but he was a progressive Republican rather than a populist. He rejected both the greenback and the free-silver solution, which blamed farmers' ills on the gold standard and vested hopes for the restoration of Jeffersonian capitalism on the monetization of plentiful silver. While he saw corporate capitalism as "civilized savagery" and "business barbarism," he showed no interest in restoring this small-scale agrarian society. Like Theodore Roosevelt, he believed that the growth of corporate capitalism and large-scale agriculture was both inevitable and potentially beneficial, and he wanted to use government to make sure that the benefits were realized for the entire society. In 1912, Uncle Henry, his son, and his grandson broke with the regular Republicans to back Theodore Roosevelt and the Bull Moose Party.

But Uncle Henry did not share the Republican Roosevelt's bellicosity or his skepticism about an international organization that would transcend the balance of power. He saw the purpose of American intervention as ridding the world of imperialist rivalry rather than gaining an American share in the spoils. Like Wilson, he believed that in a disarmed world American economic superiority would triumph. He saw World War I as a result of unresolved economic conflicts, and when it first broke out, he supported Wilson's refusal to intervene. In a visit to Wilson in 1916, Uncle Henry advocated his own version of the League of Nations: "an international fleet" that would police the seas so that "the nations of the world, wherever they might be located, could freely trade with each other without fear of molestation." Uncle Henry's views reflected the utopian impulses that the war stimulated among progressives, and his grandson would adopt a similar perspective in analyzing World War II and in proposing measures to prevent further world wars.

As a minister, Uncle Henry had offended Presbyterian church elders by his modern renderings of the Psalms and his refusal to condemn dancing. After leaving the ministry, he remained deeply religious, but in an unconventional and exploratory manner. He read widely in theology, philosophy, and mysticism, and conveyed these interests to his grandson, who became similarly devout and unconventional—a regularly practicing Episcopalian who studied other religions and dabbled in astrology, numerology, and mysticism.

Through his grandfather, young Henry was influenced by the Social Gospel, which sought the Kingdom of God on Earth through social justice. Wallace came to believe that a religious awakening was necessary to economic reform. Through religion, individuals could overcome the impetus toward competition and learn a "higher law of cooperation." Indeed, in the wake of the Crash, Wallace's impulse was to call for a new Reformation. "To enter the kingdom of heaven brought to earth," Wallace wrote, "it will be necessary to have a reformation even greater than that of Luther and Calvin." This reformation would not, however, be conventionally Protestant, but "so universal as to embrace Buddhists, Mohammedans, Jews and Protestants [and] Catholics."

As a public official, Wallace made no secret of his religious convictions, even his most bizarre ones. During his first year at the Agriculture Department, he invited the Irish mystic poet and agrarian revolutionary Æ (George Russell), to Washington. One former Agriculture Department official recalled Æ holding "philosophical conversations . . . with tense huddles of Triple A and Extension executives right in the middle of planning extremely practical courses in a time of needful haste."

During his first term in Washington, Wallace also became involved with the White Russian painter Nicholas Roerich, a mystic who had assembled a cult following in New York City. Roerich was the founder of his own religion, complete with arcane symbols and secret language. Wallace hired Roerich and his son in March 1934 to search for drought-resistant grasses in Outer Mongolia, the same place where Roerich expected the second coming of Christ. The mission's abject failure led Wallace to repudiate the artist-mystic the next year.

In the midst of Wallace's 1948 presidential campaign, columnist Westbrook Pegler printed some of Wallace's letters to Roerich and Roerich's associates. In these letters, Wallace referred to Roosevelt as "the flaming one" and "the wavering one" and the Soviet Union as "the tigers." Some of the letters are quite bizarre. In September 1933, when Wallace was angered by the Soviet rejection of the International Wheat Agreement, Wallace wrote to Roerich, "The flaming one is self-hearted toward the tigers, and I fear has made commitments of some sort. The battle against the vermin is fierce and the one refuge is the thought of the steadfast ones and that inmost conviction." In another letter to Roerich, Wallace proclaimed his otherworldliness. "Long have I been aware of the occasional fragrance from that other world which is the real world. But now I must live in the outer world and at the same time make over my mind and body to serve as fit instruments for the lord of justice."

In some respects, Wallace's mystical pursuits had little direct bearing on his political outlook. Whether in mysticism or Protestantism, Wallace was often simply expressing his conviction that society had to be shaped by higher ends than what he called the "greed of capitalism" and "the spiritual sloth of ever-increasing material pleasures." Wallace appears to have been drawn to Roerich precisely because he advocated a new universal spiritual community—a kind of religious Esperanto that could complement the economic transformation Wallace thought necessary.

Wallace was a combination of Christian socialist and farmer capitalist. He didn't want to abolish private industry, but to subject it to higher ideals. This would occur through government regulation leavened by a spiritual transformation of individuals. "Enduring social transformation," Wallace wrote, "is impossible of realization without changed human hearts." His was a religious view of social and personal transformation, but not one that necessarily required formal worship. Religion has "nothing to do with creeds or churches," Wallace insisted.

Yet his fascination with Roerich did reveal an underlying weakness in Wallace as a politician and statesman. His intense longing for the grand explanation for what was otherwise inexplicable made it difficult for him to distinguish charlatans from prophets and sheer nonsense from profound insight. When he wanted to believe something, Wallace was easily conned, as the Soviets would later discover during the Iowan's trip to Siberia. And outside the realm of his domestic expertise, he became prone to theories and doctrines based more on fantasy than fact.

Wallace's own political activity followed the example of his grandfather and father. In the 1920s, he abandoned the increasingly conservative Republican Party because of its opposition to farm price relief and its support for high tariffs. In 1924, disillusioned by both Republican Calvin Coolidge's and Democrat John Davis's indifference to farm problems, Wallace supported progressive Republican Robert La Follette's third-party candidacy; and in 1928, he backed urban Catholic Al Smith after Smith pledged price relief for farmers. But Wallace's main activity in the 1920s was organizing for a new approach to farm problems.

Working with agricultural economists, many of them protégés of his father and grandfather, and with farm organizations and sympathetic businessmen, Wallace built pressure for a series of bills to regulate farm output. The first of these tried to raise domestic prices by encouraging exports; after the Crash, the farm leaders and Wallace sought relief solely through what is now called supply management. This meant raising prices by reducing output.

Wallace championed what was called the Voluntary Domestic Allotment plan, which tried to raise prices by paying farmers to restrict their output—the payment itself to be financed by a tax on food-processing companies. Aided by county agents and farm organizations like the American Farm Bureau, the farmers would form committees that would administer the program. Wallace and the plan's author, M. L. Wilson, a protégé of Uncle Henry's, saw it not only as a way to raise prices above the cost of production but also as a first step toward a broader economic democracy.

In 1932, Roosevelt decided to embrace the domestic allotment plan. He met with Wilson and Wallace, both of whom campaigned enthusiastically for him, and after he was elected, nominated Wallace to be Secretary of Agriculture. In the excitement of the First Hundred Days, Congress created the Agricultural Adjustment Administration—or Triple A—to run the new program. Under Wallace, the Agriculture Department attracted the avant-garde of agrarian and urban intellectuals, including Wilson, Rexford Tugwell, Abe Fortas, Thurman Arnold, Milton Eisenhower, and Adlai Stevenson—not to mention Alger Hiss and a tiny Communist cell led by Lee Pressman. By 1934, the AAA was working as Wallace and Wilson had projected it. Prices were up, 70,000 farm leaders had been trained, and 4,200 county committees had formed that were administering the program. Farmers' clubs also grew out of the county committees. Journalist Gerald Johnson wrote of them, "These clubs devoted only part of their attention to the technicalities of agriculture. They were organized frankly for the enrichment of rural life culturally, as well as economically, and any subject whatever that interested farmers and their wives might be included in the program."

In January 1936, the Supreme Court threw out the AAA on the grounds that the processing tax was an illegal assessment and that the act itself was an unwarranted intrusion into private economic activity, but within two months Wallace had a new act in place in which supply management was justified by soil conservation and in which financing was provided directly by Congress. The next year Wallace also tried to remedy one of the defects of the AAA's supply management. The AAA had forbidden farmers and planters from using reduced output as a pretext for firing tenants, but many did, particularly in the South. After a visit South in 1936 convinced him of the tenants' plight, Wallace got Congress to fund a Farm Security Administration that provided loans to landless tenants to start their own farms. In all, Congress funded over 15,000 farms.

Then, in 1938, Wallace convinced Congress to pass a new Agricultural Adjustment Act that included the 1936 provisions and a new program to regulate surpluses and prevent shortages by maintaining a federal granary. The new program's advantage over the domestic allotment plan was that it was suited to conditions of both expanding and contracting world demand. Wallace had first conceived such a program in 1912, when he was inspired by the story of Joseph in the Bible.

(Joseph had advised the Pharaoh to lay away part of his crop during seven prosperous years so he would have food available for seven years of famine.)

Wallace's achievement at the Agriculture Department can best be appreciated if the fate of the AAA is contrasted with that of its industrial counterpart, the National Recovery Administration. The NRA also had a mandate to control prices and production, but it failed abysmally. In a 1982 study, political scientists Theda Skocpol and Kenneth Finegold summed up the difference: "The NRA became, over time, increasingly unwieldy, conflict-ridden, and uncertain about its basic goals and preferred means for achieving them, while the AAA (to a much greater degree) sorted out its priorities, resolved a major internal contradiction of programs and personnel, streamlined its organizational structure, and launched ambitious new plans for the future." When the Supreme Court threw out its provisions, the NRA was never revived, whereas Wallace's AAA quickly rebounded from the Supreme Court decision.

Wallace's programs certainly had their limitations, borne out by the image of farmers holding back food while people went hungry. But within the constraints of a shrinking world economy and a rudimentary welfare state, Wallace's program worked. Per capita farm income, which had dropped steadily from 1928 to 1933, rose annually from 1933 to 1938, only dropping the next year because the entire economy plunged. And the AAA also involved hundreds of thousands of farmers in planning their livelihoods. It came as close to creating economic democracy as any federal program ever has.

Wallace's achievement at the Agriculture Department must also be seen in the context of a continuing governmental commitment to agriculture. Since the Civil War, when Congress had established the Agriculture Department and passed the

Homestead Act and the Morrill Act providing for land-grant agricultural colleges, the government had been involved with agriculture. In 1914, the government began funding demonstration projects and extension services through state colleges, the purpose of which was to acquaint farmers with the latest agricultural technology, from harvesting machines to pest control and fertilizers. Henry Wallace and his grandfather and father were intimately involved with this movement to use government to socialize agricultural knowledge—to make the latest advances in plant genetics and animal husbandry science available to all farmers.

Wallace's New Deal programs provided a social mechanism to regulate the agricultural market. His programs brought the new institutional economics of Richard T. Ely, E. R. A. Seligman, and Veblen, which sought to shape the market to ethical ideals, to bear on the plight of Depression farming, and also established a long-term relationship between government and the farm market. By marshaling the best of social and natural science, Wallace's approach contributed to the greatest success story in the American economy. They vindicated the progressive vision of government.

In books and pamphlets, Wallace advocated the extension of the AAA experience to the economy as a whole. In 1937, he called for reestablishing the NRA and backed a proposal—first made by Theodore Roosevelt's administration—to require corporations to obtain federal charters. This measure was designed so that government could pressure corporations to adhere to the "general welfare."

Wallace's argument for government intervention was very similar to the argument used today by some proponents of industrial policy. Wallace contended that government had already been actively intervening in the market, through its imposition of a tariff on industrial imports, and he wanted industry to give back some of what it got. "It seems to me," Wallace wrote, "that corporations must more and more be prepared to accept the doctrine that capital and management have received from government a grant of power which entitles them to make profits on condition that certain rules of the game are observed with respect to production, prices, wages, and savings."

By the end of the 1930s, Wallace had developed a political economy that built upon the earlier progressive legacy but had been tempered and tested during the Great Depression. Like the economics of *The Promise of American Life*, it represented a viable middle ground between Marxian socialism and laissez-faire capitalism. But before Wallace could press his case further, World War I intervened.

Wallace reached the height of his power and influence in the early war years, when he served as Roosevelt's Vice President and as the chairman of the President's Board of Economic Warfare, which the White House set up to manage the import of strategic materials like rubber and tin and to prevent these materials from being exported to the Axis nations. During these years, Wallace not only had major responsibilities for managing the war, but became a key spokesman for Roosevelt's vision of what the war could accomplish. Yet just as Wallace appeared destined for national leadership—even the presidency—he succumbed to the same illusions of progressive internationalism that had doomed Croly during World War I. Like Croly, Wallace came to believe that the war itself would usher in a new era of planned prosperity and international peace.

Wallace's early support for American intervention in Europe had been a factor in Roosevelt's choosing him as his running mate in 1940. Like other progressives, Wallace saw the war as an effort to create what *Nation* editor Freda Kirchwey called a "New Deal for the World." Writing on the eve of American entry into the war, Wallace warned that overthrowing Hitler was "only half the battle . . . Ways must be found by which the potential abundance of the world can be translated into real wealth and a higher standard of living." Wallace declared that a "new order" was "waiting to be created, not the 'new order' which the Nazis talk about . . . but a new order of democracy where security, stability, efficiency, and widely distributed abundance would prevail."

As chairman of BEW and as administration spokesman, Wallace advocated applying the New Deal to the international economy. Against those who contended that the economic relationship between the United States and the poorer nations of Latin America and Africa was a "zero-sum game" in which American prosperity depended on Brazilian poverty, Wallace contended that the best way to eliminate the threat of war was to apply the New Deal's redistributive spending programs to the entire globe. By distributing wealth from the rich countries to the poor, the rich countries would increase the demand for their own goods. "By collaborating with the rest of the world to put productive resources fully to work, we shall raise our own standard of living and help to raise the standard of living of others," Wallace declared in a March 1943 speech.

Roosevelt initially shared Wallace's conception of the war. In 1940, he had said, "If the war does come, we will make it a New Deal war." And other administration members, including Secretary of the Treasury Henry Morgenthau and Under Secretary of State Sumner Welles, also backed the concept of a global New Deal. In 1942, Morgenthau commissioned Assistant Secretary of the Treasury Harry Dexter White to draw up plans for a new monetary system and a bank of reconstruction and development that would internationalize the approaches of the New Deal.

But Wallace and the other left-wing New Dealers went well beyond Roosevelt and the increasingly conservative congressional majority. Like Croly during World War I, Wallace came to think that the national planning and social responsibility inspired by the war and world leadership would become part of a new American system. "The war has brought forth a new type of industrialist who gives much promise for the future," Wallace declared in December 1942. "He is willing to cooperate with the people's government in carrying out socially desirable programs. He conducts these programs on the basis of private enterprise, and for private profit, while putting into effect the people's standards as to wages and working conditions." Even as Roosevelt himself turned away from the New Deal—describing himself as "Dr. Win-the-War" rather than "Dr. New Deal" in a December 1943 press conference—Wallace continued to believe that what he called a "new democracy" would emerge from the war.

Like Wilson and his own Uncle Henry, Wallace became enamored of the idea of an international organization. He thought that this organization—a successor to Wilson's League of Nations—could help administer an international New Deal and prevent further wars. In an April 1941 speech, entitled "Our Second Chance," Wallace blamed the failure of Wilson's League on American isolationists rather than on the President's inability to gain the assent of Britain and France to an equitable postwar settlement. After the war began, Wallace reaffirmed his support for Wilson's vision. "Now at last the nations of the world have a second chance to erect a lasting structure of peace—a peace such as that which Woodrow Wilson sought to build but which crumbled away because the world was not yet ready," he declared.

Wallace conceived of the new world organization as a supranational state with major responsibilities for encouraging economic development and keeping the peace. The new United Nations, Wallace wrote in *The New York Times Magazine* in June 1943, should have its own air force in order to "increase the chance of peace and guard against the chance of war" and should regulate air commerce and access to raw materials in order to "accelerate economic development . . . throughout the world."

Wallace's conception of a UN provoked scorn from the Republican opposition, including newly elected Connecticut congresswomen Clare Boothe Luce, who termed it "messianic Globaloney." But it also drew a mild rebuke from Roosevelt, who had begun to believe that Wallace's views on foreign policy were grounded in dreams rather than reality. Roosevelt had been Assistant Secretary of the Navy in the Wilson administration and as the Democrats' vice presidential nominee in 1920 had doggedly defended Wilson's record at Versailles, but he had become convinced that Wilson should have placed less emphasis on securing the League of Nations and more on winning great-power acceptance of a viable postwar settlement.

During the war's first years, Roosevelt repeatedly rejected Wallace's pleas to concentrate on building a new international organization. Instead, Roosevelt focused on developing a continuing alliance among what he called the "four policemen" —the United States, Great Britain, the Soviet Union, and China. Later, he incorporated his idea of the four policemen into plans for a new United Nations, embodying the four policemen in a Security Council that would make the real decisions in the UN. But he saw the General Assembly as merely a place where the smaller nations could "blow off steam." He rejected Wallace's proposal for providing the UN with an air force and giving it responsibility for international economic development.

Roosevelt's plan far more closely reflected what was possible in a postwar world where the United States, Great Britain, and the Soviet Union remained highly suspicious of each other's intentions. Wallace, like Wilson in 1919, seemed determined to leap beyond the conflicts of the moment to create a new institution that by its very creation could resolve them.

Wallace's determination to create a supranational state also contributed to his unwitting blindness toward the Soviet Union. In 1933, Wallace had opposed American recognition of the Soviet Union because of the Communist state's rejection of religion. "The Russian leadership is so utterly without religion, in our sense of the term, and so bitter regarding things we hold dear," Wallace wrote Secretary of State Cordell Hull. But during the war, Wallace swung to the opposite extreme, joining other progressives in shamelessly celebrating the Soviet Union. Wallace came to believe that the Soviet Union and the United States were converging toward a new kind of democracy—"a practical middle ground . . . between economic and political democracy." In 1942, he praised the Russians, who had two years earlier brutally subdued the Baltics, for going "further than any nation in the world in practicing ethnic democracy." He characterized the Soviet economic system, which was based on forced collectivization, as "designed not to get equality of income but to place a maximum incentive on each individual to produce his utmost."

Wallace's initial enthusiasm was probably the result of wartime support for an ally—evidenced even by Henry Luce—and a superficial understanding of Soviet economics, which he viewed as an advanced form of the New Deal. But Wallace and the progressive movement's continuing defense of Soviet socialism, even after Stalin's intentions in Eastern Europe became clear, demonstrated an unwillingness to allow reality to intrude upon their vision of international peace.

Wallace's will to believe made him an easy mark for Soviet propagandists. In May 1944, Wallace toured Siberia at Roosevelt's request. Afterward, he gushed about the prevalence of hospitals and the availability of French and American literature, comparing Soviet citizens to honest and patriotic rural Iowans. But what Wallace took for a prosperous, happy town was really a large slave-labor camp that the Russians had quickly converted for his benefit.

In contrast to Wallace, Roosevelt acknowledged the darker

side of Soviet reality, but still insisted that the United States had to bring the Soviet Union into a postwar alliance. When the Soviets in November 1944 called on the Warsaw Poles in radio broadcasts to rise against the Nazis, and then stood on the opposite bank of the Vistula as the Nazis slaughtered the Poles, Roosevelt refused to intervene for fear of wrecking post-war negotiations. Wallace, on the other hand, simply refused to believe that the Russians were at fault. When State Department official Charles Bohlen told Wallace precisely what had happened, he attributed Bohlen's version of events to his being "anti-Russian."

The best and worst of Wallace were evident in his response to Henry Luce's American Century article. Luce, the son of Christian missionaries in China, exemplified the evangelizing spirit of American capitalism. His fondest childhood memories were of American troops entering Peking to put down the Boxer Rebellion. In February 1941, Luce wrote a long editorial in *Life*, entitled "The American Century," urging Americans to enter the war on the side of the British against the Germans and Italians. Luce argued that the flame of civilization had been passed from the British to the Americans. If the United States now entered the war, it would do so as Britain's "senior part-ner." He urged Americans to create "the first American century"—a concept that drew heavily from the evangelical tradition. "It now becomes our time," Luce wrote, "to be the powerhouse from which the ideals spread throughout the world and do their mysterious work of lifting the life of man-kind from the level of beasts to what the Psalmist called a little lower than the angels."

Luce also saw the war in Europe as a threat to Anglo-American supremacy and to American access to overseas mar-kets. He warned of an America forced to rely on its own markets and resources. "We know perfectly well that there is not the slightest chance of anything faintly resembling a free economic system prevailing in this country if it prevails nowhere else," Luce wrote. On the other hand, if America prevailed in the war, Luce promised a great commercial empire. "The vision of America as the principal guarantor of the freedom of the seas, the vision of America as the dynamic leader of world trade, has within it the possibilities of such enormous progress as to stagger the imagination," Luce wrote.

In Luce's polemic, he took aim not only at Republican isolationists but also at Wallace and the progressive proponents of a global New Deal. Luce wanted to create an American Century, not in order to internationalize the New Deal, but in order to protect the economic status quo. Luce wanted Americans to use their power to create a new "world-environment" favorable to the "system of free economic enterprise," a code word for a laissez-faire capitalism free from government interference. Luce made one cryptic reference to Wallace's philosophy, attacking "the promise of adequate production for all mankind, the 'more abundant life,' " made by "demagogues and all manner of slick schemes and 'planned economies.' "

Speaking before the Free World Association in New York in May 1942, Wallace answered Luce. He accused *Time's* founder of attempting to replace a British imperial order with an American one. In contrast, Wallace portrayed the war as a battle between "free society" and "slave society" and the century that would emerge from the war as that of the "common man." An Allied victory would mean the elimination of Western imperialism. "No nation will have the God-given right to exploit other nations," Wallace promised. And it would lay the groundwork for a new international organization and a global New Deal in which "freedom from want" would be eliminated.

To Wallace's credit, he rejected Luce's vision of the war as a defense of business individualism. But if Luce's vision of the future was far too conservative—unable to anticipate the spread of social democracy and Keynesianism after the war—

Wallace's embodied all the illusions of progressive internationalism and American evangelism. Wallace saw the war, not
as a continuation of great-power conflicts that had been left
unresolved by Versailles, but as a historic contest between freedom and slavery. He saw the Soviet Union, not as an ally of
convenience, but as an unvarnished partisan in the long march
toward freedom and democracy.

Wallace viewed the war itself through the prism of the Christian Social Gospel. Democracy, he explained in his response
to Luce, "is only the true political expression of Christianity."
Hitler was "the figure of the Supreme Devil operating through
a human form . . . daring to spit straight into the eye of God
and man . . . No compromise with Satan is possible . . . The
people's revolution is on the march, and the devil and all his
angels cannot prevail against it. They cannot prevail, for on
the side of the people is the Lord." And out of the people's
victory would come a postwar millennium in which not merely
the threat of Fascism but the scourge of poverty and the iron
hand of dictatorship would be eliminated.

In 1944, as victory for the Allies neared, the Roosevelt administration was divided on how to deal with the postwar order.
On one side, Wallace, Welles, and Secretary of the Interior
Harold Ickes advocated drawing the Soviets into a new international alliance, overseen by the United Nations. They either
overlooked Soviet designs in Eastern Europe or regarded them
as an entirely legitimate response to Soviet security needs.

On the opposite side, Ambassador to the Soviet Union
Averell Harriman and his second-in-command, Sovietologist
George Kennan, urged the administration to block Soviet initiatives in Eastern Europe, even if so doing imperiled the postwar alliance between the countries. Harriman was already
beginning to draw an analogy between Soviet aggression and

Nazi aggression during the 1930s and to warn of a new Munich if the United States acceded to Soviet wishes. "If the policy is accepted that the Soviet Union has the right to penetrate her immediate neighbors for security, penetration of the next immediate neighbors becomes at a certain time equally logical," Harriman cabled in September 1944.

Roosevelt stood resolutely in the middle of these contending forces. Unlike Wallace, Roosevelt remained committed to a great-power model of diplomacy—willing to accept large nations' domination of their smaller neighbors, whether in Eastern Europe or Latin America. He told *The Saturday Evening Post*'s Forrest Davis that "if he were president of Finland, he would recommend to his people that they make peace on Russia's terms, disband their armed forces, use the savings to improve the country's well-being, and rely on their own good intentions, the self-restraint of Moscow and the moderating influence of an organized world society for security."

More concerned about global security, Roosevelt was willing to let Britain and the Soviet Union divide up Eastern and Southern Europe. Through economic aid, he sought to persuade the Soviet Union to adopt a relationship to Eastern Europe similar to the United States' "good neighbor" relationship to Latin America.

In 1944, Roosevelt's policy still prevailed, while Harriman and Wallace fought each other to a draw, but a succession of events radically altered the policy debate and Wallace's place within the administration. During the months leading up to the Democratic convention in August, conservative Democrats, fearful that Roosevelt would not survive another term, pressured him to replace Wallace on the ticket. They were joined by members of the policy elite who were fearful of Wallace's mystical and utopian proclivities. Influential columnist Walter Lippmann expressed a common concern when he wrote that Wallace's "goodness is unworldly, his heart is so detached from the realities that he has never learned to measure, as a statesman must, the relation of good and of evil in current affairs."

Before the convention, Roosevelt, unwilling to risk division, agreed to Missouri senator Harry Truman as a compromise vice presidential choice—acceptable both to labor and to oilman Edwin Pauley and the conservatives. After the election, Roosevelt made Wallace Secretary of Commerce—a position in which he was no longer intimately involved in foreign policy.

Then in April, as the Soviet Union was consolidating its hold over Poland, Franklin Roosevelt died. With Roosevelt's death, the middle ground disappeared within the administration. Wallace's allies, Ickes and Welles, soon resigned, leaving the Iowan to fight Harriman and his growing supporters within the State and War Departments virtually alone.

But the always independent Wallace would not be cowed. He spoke out in Cabinet meetings and in public used his position as Commerce Secretary to advocate close economic cooperation between the United States and the Soviet Union. This brought about a series of clashes within the Truman administration. In September 1945, Wallace and Secretary of War Henry Stimson argued in vain for the United States to share its atomic secrets (but not its actual bomb-making technology) with the Soviet Union. Over the next year, Wallace repeatedly urged Truman in vain not to cut off economic aid to the Soviet Union. Wallace also denounced Winston Churchill's "iron curtain" speech that year, charging that the British leader was trying to lure the United States into a conflict with the Soviet Union on Britain's behalf.

As the debate evolved, Wallace and his opponents were both working from historical models that didn't entirely fit the postwar period. Harriman and Secretary of the Navy James Forrestal, who complained about Wallace's "global stare," became increasingly wedded to analogies between the Soviet Union and the Nazis—analogies that implied that the Soviets had an unquenchable thirst for conquest. Harriman told Wallace that the United States was "in the same position relative to Russia in 1946 that we were relative to Germany in 1933; that the important thing is to stop Russia before she expands any further." From this view, it followed that any attempt to conciliate the Soviet Union would only lead to further advances—perhaps across Western Europe.

Wallace saw 1946 as 1919. Wallace believed that the seeds of World War II had been planted, not at Munich, but at Versailles, where the Allies failed to curb their own imperial designs through the League of Nations and where they imposed a victor's peace on Germany. In 1946, Wallace thought the victors were again laying the groundwork for a future world war—by allowing British and French imperialism to continue unchecked and by imposing a victor's peace on one of their own allies, the Soviet Union.

Wallace drew a curious analogy between the Soviet Union of the 1940s and post-Wilhelmine rather than Nazi Germany. Unlike the Nazis, Wallace argued, the Soviet Union "never preached war as an instrument of national policy." Wallace argued that the Soviet Union, reined in by an international police force and stimulated by economic incentives, would evolve into a peaceful political democracy. But Wallace warned that if the United States were to deny the Soviet Union aid and block its attempt to secure its borders, then the United States could face "the rise of other madmen at some future time."

This view of the world led Wallace to grasp subtleties that eluded the White House and the State Department. Wallace sensed how provocative and foolish it was to withhold from the Soviet Union knowledge of atomic energy. He also sympathized with anticolonial movements in Asia. He warned against returning Indochina to French rule; and he also insisted—fifteen years before it was widely acknowledged—that the Chinese Communists were not pawns of the Soviet Union. Wallace was also probably more right than wrong about economic aid to the Soviet Union. Withholding aid did not stop the Soviet Union from swallowing Eastern Europe and it cannot be credited with keeping Stalin out of Paris and Rome,

since he never demonstrated any inclination to advance beyond
Eastern Europe. At worst, economic aid might have been a
waste; at best, it could have convinced Stalin to stop short of
colonizing Eastern Europe and to effect a more congenial relationship with the United States.

But gripped by the analogy with 1919 and unwilling to abandon hope of a new international organization, Wallace continued to ignore Soviet transgressions. In 1945, Wallace downplayed Soviet imposition of a Communist government on
Poland, seeing Soviet behavior as a result of "their dire economic needs and of their disturbed sense of security." In February 1946, Wallace told former Ambassador to the Soviet
Union William Bullitt that the Soviet Union had no intention
of imposing "the Communist economic system on the Bal-
kans." He told Truman that "aside from our common language
and common literary tradition, we had no more in common
with imperialistic England than we had with Communist Russia." He continued to insist that the United States and the Soviet
Union were growing "more alike." If anything, Wallace allowed himself to be taken in by the Soviet Union in the same
way that in 1919 Wilson had allowed himself to be taken in
by the French and the British.

As he became isolated within the administration, Wallace
became confused about what he stood for. As a proponent of
supranational organization, Wallace had always been opposed
to spheres of influence. But as the Soviet puppet governments
took charge, he changed course, adopting arguments of foreign
policy realists like Walter Lippmann. Thus in his September
1946 Madison Square Garden speech, he argued that Soviet
claims in Eastern Europe were comparable to those of the
United States in Latin America. But a week later Wallace told
Truman that he wanted to continue speaking about foreign
policy in order to correct the impression that he favored spheres
of influence rather than a one-world perspective. At this point,
Truman was not interested in either version of Wallace's foreign
policy. At the insistence of Secretary of State James Byrnes,

who understandably felt his own policies being contradicted by the Secretary of Commerce, Truman fired Wallace.

Out of government for the first time since 1933, Wallace became the editor of *The New Republic*. As he served as the magazine's editorialist and later as the presidential candidate of the Progressive Party, Wallace's skepticism about the Cold War hardened into dogma. He regularly ascribed the most heinous motives to American policymakers while giving the Soviet Union the full benefit of the doubt. He blamed the February 1948 Communist coup in Czechoslovakia on the U.S. Ambassador and insisted that Czech Foreign Minister Jan Masaryk, whose mysterious death was a major political trauma for anti-Communist democrats, had committed suicide because he had cancer. He regularly accused American officials of wanting to establish a Fascist state. He attributed the 1948 Berlin crisis to an attempt by the American military to use "war hysteria" to "set up an American version of the police state in this country as a necessary part of gaining control of the entire world."

Wallace's presidential campaign proved an embarrassment. Wallace was once again victimized by his own gullibility. He refused to recognize Communist domination of the Progressive Party even after large numbers of liberals had walked out. In the final tally, Wallace got no electoral votes, and only 1.2 million of 50 million votes, half of which came from New York. By comparison, fourth-party candidate Eugene Debs, running as a Socialist in 1912, got 900,000 votes out of about 15 million cast.

After Soviet-armed North Koreans invaded South Korea in August 1950, Wallace abandoned his sanguine view of the Soviet Union. He resigned from the Progressive Party and publicly endorsed the American attempt to repel the invaders. Now Wallace identified Stalin with Hitler. But he continued to insist that the United States should work with Mao's China and oppose the perpetuation of European colonialism. Wallace declared in a 1951 lecture, "Some may say that the United States should fight in Indochina as it fought in Korea because the Truman Doctrine demands that we contain Communism at every point. I say that unless we spend as many billions for helping the people of Indochina as we do on arms to blow up the towns of Indochina, we shall surely lose in the long run."

Wallace deserves considerable credit for seeing the economic reality and the history of Western colonialism that lay beneath the Cold War. Indeed, just before he died in 1965, he again warned against American involvement in Vietnam. "It is hard to see," Wallace wrote, "how we can get out of Vietnam without serious loss financially, politically, and in terms of human lives." Wallace also had a prescient grasp of international economics—recognizing in the 1920s the importance of a free-trade regime to what had become the world's most powerful economy, and seeing in the 1940s how foreign aid and a global New Deal were essential for American postwar prosperity.

Wallace's contribution to domestic political economy was even more significant. As a progressive in the tradition of Croly and the two Roosevelts, Wallace recognized that the people, through their government, had to exercise responsibility for the general welfare. He understood that America's businessmen, if simply left to their own devices, would not necessarily lead America to the promised land, but just as easily into Florida swamps or leveraged buyouts.

As a progressive, Wallace grasped that Americans had to move beyond frontier individualism and the relentless search for short-term profit toward a more cooperative social order. The keynote of the new age, Wallace wrote in his 1934 lectures, *Statesmanship and Religion*, "must be the overwhelming realization that mankind now has such mental and spiritual powers and such control over nature that the doctrine of the struggle for existence is definitely outmoded and must be replaced by the higher law of cooperation . . . The economic and business machine must be subjected more and more to the religious, the artistic, and the deeper scientific needs of man."

But Wallace, like Croly and the pre-World War I progressives, was unable to reconcile the promise of domestic reform with the imperatives of American world leadership. Both men—and the movements they represented—fell prey to the illusions of evangelism that, in assuming leadership, Americans—and even the world—would embrace progressivism's domestic agenda. Croly suffered fatal disillusionment in 1919, as his wife read him the text of the Versailles agreement. Wallace suffered a more ignominious fate, as he chased the will-o'-the-wisps of utopian internationalism and Soviet-American convergence into the 1948 election, suffering a bitter defeat that precipitated his withdrawal from politics.

# 3

# Walter Lippmann, George Kennan, Paul Nitze, and the Origins of the Cold War

"Then you think it's just sin," Hopkins asked, "and we should
be agin it?"
"That's just about right," Kennan replied.

—Conversation between Harry Hopkins and George Kennan
in Moscow, 1945 (GEORGE KENNAN, *Memoirs 1925–1950*)

In July 1947, George Kennan, the director of the State Department's newly created Policy Planning Staff, published an article anonymously in *Foreign Affairs* entitled "The Sources of Soviet Conduct." It laid out the strategy of "containment" that Kennan had first clearly articulated in an 8,000-word telegram from Moscow the year before and had become the official American strategy. "George Kennan," Henry Kissinger wrote later, "came as close to authoring the diplomatic doctrine of his era as any diplomat in our history."

In September 1947, Walter Lippmann wrote a series of columns in which he accused Kennan of defining the U.S.-Soviet conflict so that it could be resolved only by the collapse of the Soviet Union. The strategy, Lippmann charged, committed the United States to a wartime mobilization that it could ill afford and to a diplomacy dictated entirely by the Soviet Union. It defined America's mission in negative terms, as the negation of the Soviet Union.

Reading Lippmann, Kennan suddenly realized that he had

misstated and overstated his own position. "I can still recall the feeling of bewilderment and frustration with which I read these columns," Kennan wrote in his *Memoirs*. What most disturbed Kennan was that he "profoundly agreed" with many of the views that Lippmann counterposed to his own. The following spring, lying in bed at the Bethesda Naval Hospital being treated for ulcers, Kennan wrote Lippmann a letter clarifying what he had written. Yet he never sent it.

Kennan finally did get a chance to explain when he ran into Lippmann two years later on a train trip from Washington to New York. He treated the columnist to a long monologue, leaving him little chance to respond. But by then there was no reason for disagreement. The diplomat had resigned from the Policy Planning Staff and had joined Lippmann as a critic of Washington's Cold War strategy. Kennan's place in the State Department had been taken by a former investment banker, Paul Nitze, with whom Kennan had clashed repeatedly during the year. Nitze represented the culmination of those Cold War views that Lippmann had attacked and that Kennan now repudiated.

Kennan, Lippmann, and Nitze spanned the range of sophisticated debate that divided official Washington during the first years of the Cold War after Truman had ousted Henry Wallace. Unlike Wallace, Lippmann, Kennan, and Nitze were realists who believed that American foreign policy must be based on a balance of power rather than on supranational organization or international law. Unlike the right-wing anti-Communists who envisioned the Cold War as a struggle of good against evil and God against Satan, they looked upon the United States and the U.S.S.R. as locked in a battle for power. Yet in the end they advanced very different strategies for America and different conceptions of the American Century. Nitze's conception, which prevailed, amounted to a reductio ad absurdum of realism—realism in the service of a new Cold War evangelism.

By the time he criticized Kennan's article in *Foreign Affairs*, Walter Lippmann had long been America's most influential columnist, an important political philosopher, and an adviser of Presidents and Secretaries of State. He was not above making policy as well as influencing it through his writing. In 1940, anxious about Britain's survival in the face of the Nazi submarine onslaught, Lippmann convinced the British Ambassador to trade English bases in the Atlantic for American destroyers and then sold the deal to the Roosevelt administration and the public in his column.

Lippmann's views were by no means conventional. He was a realist and agnostic in an era of renewed American evangelism, a progressive at a time when liberals sought to emulate Soviet socialism and conservatives wanted to undo liberalism. He had been one of the first progressives to denounce the Soviet dictatorship, yet he advocated American recognition of the Soviet Union throughout the 1920s, and after World War II pressed for an accommodation with America's former wartime ally. In the 1930s, he was the darling of anti–New Deal Republicans; in the 1960s, he became a hero of antiwar Democrats.

The key to Lippmann's outlook was his objectivity, which, borrowing from Croly, he called disinterestedness. He never allowed himself to become so attached to a politician that he abandoned his critical perspective. He was one of the few intellectuals of his generation who were swept up neither by Soviet Bolshevism nor by Cold War anti-Communism. He regarded Fascism and Communism—the great ideologies of the period between the two world wars—as historical rationalizations rather than genuine theories of history. He envisioned America as an island nation whose peculiar history and foreign relations reflected geography rather than God's providence.

And he saw the conflicts among nations as the result of inequalities of power rather than of virtue.

Lippmann's perspective was partly a product of his background, but also of his experiences during World War I. Lippmann, born in 1889, was the only child of a wealthy German-Jewish family in New York. Lippmann's parents were second-generation Americans who raised their son to assimilate into the American upper class. Educated at private schools and at Harvard, Lippmann later became the only Jewish member of Harvard's Board of Overseers and one of the few Jewish members of exclusive New York and Washington social clubs.

Like other German-American Jews of his generation, he adopted a manner designed to distinguish himself from the stereotype of the vulgar, loud Eastern European Jew. (In 1923, he would sympathize with Harvard president Lawrence Lowell's attempt to set quotas on Jewish admissions to Harvard.) Lippmann was reserved and aloof, fearful of chaos, open display of emotion, and deep political passion. He was an agnostic, and in his *Preface to Morals* defended what is now called secular humanism. And he projected the same values onto the great conflicts of nation and world. He distrusted popular democracy and craved stability. He was skeptical of idealism and ideology. He was inclined to look past the great political passions of the moment toward the historical forces and geographical realities that lay beneath them.

Lippmann was a member of the Harvard Class of 1910, along with the journalist John Reed, the author of *Ten Days That Shook the World*, and poet T. S. Eliot. He quickly made a name for himself on campus as a social critic and fledgling philosopher. He and Reed founded Harvard's Socialist Club, and Lippmann became a favorite student of philosophers George Santayana and William James. After graduation, Reed captured in verse the positive and negative sides of Lippmann's reserve:

Lippmann,—calm, inscrutable,
Thinking and writing clearly, soundly, well;

All snarls of falseness swiftly piercing through,
His keen mind leaps like lightning to the True;
His face is almost placid—but his eye—
There is a vision born to prophecy!
He sits in silence, as one who has said:
"I waste not living words among the dead!"
Our all-unchallenged Chief! But . . . one
Who builds a world and leaves out all the fun,—
Who dreams a pageant, gorgeous, infinite,
And then leaves all the color out of it,—
Who wants to make the human race and me,
March to a geometric Q.E.D.

Out of college, Lippmann went to work briefly for muck-raking journalist Lincoln Steffens and then served for four months as the assistant to the newly elected socialist mayor of Schenectady, resigning because the mayor seemed more con-cerned with ensuring his reelection than with advancing a rad-ical program. Even then, however, Lippmann was a far cry from a working-class socialist like Eugene Debs or Big Bill Haywood. At Harvard, Lippmann had become interested in the Fabian socialism of George Bernard Shaw and Sidney and Be-atrice Webb—an elite socialism of enlightened managers who would administer society and industry on behalf of the working class. Lippmann shared the American socialists' concern for poverty and their opposition to capitalist greed and immorality; he also supported creative governmental power; but he had no faith in the working class's ability to govern itself and he retained a skepticism about vesting absolute power in a cen-tralized state. Lippmann's socialism was really a variation of middle-class progressivism, very similar to what Croly advo-cated in *The Promise of American Life*. In 1912, Lippmann voted for Wilson rather than for Debs, and in his first book, *A Preface to Politics*, published in 1913, he explicitly renounced socialism, warning that it would result in "that great bureaucratic tyranny which Chesteron and Belloc call the 'servile state.' "

In 1914, Lippmann joined Croly as an editor of *The New Republic*. Like the other editors, Lippmann was caught off guard by the outbreak of war in Europe that August. As he admitted later, he believed that war "was an affair that 'militarists' talked about and not something seriously-minded progressive democrats paid any attention to." But after a year of war Lippmann was promoting Anglo-American unity against Germany. His aim was not making the world safe for democracy, but preserving the Anglo-American maritime alliance on which American freedom of the seas and commerce depended.

While tilting toward Great Britain, Lippmann favored the United States taking the steps toward a new international organization that would stabilize relations among nations. When Wilson endorsed the proposal for a League to Enforce the Peace in May 1915, Lippmann called the President's speech "a decisive turning point in the history of the modern world. There is something intensely inspiring to Americans in the thought that when they surrender their isolation they do it not to engage in diplomatic intrigue but to internationalize world politics." Like Henry Wallace's grandfather, Lippmann looked toward supranational organization as a way to end war altogether.

In 1916, Lippmann was one of the few progressives who clearly saw—in view of the Anglo-American alliance—that the United States was heading inexorably to war. While Charles Beard, Randolph Bourne, and other progressives backed Wilson in the 1916 presidential election because they thought he would keep the country out of war, Lippmann perceptively wrote Croly, "What we are electing is a war president, not someone who kept us out of war." When the Germans renewed submarine warfare against American shipping in January 1917, which they had suspended the year before because of American protests, Lippmann called for war. "Our own existence and the world's order depend on the defeat of that anarchy which the Germans misname 'freedom of the seas,'" Lippmann wrote the next month. "The world's highway shall not be closed to Western allies if America has the power to prevent it."

Soon Lippmann left *The New Republic* to become an assistant to the Secretary of War, Newton Baker, and in Washington he met a rising young politician, Franklin Roosevelt. In October 1917, at the behest of Wilson's chief aide, Colonel Edward House, Lippmann became the secretary of "the Inquiry," a group of scholars and other policy experts who were entrusted with drafting the terms the United States would propose for ending the war. Three months later, Lippmann furnished the White House with a draft of peace terms that became the basis for Wilson's "Fourteen Points," which the President announced to Congress in January 1918. These included freedom of the seas, open diplomacy, and the reduction of tariffs, as well as the creation of a "general association of nations," the adjustment of colonial claims taking into account "the interests of the population concerned," and the settlement of outstanding European territorial disputes.

But Lippmann was not to play a role in the actual peace negotiations at Versailles. By the time the talks began in January 1919, Wilson was no longer relying on Lippmann's sponsor, Colonel House, for advice. After helping House present the Fourteen Points to the French and British negotiators, Lippmann found his services were no longer needed, and in January 1919, he left Paris to return to New York and to *The New Republic*, where, along with Croly, he greeted the announcement of the treaty's terms—the impossible reparations burden it imposed on Germany and the "Balkanization" of Austria-Hungary—with bitterness and disbelief. Like Croly, Lippmann believed that the treaty laid the groundwork for another war. "It will require at least a generation of force to secure the execution of this treaty," Lippmann declared in a speech in Boston. Lippmann himself wrote *The New Republic*'s editorial opposing the treaty and secretly aided the Senate Republicans trying to block its ratification.

Lippmann's assessment of Wilson's League of Nations would vary over the next decades, but Lippmann remained critical of Wilson for ignoring the realities of power among nations and for framing American objectives in what he called "idealistic" terms. The experience of World War I and Versailles reinforced Lippmann's tendency to discount moralism and ideology in analyzing America's aims and those of other nations.

In January 1922, Lippmann resigned from *The New Republic* to write editorials for the New York *World*, rising eventually to become the newspaper's executive editor. When the *World* folded in 1931, he began writing a syndicated column for the *New York Herald Tribune*. During these decades, Lippmann developed a strain of progressivism that was markedly different from Croly's in the 1920s and from that of the new generation of progressives who wrote for *The New Republic* and *The Nation* in favor of central economic planning. Croly, disillusioned with the role of business during the 1920s, had come to espouse a more democratic progressivism, but Lippmann turned even more toward the elitist bent of Croly's *Promise*. Lippmann, who never held popular democracy in high esteem, learned from the war how easily the government could manipulate public opinion. In two books written in the 1920s, *Public Opinion* and *The Phantom Public*, Lippmann argued that the public, because of its limited access to information, was inherently incapable of making decisions about American policy. In *Public Opinion*, he argued for government through specially organized "intelligence bureaus"—a proposal that sounded as if it had been lifted directly out of the works of Auguste Comte.*

* Herbert Croly valued Lippmann as a journalist rather than as a philosopher, complaining in 1930 that Lippmann's "journalistic habit of mind" made it impossible for him to do justice to the subject matter of *A Preface to Morals*. Lippmann's works on public opinion bear out Croly's assessment. They stand up as political essays, not as philosophy. In both *Public Opinion* and *The Phantom Public*, Lippmann encumbered his theory of journalism with questionable theories borrowed from contemporary Anglo-American philosophers. These philosophers, including Bertrand Russell and C. I. Lewis, argued that persons constructed reality out of sense data. Thus each person's reality was inherently different, because it reflected his or her own limited perspective on reality. Lippmann used this metaphysical argument to suggest that the American

Lippmann did not share the positive view that many progressives (although not Croly) had of the Soviet Union. While he opposed Wilson's and the Allies' attempt to erect a *cordon sanitaire* around the Soviet Union and advocated American recognition of the Bolshevik government, he had no illusions about the regime itself, describing it along with the governments of Germany and Italy as "primitive tyrannies" driven by mobilization for war. Unlike leftists of the 1920s and 1930s, he didn't think that the United States would do well to emulate Soviet national economic planning. Influenced by the Austrian critics Friedrich von Hayek and Ludwig von Mises, Lippmann believed that full-scale national economic planning—where the state itself becomes the employer of the citizenry—was inherently incompatible with political liberty. It vests insuperable power in state officials to perpetuate their own rule.

Lippmann's fears about centralization were carried over to the New Deal. While he supported Roosevelt's emergency measures during his First Hundred Days, he was highly critical of the Second New Deal of 1935 and Roosevelt's Court-packing scheme—seeing the President's attempt to curb the judiciary and increase the power of the executive as steps toward an American collectivism. In his major work of the 1930s, *The Good Society*, Lippmann tried to reconcile his progressivism with his fear of political and economic centralization. While warning against attempts to replace private industry with government, Lippmann also rejected "the political dogma of laissez-faire." He urged government support for conservation, education, social welfare, and labor bargaining rights and the use of Keynesian countercyclical fiscal policy to prevent future depressions. (Lippmann, who had first met Keynes in 1919, championed his economic theories in the 1930s.) But he stopped short of endorsing the kind of government supervision of corporations

---

populace had an imperfect grasp of political reality, but in fact it could be used to demonstrate that no one, including the members of Lippmann's intelligence bureaus, had a grasp of reality. The problem was that these metaphysical theories were open to the skeptic's contention that if one could experience only sense data, one had no basis for judging what reality was. Reality itself vanishes.

favored by Theodore Roosevelt and left-wing New Dealers like Henry Wallace and Rexford Tugwell.

At the time, Lippmann's prescriptions and warnings fell between the political cracks. Many of the bankers and businessmen to whom Lippmann had been close in the 1920s wanted to eliminate the New Deal altogether, while liberals and leftists such as popular economist Stuart Chase and *New Republic* editor George Soule wanted to combine Soviet-style national economic planning with parliamentary democracy. But in fact Lippmann's views in *The Good Society* represented the underlying trend of the Roosevelt administration and would become the guideline for Democratic liberals and Republican moderates for the next three decades—to be abandoned only in the 1980s with the return of laissez-faire conservatism.

During Hitler's first years in power, Lippmann deferred to the strong isolationist feelings in the United States. He also displayed his cultivated disinterest through his refusal to base foreign policy on a nation's internal practices. When he described the Nazi persecution of the Jews, Lippmann's realism obscured the true horror of reality. "By satisfying the lust of the Nazis who feel they must conquer somebody," Lippmann wrote in 1933 in his column, the persecution of the Jews "is a kind of lightning rod which protects Europe." As Hitler began to arm for battle, Lippmann worried aloud that the United States would face another world war. Writing in *Foreign Affairs* in 1937, Lippmann warned that if Britain lost control of the Atlantic, "all that is familiar and taken for granted, like the air we breathe, would suddenly be drastically altered." Lippmann never came to terms with the Holocaust. It was his most grievous failing—moral and personal.

In 1938, Lippmann criticized the Munich agreement as a misguided and cowardly attempt to turn Hitler toward the East and toward war with the Soviet Union. When war finally broke out in Europe, Lippmann began advocating intervention—cautiously in his column, but more vigorously behind the scenes to his administration connections. He also urged the United States to reach an agreement on China with the Japanese so that it could concentrate on the threat from Hitler, but when the Japanese took advantage of the German attack on the Soviet Union to move into Southeast Asia, Lippmann changed course and backed the administration's sanctions against the Japanese.

As he had done during the debate over American entry into World War I, Lippmann urged intervention on realistic grounds, arguing that a Nazi victory over Great Britain would threaten Anglo-American control of the seas and choke off trade routes. He became concerned when the administration, led by Wallace and Welles, framed the war as another crusade for democracy. In 1942, he began working on a book that would express his misgivings. *U.S. Foreign Policy: Shield of the Republic* was published the next spring, and it remains one of the outstanding works on American foreign policy.

In this book, Lippmann argued that American foreign policy should be based directly on America's capabilities and "vital interests" rather than on the "mirages" of idealism. In *The Promise of American Life*, Croly had rewritten the history of American politics; now Lippmann rewrote the history of American diplomacy. He divided that history into three stages. In the first, beginning with the American Revolution and ending with the Monroe Doctrine of 1823, American leaders decried "entangling alliances" with European powers, but in fact depended upon temporary or even permanent alliances to achieve their goals. As Lippmann recounted, President James Monroe and his Secretary of State, John Quincy Adams, committed themselves to preventing further foreign colonization of the Western Hemisphere only after obtaining the tacit consent of Britain and the British Navy. Otherwise, the United States would not have been able to back up its words.

From 1823 to 1898, the nation lived in a "state of illusory isolation." Americans believed that they could keep their commitments without "entangling alliances," whereas in fact the defense of the hemisphere required the support of British sea power. But at the turn of the century, America's situation changed utterly. Germany began to challenge Britain's control of the seas and to make incursions into Asia, Africa, and Latin America. As a result of the war against Spain in 1898, the United States emerged as a global power, extending its perimeter of commitments from the Western Hemisphere to the Philippines. In 1901, emboldened by its success at Manila, the United States even pledged to uphold the territorial integrity of China, albeit with British cooperation.

According to Lippmann, Theodore Roosevelt understood that America, to meet its commitments, had to have the necessary military and economic power and political support at home, and where its own power would not suffice, it had to have the backing of other great powers. Roosevelt rushed to build a strong navy, began constructing the Panama Canal (which linked defense of the Atlantic and that of the Pacific), and forged an alliance with Britain to uphold America's commitments. But Roosevelt's successors, William Howard Taft and Woodrow Wilson, did not understand this principle of solvency, or balancing of ends and means.* "Both were idealists who habitually rejected the premises of the politics of power," Lippmann wrote. "In them the idealism which prompts Americans to make large and resounding commitments was combined with the pacifism which causes Americans to shrink from the measures of force that are needed to support the commitments . . . Both abhorred as inherently vicious and unnecessary, and as contrary to American principles, the formation of alli-

* In *The Promise of American Life*, Croly made a very similar critique of American foreign policy. Urging Americans to abandon the principle of isolation, Croly lamented that "the American habit is to proclaim doctrines and policies, without considering either the implications, the machinery necessary to carry them out, or the weight of the resulting responsibilities."

ances. But both favored a League of Nations in which the
United States assumed the obligation to enforce peace."

After Theodore Roosevelt, Lippmann argued, American foreign policy had become "insolvent"—it failed to match its capabilities to its commitments, either through the threat of
force or the power of alliances. Lippmann attacked the very
premises of Wilsonian diplomacy. Wilson had tried to rein in
the great powers through a system of "collective security," but,
Lippmann now argued, collective security had to be based on
a preexisting alliance among the great powers. An international
organization like the League of Nations "could not be maintained unless within it there existed an alliance of strong and
dependable powers."

Lippmann had even greater contempt for the isolationists of
the 1920s and 1930s. They had agreed to limit American naval
power to less than that of Japan while maintaining American
commitment to the territorial integrity of China. Then, in the
1930s, they had shunned "entangling alliances" with their former allies in Europe. "The isolationist party adhered, on the
whole, to our vast trans-oceanic commitments," Lippmann
wrote. "They devoted their efforts to opposing the alliances
which, as is now obvious, we needed in order to validate the
commitments."

Lippmann argued that Americans had to recognize that their
commitments were, historically, the defense of the Atlantic
community and the Western Pacific against hostile powers.
Lippmann warned against replacing these concrete ends with
"a set of ideals which were incompatible with all the means
of achieving any ideals." These included the ideals of peace,
disarmament, global democracy, and collective security. And
Lippmann insisted Americans had to acquire the power to meet
these commitments—through their own arms and through alliances with other great powers. American foreign policy had
to become "solvent."

In *U.S. Foreign Policy: Shield of the Republic*, Lippmann applied
these principles to the question of what kind of settlement the

United States should seek from World War II. He rejected out of hand the Wilsonian approach of Wallace and Welles. Instead, Lippmann urged that a postwar peace be based on a "nuclear alliance" among the United States, Great Britain, and the Soviet Union. Lippmann maintained that regardless of contending ideologies, the Soviet Union had been a "natural ally" of the United States since the Revolutionary War. "Historic experiences show . . . that Russia and the United States . . . have always been antagonistic in their political ideology, always suspicious that close contact would be subversive. Yet each has always opposed the dismemberment of the other." Moreover, Lippmann warned that "a settlement which was such that it could be maintained only by aligning American, and therefore also British, military power against Russia in Europe would set the stage inexorably for a third World War in Europe and in Asia as well."

Lippmann's prescription for a postwar settlement was very similar to Roosevelt's conception of the "four policemen"— and perhaps even had some influence on the President. In 1943, Lippmann's support for a U.S.-Soviet alliance seemed far from controversial. But the way he understood the U.S.-Soviet relationship—as an alliance *in spite of* Soviet ideology and internal oppression—and his rejection of both "one world" and isolationist prescriptions set him off from large numbers of Americans on the left and the right. As U.S.-Soviet relations chilled, these differences would become more pronounced.

Lippmann's analysis provided a primer in how to think about American foreign policy, but it had some weaknesses. As it would turn out, Lippmann was overly optimistic about what it would take to reach a postwar agreement with the Soviet Union. In 1943, he thought it would be sufficient to assure the neutralization of Eastern Europe. In his next book, *U.S. War Aims*, published in 1944, Lippmann conceded that the Soviet Union would have to enjoy hegemony in Eastern Europe, which would have to be part of a "Soviet orbit" in the way that Latin America was part of the United States' sphere of influence. Wanting to square his proposals with American support for democracy, and with his own assumption that over the long run only Soviet democratization could ensure a lasting peace, he continued to underrate the Soviet regime's determination to subjugate its citizens and to dominate rather than control the Soviet Union's neighbors.

Lippmann also underestimated the underlying popular opposition to his own approach. He argued that his realism was in line with the "common sense" of the majority of Americans. For instance, he suggested that if Wilson had explained to the public his real reasons for entering World War I—protecting the Atlantic highway rather than making the world safe for democracy—the public would have been far more amenable afterward to an interventionist foreign policy. But as the Cold War years would reveal, most Americans, and certainly most of their political representatives, were unwilling or unable to accept the premises of a realistic foreign policy.

George Kennan rose from being a truculent, unhappy, and obscure aide at the U.S. embassy in Moscow—given to bouts of depression and threats of resignation—to become the most famous diplomat of his generation and an architect of America's Cold War strategy. His rise was the product of his persistence, eloquence, and original point of view. These were the same qualities that would eventually lead to his fall from power.

Kennan was always the loner, the outsider, and the dissenter. He was born in Milwaukee in 1904, the youngest child of a railroad attorney. His mother died immediately after his birth, and he was raised by a distant father, already fifty-two at the time Kennan was born, and an indifferent stepmother. He spent much of his youth reading and imagining that he was somewhere other than where he was. His father sent him to St. John's Military Academy in Wisconsin and then to Princeton, where Kennan kept largely to himself, refusing to join one of the social clubs that functioned like fraternities. He was, he writes in his *Memoirs*, "an oddball on campus, not eccentric, not ridiculed or disliked, just imperfectly visible to the naked eye."

After graduation, Kennan applied to the newly established Foreign Service, and was one of eighteen admitted out of several hundred applicants who took a competitive examination. He served two years in Europe, and then, moved by the example of his grandfather's cousin, the first George Kennan, a famous writer-explorer who had exposed the Czar's prison camps in Siberia, he applied to become a Russian specialist. In 1930, Kennan was posted to the American consulate at Riga, Latvia, where he learned Russian and also absorbed the White Russian hatred of the Bolshevik regime, and then to Berlin, where, under instructions from his State Department superior, he studied pre-Bolshevik history and culture. In 1933, when the United States established diplomatic relations with the Soviet Union, he secured an appointment as an aide to the new ambassador, William Bullitt.

Kennan brought an unusual political sensibility to his job. Like Lippmann, he identified himself as a member of a governing class, but Kennan's affinities were as much European as American. His heroes were Gibbon, Tocqueville, and Chekhov. Like Ortega y Gasset and Brooks and Henry Adams, he disdained popular democracy as a threat to higher culture. He saw the Soviet Union in this peculiar light—detesting it, not for its lack of democracy, but for its totalitarian suppression of "spiritual and cultural development." He saw the conflict with the Soviet Union, not as one between freedom and slavery, but as one between civilization and barbarism.

Kennan displayed little allegiance to his family's Presbyterian background, but he liked to tell the story of the exchange that he had with Franklin Roosevelt's closest aide, Harry Hopkins, when Hopkins, several weeks after the President's death in April 1945, visited Moscow to calm the growing tensions between the U.S.S.R. and the Truman administration. Hopkins had wanted to reach an agreement with Stalin on Poland, but Kennan, seeing the Soviets as evil incarnate, insisted that the United States have nothing to do with an arrangement that allowed the Soviets to dominate its neighbor. "Then you think it's just sin, and we should be agin it?" Hopkins asked Kennan. "That's just about right," Kennan replied.

From his years in Riga and Berlin, Kennan acquired a contradictory view of the Soviet state and its foreign policy. Was the Soviet Union an updated version of Czarist Russia—a nation-state with limited imperial ambitions? Or was the Soviet Union a revolutionary state bent on world domination? The Kennan trained in Berlin saw the Soviet Union as a variation on Czarist Russia rather than a new revolutionary regime that had radically broken with the past. He saw the emerging class distinctions of Soviet society as "a mirror image of the feudal institutions Russia had so recently rejected." Unlike other officials and analysts, he never took Soviet Marxism seriously, seeing it, he said later, as a "pseudo-science, replete with artificial heroes and villains."

The Kennan who served in Riga saw the Soviet government as a revolutionary regime bent on world domination. He opposed American recognition of the Bolshevik regime, explaining in a letter to a friend in 1931 his belief that

the present system of Soviet Russia is unalterably opposed to our traditional system, that there can be no possible middle ground or compromise between the two, that any attempts to find such a middle ground, by the resumption of diplomatic relations or otherwise, are bound to be unsuccessful, that the two systems cannot even exist together in the same world unless an economic cordon is put around one or the other of them, and that within twenty or thirty years either Russia will be capitalist or we shall be communist.

When Kennan was in the Soviet Union during the 1930s, his hatred of Russia knew no bounds, overshadowing his insights into Soviet society and foreign policy. He even preferred Nazis to Bolsheviks. In 1935, he minimized the threat of Nazi Germany (it would take the "wildest stretch of the imagination" to conceive of Hitler expanding eastward, he wrote), while warning that the Bolsheviks were "revolutionary communists" and the "most unalterable opponent of any peace in the West." After the Nazi invasion of the Soviet Union in 1941, he opposed aiding the Soviet Union. In his *Memoirs*, Kennan summed up his attitude toward the Soviet Union. "Never . . . did I consider the Soviet Union a fit ally or associate, actual or potential, for this country."

In June 1944, after serving in Washington, Berlin, Lisbon, and London, Kennan returned to Moscow as Ambassador Averell Harriman's second-in-command. It was a pivotal time in U.S.-Soviet relations. That October, negotiations took place between Stalin and British Prime Minister Winston Churchill in Moscow, with Harriman present, during which Britain accepted Soviet hegemony in Eastern Europe in exchange for continuing British domination of the Mediterranean, including Greece. But just as Churchill never divulged to his public what he had done, Roosevelt never justified or explained to Congress or the American public the arrangement Churchill had worked out, setting the stage for massive disillusionment with the Soviet Union when it appeared to be violating wartime agreements.

In the United States, the administration and Congress were split over postwar policy toward the Soviet Union. The realists, including Roosevelt and Lippmann, hoped to draw the Soviet Union into a great-power alliance after World War II—if necessary, through granting the Russians territorial concessions in Eastern Europe. The neo-Wilsonians, including Wallace and

Welles, vested hope for a postwar settlement in the United Nations, while refusing to believe that the Soviet Union had designs on Eastern Europe. The neo-isolationists and hard-line anti-Communists, including Republican Majority Leader Robert Taft and *Time* editor Whittaker Chambers, rejected any alliance with or concession to the Soviet Union.

Immediately after Kennan's return, he wrote an extended report, "Russia—Seven Years Later," which he sent back to Washington.* Unlike his earlier or later writings, it rested on a more historical view of the Soviet Union. Kennan did not present Russia as a Marxist megapower determined to take over the world, but rather as an imperial state determined to prevent further threats against its territory. And he presented Stalin as the successor of the Czars. After the purges of the 1930s, Kennan wrote, Stalin "settled firmly back into the throne of Peter the Great and Ivan the Terrible . . . The ship of state had been cut loose from the bonds of Communist dogma."

Kennan attributed Soviet designs in Eastern Europe to traditional fears of invasion. "The men in the Kremlin have never abandoned their faith in that program of territorial expansion which had once so strongly commended itself to Czarist diplomatists," he wrote. This program "was intended to prevent the formation in Central and Eastern Europe of any power or coalition of powers capable of challenging Russian security." Russia's historic fear of invasion had been reinforced by the Bolshevik experience after World War I. "The Soviet leaders have never forgotten the weak and vulnerable position in which the Soviet regime found itself in the early days of its power," Kennan wrote.

Although Kennan's reasoning in these memoranda implicitly supported Roosevelt's and Lippmann's argument for a Soviet-American postwar alliance based upon the mutual recognition

* In his *Memoirs 1925–1950*, written when he had abandoned his postwar views, Kennan describes this essay as "a better paper, broader, more balanced and more specific than the so-called X-Article."

of spheres of influence, the diplomat didn't draw these conclusions. Instead, driven by his own hostility to the Soviet Union, he concluded that the United States should threaten the Soviet Union with the loss of aid and diplomatic cooperation if it did not grant full independence to Eastern Europe. The next year, he spelled out this position in a report he sent back to the State Department, entitled "Russia's International Position at the Close of the War with Germany."

In this paper, Kennan again drew an analogy between the Stalin regime and "Czardom's policies of western expansion in the eighteenth and nineteenth centuries," but he took the analogy one step forward. Just as the Czars' attempt to absorb these "indigestible" areas laid the foundation for their own overthrow, so too the Soviet expansion would lead imminently to the collapse of the Bolshevik regime. Kennan predicted that "another five or ten years should find Russia overshadowed again by those clouds of civil disintegration which darkened the Russian sky at the outset of this century."

Kennan called on the United States to hasten this disintegration by denying the Soviet Union "moral and material support" for the consolidation of Russian power through Eastern and Central Europe. If it did this, "Russia would probably not be able to maintain its hold successfully for any length of time over *all* the territory over which it has today staked a claim."

But why should the United States seek to prevent Communist governments in Poland, Romania, and Bulgaria, which Stalin and Churchill had agreed to in 1944? Kennan did not provide an answer in his 1945 memorandum, because within the terms of his own analysis he did not have one. But in the 8,000-word telegram that he sent back in response to a routine administration request for information about Soviet foreign policy, Kennan shifted the grounds of his analysis, and in so doing laid the basis for what would be called his containment strategy.

In this missive, later dubbed the "Long Telegram," Kennan took aim at both the remaining realists who sought an accommodation with the Soviet Union in spite of its policy toward

Eastern Europe and the left-wing internationalists like Wallace who sought to justify or explain away Soviet behavior. Kennan tried to show that unless the United States adopted an active policy of containment, the Soviet Union could potentially threaten not merely Poland but the United States itself.

Kennan now rejected what he had written a year before. Instead of seeing Soviet behavior in Eastern Europe dictated by insecurity engendered by previous invasions and encirclement, he now spoke of Soviet fears as mere pretext. "To speak of possibility of intervention against USSR today," Kennan wrote, "is sheerest nonsense." Instead, Russian insecurity was the product of "inner-Russian necessities." While Kennan didn't impute the Marxist quest for world Communism to the Soviet Union, he did imply that the Soviet leadership had limitless ambitions. "Whenever it is considered timely and promising, efforts will be made to advance official limits of Soviet power," he wrote. "This is only in line with basic Soviet instinct that there can be no compromise with rival power and that constructive work can start only when Communist power is dominant."

As he had done in 1931, Kennan portrayed a Soviet Union bent on destroying the United States:

> In summary, we have here a political force committed fanatically to the belief that with US there can be no permanent modus vivendi, that it is desirable and necessary that the internal harmony of our society be disrupted, our traditional way of life be destroyed, the international authority of our state be broken if Soviet power is to be secure.

But even though Kennan portrayed the Soviet Union as a threat to Western security, he stopped short of counseling a military response. Instead, he defined the threat in political terms and called for the West to counter it by internal measures. "Much depends on the health and vigor of our own society. World communism is like a malignant parasite which feeds only on diseased tissue," Kennan wrote. "Every courageous and incisive measure to solve internal problems of our own society . . . is a diplomatic victory over Moscow worth a thousand diplomatic notes and joint communiqués."

Kennan's analysis in the Long Telegram stood up well against that of Wallace and those leftists who were determined to ignore Soviet advances in Eastern Europe. But Kennan overstated Soviet aims in Eastern Europe and in the rest of the world. As scholarship has now confirmed, Stalin was determined to dominate the Baltics, Poland, Bulgaria, Romania, and East Germany, but he held off Communists in Hungary, Czechoslovakia, Greece, and Yugoslavia. (Yugoslavia's Tito simply ignored him.) Stalin told Communists in France and Italy to abandon any plans of winning state power, whether through insurrection or election.*

Where Stalin moved beyond his initial reach, he did so either because he felt threatened by the United States or by dissension within Communist ranks. Stalin's takeovers in Hungary and Czechoslovakia came after the United States made clear that it planned to divide Europe and to rebuild Western Europe and the Western zone of Germany. Stalin repeatedly tried to stop the Greek Communists, who were aided largely by the Yugoslavs. The Soviets finally backed the Greek Communist bid for power in order to compete with Tito, but they didn't extend military aid until July 1947, after the Truman administration sent military aid to the conservative Greek government. As Kennan had earlier observed, Stalin's Russia acted exactly like the Russia of the Czars. It was an imperial power with real but limited aspirations in Europe. But although Kennan would later acknowledge this, he allowed himself to feed contrary fears in those early postwar years.

Kennan was also tragically mistaken in dismissing Soviet

* On this subject, see Charles Gati, *Hungary and the Soviet Bloc* (Durham: Duke University Press, 1986); Robert H. McNeal, *Stalin: Man and Ruler* (New York: New York University Press, 1988); and Peter Stavrakis, *Moscow and Greek Communism, 1944–1949* (Ithaca: Cornell University Press, 1989).

fears as mere pretext. The Cold War was largely triggered by each country's fearing the worst of the other without taking the other's fears of it seriously. Eight months after Kennan sent his telegram to the State Department, the Soviet Ambassador to the United States, Nikolai Novikov, sent a telegram to the Soviet Foreign Minister in Moscow that almost exactly mirrored Kennan's. Novikov warned that the United States, in "striving for world supremacy," was preparing for war against the Soviet Union, "which in the eyes of the American imperialists is the main obstacle in the path of the United States to world domination."

Kennan's telegram arrived at the critical juncture in the debate over U.S.-Soviet policy. Realists were on the defensive, and Wallace himself was isolated. The war's end had brought a resurgence of Republican isolationism and conservative anti-Communism, making the realistic strategy politically unpopular, if not untenable. When Truman's Secretary of State, James Byrnes, tried to make a deal that would allow the Soviet Union control of Bulgaria and Romania, he was widely denounced in Congress as an appeaser.

At the same time, many would-be realists within the administration, such as Under Secretary of State Dean Acheson, became increasingly piqued with the Soviet Union—not because of its intransigence in Poland or Romania, but because it seemed determined to impose on Germany and even on Japan the kind of victor's peace that had wrecked the settlement of World War I and helped to precipitate World War II.

Acheson first became angry when he led a State Department negotiating team in 1945 to decide on funding for the United Nations Relief and Rehabilitation Administration. "As far as the Russians were concerned, the organization existed to give prizes for fighting Hitler," Acheson wrote in his memoir, *Present at the Creation*. According to Paul Nitze, Acheson finally lost his patience with the Soviets when they refused to modify the Allied agreement to allow Japan to increase its level of industry.

Kennan's telegram was seized upon by those like Secretary of the Navy James Forrestal who were advocating a hard line against the Soviet Union. Saying, "We must prepare for war," Forrestal made the telegram required reading for military officers under him and from that moment became Kennan's patron within the Truman administration. Even Truman read the Long Telegram. That spring of 1946, Kennan, a minor celebrity, was summoned back to Washington, where he was appointed a lecturer at the War College and sent on a lecture tour to promote the administration's foreign policy. "My reputation was made. My voice now carried," Kennan recalled in his *Memoirs*.

Back in the United States, Kennan threw himself into the factional battles of the Truman administration. In October, after Truman had fired Wallace, Kennan publicly attacked the former Commerce Secretary for "the warmth of his sympathy for the cause of Russian communism" and for "fatuous gestures of appeasement." He lent a hand in and profusely praised a provocative report on U.S.-Soviet relations prepared after Wallace's ouster by Truman's Special Counsel, Clark Clifford, and Special Assistant George Elsey. The Clifford-Elsey report asserted that the Soviet Union was preparing for a military conflict with the United States and might "fight at any time for the twofold purpose of expanding the territory under communist control and weakening its potential capitalist opponents."

In early 1947, Kennan prepared for Forrestal a paper on Soviet strategy expanding on the Long Telegram, and with the approval of the State Department, submitted it for publication in *Foreign Affairs*, where it was published anonymously (signed "X") in the July 1947 issue. Even more explicitly than in the Long Telegram, Kennan argued that Soviet expansion in Eastern Europe had nothing to do with historic fears of invasion. "There is ample evidence that the stress laid in Moscow on the menace confronting Soviet society from the world outside its borders is founded not in the realities of foreign antagonism but in the necessity of explaining away the maintenance of dictatorial authority at home," Kennan wrote.

Kennan also made more explicit his own strategy of containment, but this time (perhaps because of his immediate audience) appeared to emphasize military "counter-force" rather than political will:

> The Soviet pressure against the free institutions of the Western world is something that can be contained by the adroit and vigilant application of counter-force at a series of constantly shifting geographical and political points, corresponding to the shifts and maneuvers of Soviet policy, but which cannot be charmed or talked out of existence.

Such a strategy, Kennan asserted, would result in "either the breakup or the gradual mellowing of Soviet power."

In May 1947, before the article appeared, Kennan was appointed director of the newly established State Department Policy Planning Staff, where he wrote speeches and policy directives for Secretary of State George Marshall. Along with Nitze, who was working in the Office of International Trade Policy, Kennan helped to inspire the Marshall Plan, which sent billions to revive Western Europe's economy.

When the article appeared that summer, *New York Times* columnist Arthur Krock revealed that Kennan was its author. Now Kennan became a national figure. The article was excerpted in both *Life* and *Reader's Digest*. And "containment" became the official term for U.S. strategy. But at the height of his fame, Kennan began to experience misgivings about the foreign policy his writings had helped to spawn. The agent of his disillusion was none other than Walter Lippmann.

In the first postwar years, Lippmann had continued to press for a continuation of the wartime alliance among the United States, Great Britain, and the Soviet Union. He had hoped that by bringing the Russians into the Marshall Plan, the United States could lay the basis for a settlement in Europe, but was disappointed when the Soviets, angered by American insistence that it contribute to rather than receive Plan funding, walked out of talks in June 1947. That summer, vacationing in Maine, Lippmann read Kennan's article in *Foreign Affairs* and decided to write a response; it would run in twelve columns in September.

Lippmann took particular umbrage at Kennan's strategy of applying "counter-force at a series of constantly shifting geographical and political points." Such a strategy violated Lippmann's principle of solvency by forcing the United States to develop a military force sufficient to counter Soviet or Communist incursions anywhere in the world. "How, for example, under the Constitution of the United States is Mr. X going to work out an arrangement by which the Department of State has the money and the military power always available in sufficient amounts to apply 'counterforce' at constantly shifting points all over the world?" Lippmann asked. For Lippmann, such a strategy meant the militarization of American society to fight what he called a "Cold War." Just as Kennan had coined the term "containment" in his essay, Lippmann introduced the term "Cold War" into the American political lexicon.

Lippmann did not believe that it was necessary to fight this kind of war against the Soviet Union. He accused Kennan of treating Russia as a Marxist state aiming for world rule rather than as a successor to the prerevolutionary Czarist regimes that, seeking to protect their flank against Central European foes, had also expanded into Eastern Europe. "Mr. X has neglected even to mention the fact," Lippmann wrote, "that the Soviet Union is the successor of the Russian empire and that Stalin is not only the heir of Marx and of Lenin but of Peter the Great, and the Czars of all the Russians."

Lippmann rejected both ways in which Kennan had framed the Soviet threat: either as omnipresent military force or as (in the Long Telegram) a "malignant parasite" that could invade the body of Western civilization. Lippmann downplayed both the military ambition of the Soviet Union and the appeal of Soviet Marxism to the United States or Western Europe. The Soviet threat, if any, consisted of the presence of its armies in Central Europe facing those of the United States and Great Britain. Lippmann's way of dealing with the Soviet Union was through trying to negotiate a settlement by which all the Allied armies from World War II would withdraw from Central Europe, leaving Germany united but neutral. To win Soviet consent, the United States should, if necessary, offer a "ransom." By contrast, he charged, Kennan's strategy was based on accepting the division of Europe in the hope that within ten or fifteen years the Russian regime would mellow or collapse under American pressure. "At the root" of Kennan's analysis, Lippmann charged, was "disbelief in the settlement of the issues raised by this war."

Lippmann's analysis challenged above all the conception of America's place in the world that Kennan and the other Cold War planners were increasingly accepting. Lippmann charged that Kennan, on the basis of a mistaken analysis of the Soviet Union, was dragging America into a military and "ideological crusade" that would transform American society beyond recognition. Worst of all, Kennan was allowing what he imagined to be Soviet foreign policy to dictate America's mission in the world. "It is not leadership to adapt ourselves to the shifts and maneuvers of Soviet policy," Lippmann wrote.

Kennan was deeply disturbed by Lippmann's criticism—not least because it was based on analyses of Soviet behavior that

Kennan himself had made three years before. Kennan also realized that Lippmann had seized upon a disastrous ambiguity in his essay to imply that he favored a primarily military doctrine of containment directed wherever Communism should rear its head. Kennan could justifiably tell himself that he didn't support the strategy that Lippmann attributed to him, but he realized that he had nonetheless given that impression. But most important, Lippmann's essay crystallized growing doubts in Kennan's mind about how the Truman administration was applying his strategy of containment.

Kennan's first hint of difference with the Truman administration's policies had come in March 1947, when the United States decided to aid the Greek government against a Communist insurgency. Kennan backed the initial request for aid, but objected to the way that Truman and Acheson, eager to win congressional backing, publicly formulated the request. To win support from a reluctant, Republican-controlled Congress, Truman dramatized the Greek threat, portraying it as the first step of a global Communist military offensive, and as a conflict between freedom and slavery:

> The disappearance of Greece as an independent state would have a profound effect upon those countries in Europe whose peoples are struggling . . . to maintain their freedoms . . . collapse of free institutions and loss of independence would be disastrous not only for them but for the world . . . should we fail to aid Greece and Turkey in this fateful hour, the effect will be far-reaching to the West as well as to the East.

Kennan was particularly annoyed at one passage in Truman's speech announcing what would be called the Truman Doctrine. Truman said, "I believe it must be the policy of the United States to support free peoples who are resisting subjugation by armed minorities or by outside pressures. I believe we must assist free peoples to work out their own destinies in their own way." In his *Memoirs*, Kennan explained: "This passage, and others as well, placed our aid to Greece in the framework of a universal policy rather than in that of a specific decision addressed to a specific set of circumstances." Kennan also objected to dividing the world "into Communist and 'free world' components, to avoid specific recognition of specific differences among countries on either side."

In the last months of 1947, as he groaned under an attack of ulcers that would soon hospitalize him, Kennan reconceptualized his view of the Soviet Union and his doctrine of containment in the light of Lippmann's criticisms. Kennan returned to the view of Soviet intentions that he had presented in 1944 in "Russia—Seven Years Later." Now he saw the Soviet Union as a nation within a complex international balance of power, responding to provocation as much as creating provocations of its own. The next year, for instance, Kennan imputed the Soviet coup in Czechoslovakia and the Berlin blockade to Western attempts to create a de facto division of Europe through the Marshall Plan, the development of a West German state, and the creation of a Western European military alliance. Later, he would see the Korean War as in part a Soviet response to America's separate peace with Japan and the continuation of American military bases on Japanese soil.

Kennan also made explicit what had been implicit in his earlier views: that he did not believe that the Soviet Union threatened Western Europe militarily. "We do not think the Russians, since the termination of the war, have had any serious intentions of resorting to arms," Kennan told a War College audience. He advocated using the Marshall Plan to inoculate Western Europe against Communist political subversion, and he now joined Lippmann in pressing for negotiations toward the unification and neutralization of Germany and the withdrawal of both American and Soviet armies.

Kennan clarified his military strategy. He didn't think that the United States needed or was able to counter Soviet or Communist advances everywhere. Instead, he told a War College audience, it should limit itself to defending the concentrations of military and industrial power in Western Europe and Japan. And he rejected the need for a military buildup aimed at matching Soviet conventional forces. Instead, he thought the United States merely needed highly mobile divisions capable of intervening in the case of isolated crises. He was adamant in opposing American intervention in China. A Communist China, Kennan argued, would eventually prove a thorn in the Soviet side. "I can't say to you whether Titoism is going to spread in Europe," he prophetically told a War College audience in 1948, but "I am almost certain that it is going to spread in Asia."

Over the next two years, Kennan repeatedly dissented from administration policy. In November 1947, he proposed secret negotiations with the Soviet Union aimed at a neutral Central Europe. He objected to the plan for setting up NATO (the North Atlantic Treaty Organization) as an anti-Soviet alliance and to plans to establish an independent West German government. In November 1948, he warned Secretary of State Marshall that NATO's formation reflected "a general preoccupation with military affairs, to the detriment of economic recovery and of the necessity for seeking a peaceful solution to Europe's difficulties."

Kennan also advanced his own plan for negotiating a neutral, unified Germany with the Soviet Union, but Acheson, who became Secretary of State at the beginning of 1949, dismissed Kennan's initiative. Kennan then argued unsuccessfully for including the Soviet Union in the final settlement of the Pacific war and for withdrawing American troops from Japan. By 1949, he felt totally isolated within the administration. He wrote in his diary in November:

The heart of the difficulty lies in the fact that my concept
of the manner in which our diplomatic effort should be
conducted is not shared by any of the other senior officials
of the department; and that the Secretary is actually dependent on these officials, for better or for worse, for the
execution of any foreign policy at all.

Kennan's defeat was partly his own fault. In his Long Telegram
and X article, he had helped to formulate the doctrine that
guided the United States in the late 1940s. The militarization
of containment, which he deplored, followed nevertheless from
his warnings about Soviet expansion. But Kennan would probably have been defeated no matter how eloquently he stated
his position. By the late 1940s, America's Cold War policy had
in great part become a hostage to domestic politics.

Domestically, the administration, in attempting to win support for the Truman Doctrine and the Marshall Plan from a
Republican-controlled and penurious Congress, shamelessly
exaggerated the Soviet threat to Western Europe and, by extension, to the United States. The Marshall Plan, for instance,
was intended as much to prevent the recurrence of another
depression by reviving European markets for American goods
as to insulate Western Europe against Communism, but administration policymakers—worried about isolationist opposition
to foreign aid—justified it as a Cold War measure. A committee
chaired by Secretary of Commerce and former Ambassador to
the Soviet Union Averell Harriman reported that aid was necessary because

the first major battle in the Cold War is being fought in
Western Europe. It is cold only in the sense that guns
aren't smoking and bombs and guided missiles are not
exploding. In every other respect the ideological war of
the Communists is as ruthless and as determined a drive
to achieve world domination as a hot war.

The Republicans were eager to up the anti-Communist ante, as was FBI Director J. Edgar Hoover, whose appropriations depended upon fanning fear of the Red Menace. By the late 1940s, America was in the throes of a full-scale Red Scare, and Truman and Acheson (who had defended his longtime associate Alger Hiss) were on the defensive. In this overheated atmosphere, any gesture at negotiations with the Soviet Union would have been instantly denounced as appeasement.

Events themselves seemed to lend credence to the fears of Communist world domination. Wartime illusions about Soviet democratization were shattered by the savage repression that followed the war's end. When the Communists won power in China in 1949, a year after the Soviet Union had consolidated its hold over Eastern Europe, it seemed as if the world was turning Red. Arguments by Kennan and even Acheson that the Soviets had initially opposed and would one day rue the Chinese Communist success went unheeded; for their part, the Republicans tried to blame the loss of China on Democratic appeasement. Then in September 1949 the Soviets tested an atomic bomb. Even sober policymakers, with access to government intelligence, began to imagine the United States locked in a life-or-death struggle.

In March 1950, Robert Lovett, who had been Marshall's Under Secretary of State and would become Secretary of Defense, met with State Department officials to assess the Soviet threat. Lovett's private words of 1950 echoed the public exhortations of 1947. "We must realize that we are now in a mortal conflict; that we are now in a war worse than any we have ever experienced. Just because there is not much shooting as yet does not mean that we are in a Cold War. It is not a Cold War; it is a hot war. The only difference between this and previous hot wars is that death comes slowly and in a different fashion."

When the policy elite joined in spouting the rhetoric of the Republican right, Kennan was entirely alone. His words no longer had any impact on administration policy. He resigned as director of the Policy Planning Staff in September 1949. The immediate reason was that Acheson decreed that his staff's papers would no longer be routed directly to the Secretary of State, but would be reviewed first by lesser officials. Kennan was replaced by his deputy, Paul Nitze, who, ironically, embodied exactly those views—and more—that Lippmann had imputed to Kennan in his criticisms of the X article. Nitze's ascension meant that both Lippmann and Kennan had been eclipsed.

Like them, Paul Nitze fancied himself a realist concerned with the balance of power and immune to ideological crusades. But his fascination with the quantification of power contributed to a new Cold War theology in which the United States was always at the verge of being obliterated by a Soviet nuclear attack. Nitze's approach to the Cold War became the reductio ad absurdum of Lippmann's and Kennan's realism. It was realism in the service of an evangelical vision of America fighting for God's way against a satanic enemy.

Nitze, born in 1907, grew up in the neighborhood of the University of Chicago, where his father was a professor of Romance languages. Both Nitze's parents were of German extraction, and to Nitze's consternation, his uncle, Paul Hilken, was a German agent and saboteur in the United States during World War I. Nitze himself recalled first becoming interested in world politics when he played the role of German Foreign Minister Walther Rathenau in a sixth-grade play about Versailles. "I shared his view that the peace treaty lacked justice, consistency, and proper purpose," Nitze wrote later in his memoirs.

Nitze attended Hotchkiss and Harvard, where he met Charles "Chip" Bohlen, a close friend of Kennan's in the Foreign Service and Roosevelt's translator at Yalta. After graduation, Nitze joined the Wall Street investment banking firm Dillon, Read & Co. But he remained fascinated by world affairs. After a trip to Germany in 1937, where he read Oswald Spengler's *Decline of the West*, Nitze decided to take a year off from business and read history and politics at Harvard. Afterward, Nitze returned to investment banking, but his primary interest lay elsewhere. In 1940, when Roosevelt asked Dillon, Read's managing partner, James Forrestal, to come to Washington and set up a brain trust, Nitze followed him.

In the 1930s, Nitze was sympathetic to Hitler, impressed by his economic achievements. At one dinner-party conversation that made its way into FBI files, Nitze even argued that he would rather see the United States under Nazi than British rule. Nitze and Forrestal both believed that the Bolshevik government was a far greater menace than the Nazis. Even as Nitze helped Forrestal design a selective service system, he opposed entry into the war in Europe. But when the Japanese bombed Pearl Harbor and Germany declared war on the United States, Nitze enthusiastically backed the government war effort.

For the first war years, Nitze worked as a staff member of Henry Wallace's Board of Economic Warfare (BEW), supervising the imports and exports of strategic materials from Latin America. In 1944, Nitze became a member of the Strategic Bombing Survey, which studied the impact of aerial bombardment on Germany and Japan, including the effects of the atomic bombs dropped on Hiroshima and Nagasaki. He emerged from the experience with the notion that atomic warfare was an extension of, rather than a break with, conventional warfare. He was impressed by the survival rate of the Japanese who had time to climb into air-raid tunnels. In 1946, when he returned to the United States, he advised New York city planner Robert Moses to put bomb shelters in all new city buildings. "Paul, you're absolutely mad," Moses responded.

That year, Nitze became deputy director of the Office of International Trade Policy in the State Department under Will Clayton, where he helped lay the foundation for the Marshall

Plan. Estimating that America would run a $5 billion trade surplus for 1947, primarily with Europe, Nitze reasoned that if wealth continued flowing out of Europe at this rate, the Western European nations would be bankrupt by 1952, and the United States would have nowhere to sell its goods. In a memo to Clayton, he recommended a massive aid program. When the final decision on the Marshall Plan was reached in May 1947, it was based as much on Nitze's reasoning as on the reasoning of those who were concerned that an impoverished Europe would be vulnerable to Communist subversion. And he contributed the method by which the Marshall Plan administrators calculated Europe's financial needs.

But while Nitze's job didn't directly concern U.S.-Soviet relations, he remained vitally concerned about the growing conflict. Nitze retained a fierce hatred of the Bolsheviks and was always ready to believe the worst about their intentions. In February 1946, for instance, Nitze read the translation of a speech that Stalin delivered proposing three new five-year plans. It was an amazingly innocuous speech. Stalin blamed the war on the "unevenness of development in capitalist countries"—a standard Marxist analysis—but also described the United States and Britain as "freedom-loving states." Yet Nitze read the speech as a "declaration of war" against the United States. "I went over to see Forrestal about it; he fully concurred in my opinion," he reported in his memoirs. When Nitze told Acheson his interpretation of the speech, however, Acheson said, "Paul, you see hobgoblins under the bed. They aren't there. Forget it."

Nitze also took sides in the growing debate in 1948 between Marshall and Forrestal, who had become Secretary of Defense in 1947 when the new Cabinet position was created. Marshall favored concentrating American resources on economic recovery in Europe in the hope that the Europeans could learn to defend themselves against both the political and the military threat of Communism, but Forrestal favored military preparation for a possible war with the Soviet Union or for deterring the Soviets from initiating one. Nitze shared Forrestal's fear of war, but he had a much more expansive view of the budget than either Marshall or Forrestal. Nitze believed that if Americans were convinced of the Soviet threat, they would support a much larger military and foreign aid budget, making it possible for the United States to rebuild Europe and to prepare for war. He got a chance to argue his case in August 1949.

Nitze had first met George Kennan on a train ride from New York to Washington in 1944, when Kennan was just about to leave to return to Moscow. Nitze was impressed by Kennan's warnings about the Soviet Union, and Kennan liked him. When Kennan set up his Policy Planning Staff in 1947, he asked Acheson, who was then Under Secretary of State, to include Nitze. Acheson, who was worried that Nitze lacked a broader vision, vetoed the choice. In the summer of 1949, however, Acheson, who became impressed with Nitze's work on the Marshall Plan, finally approved Kennan's request to make him his deputy. When Kennan announced his resignation in September, Nitze was designated as his successor.

By this time, it had become obvious that Nitze and Kennan had grown apart in their views. Kennan gave priority to political containment. He did not believe large-scale war between the two superpowers was imminent. Kennan thought that in assessing the Soviet threat, what was important was gauging, through history and politics, what the Soviets might do, and then meeting that challenge. Nitze believed that the military balance was the basis for overall containment. He believed that the United States must base its strategy simply on what the Soviet Union was capable of doing; in assessing the Soviet military threat, Nitze was inclined to take the most pessimistic estimate.

Later, Kennan explained to journalist Strobe Talbott how Nitze operated:

Paul was in one sense like a child. He was willing to believe only what he could see before him. He felt comfortable with something only if it could be statistically expressed. He loved anything that could be reduced to numbers. He was mesmerized by them . . . Of course, the numbers were predicated on a total theoretical hostility that had to be assumed to give these figures meaning . . . When there was talk of intentions, as opposed to capabilities, he would say, "How can you measure intentions? We can't be bothered to get into psychology; we have to face the Russians as competitors, militarily. That's where I come in."

Nitze's differences with Kennan crystallized that September after the United States discovered that the Soviet Union had exploded an atomic bomb. Acheson called Nitze and Kennan into his office to gain advice on how the Soviet nuclear capability affected American strategy, and whether the United States should now go ahead with building a thermonuclear H-bomb, called the "super." In meetings of the Policy Planning Staff, the two men squared off. Nitze argued that the United States should now undertake a civilian defense program and should build the super. "The burden of proof should fall on those who say that there would be no power advantage to the country developing it," he said at a November 3 meeting of the Policy Planning Staff.

Kennan took the opposite tack. He argued that now that the Soviet Union had acquired nuclear weapons, they were useless as weapons since neither nation would risk its own destruction by using them. He saw the weapons themselves as a threat to civilization that had to be resisted as wholeheartedly as Soviet Communism. Kennan thought the United States should maintain a sufficient number of atomic weapons to provide a deterrence against attack while attempting to reach an arms agreement with the Soviet Union banning or drastically limiting the weapons. Kennan rejected the view that the Soviet Union would attempt to use them first in war; and he wanted the United States to join the Soviet Union in pledging no first use. At the November 3 meeting, Kennan argued that if the United

States were to initiate building the H-bomb without trying to negotiate arms control, "wouldn't we be pushing the Russians against a closed door and demanding that they go through it?"

If building the super was an isolated question of policy, Nitze probably had the better of the argument. The Soviet Union had already begun building an H-bomb, and if the United States had not gone ahead with its own, the Soviets might have been able to use their superiority in a crisis to pressure the United States to back down. But as Kennan sensed, far more than the bomb itself was at stake in the debate. Nitze's argument—and the argument of those who supported him—rested on two premises that would come to characterize American Cold War strategy for much of the next four decades.

First, Nitze assumed that in seeking to contain the Soviet Union, what counted above all was matching or exceeding their military capabilities, regardless of what one might think they might do with these capabilities. This was necessary not only to counter any contingency but also (in the case of American nuclear superiority) to be able to exert pressure on the Soviets. From this followed the arms race. Second, Nitze and his supporters assumed that it would be impossible to negotiate meaningfully with the Soviet Union, whether on arms control or on Germany, so long as it remained a Communist state. Thus, Nitze and Acheson never considered Kennan's proposal to negotiate arms control with the Soviet Union prior to building the H-bomb. They equally rejected (and with good reason) Kennan's prediction in his *Foreign Affairs* article that the Soviet Union would soon collapse or mellow under the pressure of containment. Those who favored the H-bomb viewed the world as riven inexorably by military confrontation between the United States and the Soviet Union.

Seeing the world through the prism of military capability encouraged policymakers like Nitze to assume the worst about the size of the Soviet arsenal and about whether it would be used. Thus, Nitze and others didn't stop at comparing the strength of American and Soviet forces. Nitze first assumed that the Soviets had undertaken a nuclear first strike, and then measured whether the United States would be able afterward to withstand Soviet power. If it could not, then the United States was in danger. Over the next three decades, Nitze became the principal proponent of what his critics called "threat inflation"—discovering the "missile gap" of the late 1950s and the "window of vulnerability" of the late 1970s.

Kennan lost the debate over the H-bomb. On January 31, Truman decided to go ahead with building it. The next month, Nitze and Kennan, now serving as Counselor to the State Department, offered Acheson widely divergent estimates of the world situation. Nitze warned that the Soviet Union could be about to start a major war in Europe. According to Nitze, the danger of war "seemed considerably greater than last fall . . . There are an increasing number of signs of toughness on the part of the Kremlin. The informal opinion of the Joint Chiefs now is that the Soviet Union could begin a major attack from a standing start." Nitze characterized the Soviet Union as being guided by a "messianic faith" spurring it "to assist the transformation of the Marxist blueprint into reality."

Kennan countered that "there is little justification for the impression that the 'Cold War,' by virtue of events outside of our control, has suddenly taken some drastic turn to our disadvantage." He insisted that the Russians have "no intention of launching a military attack on the rest of Europe at this juncture. Our best hope of avoiding catastrophe lay in . . . concentrating on the strengthening of the resistance of other countries to Soviet political aggression." Indulging in his own kind of overstatement, Kennan once more used the metaphor of an infectious illness to characterize Communism. "Primarily Communism had to be viewed as a crisis of our own civilization, and the principal antidote lay in overcoming the weaknesses of our own institutions."

At the same meeting in which Truman approved building the H-bomb, he also commissioned his National Security Council to draft a new Cold War strategy statement that would reflect the Soviet acquisition of the atomic bomb. Acheson and Nitze maneuvered responsibility for the new draft out of the NSC and onto a joint State and Defense Department committee that Nitze could chair. But to gain full control, they had to fight Secretary of Defense Louis Johnson for the right to define American defense priorities and the nature of the conflict between the United States and the Soviet Union.

Since 1947, the Truman administration, fearing deficits, had been pledged to a $14 billion ceiling on defense expenditures. Johnson, a political appointee who had dreams of running for President, was committed to upholding Truman's pledge, but Nitze believed that in order to meet the Soviet threat, the United States would at least have to quadruple its defense budget. Nitze would have preferred to finance the new expenditures through higher taxes, but he was convinced by Truman's Keynesian economic adviser, Leon Keyserling, that budget deficits from military spending would actually stimulate rather than stifle the economy. (Keyserling himself preferred increasing social rather than military expenditures.)

At the first meeting of the new committee, Defense Department representative Major General Truman Landon presented a paper portraying the U.S.-Soviet military balance as favorable to the United States and calling for the United States to keep beneath the $14 billion ceiling. Nitze and his allies launched an attack on Landon's paper, which Landon himself, who did not share Johnson's budgetary priorities, failed to resist. Nitze gained control of writing the document. NSC-68 was drafted by Nitze's assistant Robert Tufts, but the final wording and the ideas belonged to Nitze.

The argument of NSC-68 repudiated everything Lippmann and later Kennan had argued. In the name of realism, it was a brief for an evangelical anti-Communism—an ideological crusade against Soviet Communism. It promoted a war psychology, encouraging Americans to subordinate their quest for domestic well-being to the struggle against international Communism. Its portrayal of the Soviet Union reflected the same kind of misdirected paranoia that Kennan had attributed to the Soviets.

NSC-68 portrayed the Soviet Union as if it had emerged without a history in 1917. No hint of Russia's Czarist past or of past alliances between the United States and Russia could be found in the document. Russia was presented as a Marxist nation guided by a messianic ideology of world conquest. "The Soviet Union," the document announced, "is animated by a new fanatic faith, antithetical to our own, and seeks to impose its absolute authority over the rest of the world." The document also failed to acknowledge any division, either existing or potential, within the Communist camp. Instead, the Soviet Union was represented as the leader of a monolithic "international communist movement" arrayed against the "free world."

Nitze's document depicted the conflict between the United States and the Soviet Union as a contest between "freedom" and "slavery," echoing Wallace's characterization of World War II as a battle between "free society" and "slave society." According to NSC-68, the United States itself was in "mortal danger" and "the deepest peril" from the Soviet threat. "The integrity and vitality of our system is in greater jeopardy than ever before in our history," the document stated. Paramount was the military threat. Using highly exaggerated and tendentious estimates of the Soviet military and economy and worst-case projections of the American economy, the document asserted that if defense expenditures continued at their current level, the Soviet Union would be able to defeat the United States by 1954 in an "initial surprise atomic attack."*

In addition, the document echoed and amplified J. Edgar

---

* In 1990, Soviet and American historians met to compare notes about the origins of the Cold War. According to Stephen Ambrose, writing in *The New York Times* (December 27, 1990), one of the things Soviet historians told the Americans was that "in the early 1950's, American intelligence grossly overestimated the Soviet nuclear arsenal. At a time when the U.S. had about 1,000 atomic bombs, the Soviets had 20 or 30, with no delivery capability. The Soviet leaders were terrified of a U.S. first strike, which they were incapable of preventing. At no time did the Red Army contemplate, much less plan for, what the West most feared: a Red Army offensive over the Elbe River and through West Germany."

Hoover's fright-mongering of an omnipresent Communist subversion. "The preferred technique is to subvert by infiltration and intimidation. Every institution of our society is an instrument which it is sought to stultify and turn against our purposes. Those that touch most closely our material and moral strength are obviously prime targets, labor unions, civic enterprises, schools, churches and all media for influencing opinion."

NSC-68 saw no hope for successful negotiations between the United States and the Soviet Union. "We can expect no lasting abatement of the crisis unless and until a change occurs in the nature of the Soviet system," the document declared. Its strategy for containment was exactly that which Lippmann had earlier attributed to Kennan. According to NSC-68, the United States could not permit Communist expansion anywhere. "Any substantial further extension of the area under the domination of the Kremlin would raise the possibility that no coalition adequate to confront the Kremlin could be assembled." In more metaphysical terms, it stated that "a defeat of free institutions anywhere is a defeat of free institutions everywhere." There was a straight line between these assertions and America's later involvement and defeat in Vietnam.

To gain military superiority over the Soviet Union, and to mount a global defense of the "free world," NSC-68 called for "greatly increased general air, ground and sea strength, and increased air defense and civil defense programs." On Acheson's advice, Nitze did not put numbers in NSC-68 for fear of alarming the President and Congress. Nitze also deferred to politics and omitted pleas for new taxes, arguing instead on Keynesian grounds that the new expenditures would "increase the gross national product by more than the amount being absorbed for additional military foreign assistance purposes."

In conclusion, NSC-68 called on the American people to assume a war footing. "The whole success of the proposed program hangs ultimately on recognition by this Government, the American people, and all free people, that the Cold War is in fact a real war in which the survival of the free world is at stake."

During the drafting of NSC-68, Nitze invited policy experts to address the committee, but even though Nitze was not a specialist in the Soviet Union—he did not even know Russian—he did not invite any experts on the Soviet Union to visit the committee. Kennan himself was in Latin America and was not consulted. But Bohlen, upon returning from France, obtained a copy of Nitze's draft and sent him polite but scathing criticisms. Bohlen questioned the document's statement that "the fundamental design of the Kremlin is the domination of the world." Bohlen continued:

> If by this is meant that this is the chief purpose and, as it were, the raison d'être of the Kremlin, this carries the implication that all other considerations are subordinate to this major purpose and that great risks would be run for the sake of its achievement. It tends, therefore, to over-simplify the problem and, in my opinion, leads inevitably to the conclusion that war is inevitable, which then renders [moot]* the statement of our objectives, i.e. the frustration of the Soviet design by peaceful means and the possibility of bringing about thereby a reorientation of Soviet policy to an extent which would permit the peaceful coexistence of the two systems.

Bohlen also commented on Nitze's commitment to contain Communism wherever it appears. If this criterion of defense were used, Bohlen warned, "it would seem to entail a defense establishment beyond anything that is reasonable since in order to defend the areas of the world not now under Soviet domination . . . would appear to imply a defense establishment in time of peace which would involve almost full-time war mo-

* The term "moot" or same equivalent is omitted from Bohlen's sentence, but is clearly implied.

bilization in the United States and the Atlantic pact countries." Indeed, this was exactly what Nitze had in mind.

Bohlen wryly described the "section on a free versus slave society" as "worth retaining as supplementary reading." "This might be very good material for publication, speeches, or other media but tends to detract the reader's attention from the central core of this paper," he wrote. But Nitze retained those sections and made only one cosmetic change in the draft, rewriting a sentence that had explicitly stated the Soviet Union's goal to be the domination of the world, while retaining different formulations of the same idea throughout the document.

Acheson, to whom Nitze submitted the document at the end of March, recognized that it was based on an exaggeration of the Soviet threat, but he saw its hyperbole as a useful weapon in the battle to convince Truman and the rest of the Cabinet to accept the document's substantive recommendations. "The purpose of NSC 68," Acheson wrote in his memoirs, "was to bludgeon the mass mind of 'top government' that not only could the President make a decision but that the decision could be carried out." But Nitze didn't seem to share Acheson's cynical approach. Four decades later, Nitze was still defending the integrity and accuracy of the formulations in NSC-68. Nitze, the realist, became swept up in the fear generated by his own numerical projections. He came to believe the apocalyptical warnings in his own document.

Acheson passed NSC-68 on to Truman for his signature on April 7, but the President, reluctant to endorse such sweeping increases in the military, let the document sit on his desk. He might never have signed it had it not been for the Korean War, which broke out two months later. The Korean War was the final link in the chain of confirmation that led to the acceptance by the public and the policymaking elite of Cold War evangelism. It seemed to suggest exactly what Nitze had predicted: the beginning of a large-scale war with the Soviet Union.

Yet the Korean War, like the war in Greece and the later war in Vietnam, defied easy explanations. It was rooted in the

Korean peninsula's past, when the country was colonized by the Japanese before being partitioned by the victorious Allies. According to recent Soviet disclosures, Stalin had initially tried to discourage the North Koreans from invading the South, but had finally endorsed the action after his rival as Communist leader, Mao Zedong, gave the North Koreans his blessing. When the war began, the Truman administration refused to take advantage of repeated opportunities—well noted by Kennan at the time—to divide the Soviets and the Chinese and return to the *status quo ante bellum*. Indeed, Kennan argued at the time that the United States should regard the conflict as a "civil war," but NSC-68's view of the Communist monolith had won out.

The formal adoption of NSC-68 by the Truman administration that fall signaled the end of the debate on U.S.-Soviet policy that had begun when Lippmann published *U.S. Foreign Policy: Shield of the Republic* in 1943. Lippmann and Kennan had lost. The vision of America and its role in the world that ultimately emerged from the late 1940s bore little resemblance to the one that Lippmann had described in *The Good Society*. What Lippmann had said then of the Soviet Union—that it was a society driven by the fear of and preparation for war—had become true of the United States too.

For the next fifteen years—until the war in Vietnam revealed the underside of NSC-68—the debate in Washington would be over the details rather than the thrust of that document— how rapidly to expand the military, the extent of the Soviet threat, and whether America was taking seriously its role as the defender of God and freedom.

# 4

# Whittaker Chambers

## The Cold War as Armageddon

In this fiction, everything, everybody is either all good or all bad, without any of those intermediate shades which, in life, complicate reality and perplex the eye that seeks to probe it truly.

—WHITTAKER CHAMBERS, review of *Atlas Shrugged*, 1957

On August 3, 1948, a pudgy, unkempt man sat at the witness table at a hearing of the House Un-American Activities Committee. The committee had called him as an afterthought—to back up the testimony three days earlier of Elizabeth Bentley, dubbed the "Red Spy Queen" by the tabloids, who had claimed that thirty-two government officials in the Roosevelt administration had supplied her with documents which she had passed on to Soviet intelligence. When the committee's chairman, Karl Mundt, learned that a *Time* senior editor had told the FBI of Communist infiltration of government, he had had him subpoenaed as a supplementary witness.

That sultry summer morning, Whittaker Chambers, speaking in a monotone, told the committee that, as a member of the Communist Party, he had been responsible for overseeing the activities of a Communist "underground organization" within the government. Three of the men in the group had been named publicly by other witnesses, including Bentley, but Alger Hiss, who was far more prominent than the others, had not been. Hiss had served in Wallace's Agriculture Department, but had then risen to a position of influence within the State Department, helping to organize the United States side of the Yalta conference. Upon leaving government in 1947, he had become president of the Carnegie Endowment for International Peace.

As the committee learned, Chambers believed that international Communism was on the verge of destroying the free world. "I am proud to appear before the committee," said Chambers in conclusion. "The publicity, inseparable from such testimony, has darkened and no doubt will continue to darken my effort to integrate myself in the community of free men. But this is a small price to pay if my testimony helps to make Americans recognize at last they are at grips with a secret, sinister, and enormously powerful force whose tireless purpose is their enslavement." Chambers called on other Communists and former Communists to come forward "while there is still time."

Chambers's testimony began two years of hearings and trials, which concluded on January 21, 1950, when Hiss was convicted of perjury for denying that he had passed secret government documents to Chambers. In the process, the politics of the nation were profoundly altered. More than any other event, the Hiss-Chambers case gave credence to charges by FBI Director Hoover and by Wisconsin senator Joseph McCarthy that the nation was in danger from a secret Communist conspiracy aimed at infiltrating the highest levels of government. And it helped to lay the basis for a new conservative political movement in the country dedicated to combating this Communist menace.

The new movement would derive much of its worldview from Chambers's testimony and from his autobiography, *Witness*, which he completed in 1952. In *Witness*, Chambers portrayed the struggle against Communism as a "great war of faith." The book's religious anti-Communism captured the imagination of a new generation of conservatives. The young William F. Buckley, Jr., was "shaken" by *Witness*'s "conjunction of style, analysis, romance, and historicity." Ronald

Reagan found his doubts about liberalism confirmed and mag-
nified. Three decades later, Reagan would still be quoting
Chambers's warning that "the crisis of the Western world exists
to the degree to which the West is indifferent to God, the degree
to which it collaborates in Communism's attempt to make man
stand alone without God."

But while Chambers became a kind of guru to the new
conservatives, he became increasingly uncomfortable as a
member of their movement. He recoiled from the reflection of
his own views in their writings and actions. He found their
rejection of political compromise self-defeating and their extreme anti-Communism irrational and potentially threatening
to the very civilization they were attempting to defend.

It wasn't that the new conservatives hadn't read Chambers
correctly; it was that Chambers was of two minds. While he
epitomized the absolutist and the extremist, whether as a Soviet
spy or as the anti-Communist of *Witness*, he was also a man
of considerable political and intellectual sophistication. As a
Communist, he had spent nearly fifteen years trying to understand how a movement on the margins of the society could
capture the mainstream. By the time he became a conservative,
he had already learned from Lenin that a fledgling movement
must hew to a careful path between opportunism and sectarianism if it is to succeed. Chambers was well aware of the
pitfalls of the soapbox and the third party, but few of his com-
rades on the political right were.

Chambers was also a man of prodigious learning, who was
fluent in German and French, had a reading knowledge of
Russian, Italian, and Spanish, and, according to some accounts,
could also read Hungarian and Chinese. While he could be
doctrinaire in his political views, he had the intellectual's penchant for understanding rather than simply dismissing the
avant-garde, from the existentialists to Allen Ginsberg and Britain's Angry Young Men.

Chambers appreciated the historical paradox of trying to develop a conservative politics in a nation that had never had an

*ancien régime.* For the last decade of his life, as an editor and
contributor to *National Review,* the most important conservative
publication of the time, and as a close friend of William F.
Buckley, Jr., its founder, Chambers waged a quiet struggle to
make conservatives more realistic about their politics and even
about their view of the Soviet Union.

Along with Max Eastman and James Burnham, who also ended
up writing for *National Review,* Chambers belonged to a particular generation of Americans who came of age in the 1920s
rather than the 1930s. They entered the left as radical individualists and bohemian intellectuals, through an interest in the
arts and philosophy rather than through the experience of exploitation or poverty or political organization. Their individualism colored and finally subverted their commitment to
Communism—and in some cases, to the left itself.

But Chambers was more eccentric and alienated than Eastman or Burnham. While they were excelling at Harvard and
Princeton, Chambers was getting bounced from Columbia as
a junior for publishing a blasphemous play in the school's
literary magazine. While they achieved public acclaim quickly,
Chambers chose to labor in the netherworld of the Communist
underground.

Chambers was brought up in a troubled, bohemian family
ill at ease in a Long Island fishing village. His father temporarily
left the family for a homosexual lover, and his younger brother
committed suicide. Chambers was plagued by doubt and guilt,
reinforced after he left Columbia by sporadic, secret homosexual adventures. Chambers's anguish probably made him more
receptive, whether as a Communist or as an anti-Communist,
to overly simple melodramatic world systems. It also lent passion to his writing.

In 1932, after a brief career as a short-story writer and editor on *The Daily Worker* and *The New Masses*, Chambers became a Soviet secret agent, serving as a courier and organizing a network of pro-Soviet or Communist officials in the Roosevelt administration. It was in this capacity, according to Chambers, that he worked with Alger Hiss. By 1937, Chambers was becoming disillusioned with the Soviet Union, but he also feared for his life. Having been accused by a political opponent of being a "Trotskyite," Chambers had been summoned to Moscow in 1937, the time of the Great Purge. He stalled; and when one of his associates disappeared and another was arrested in Moscow, he decided in 1938 to make a break from the party.

In 1939, Chambers decided to warn Assistant Secretary of State Adolf A. Berle of the Communist infiltration. Chambers met with Berle the day after the Germans invaded Poland and provided him with the names of Communists in the State and Treasury Departments. When nothing came of his visit, Chambers attributed the administration's failure to act to Communist influence. He realized, he wrote in *Witness*, that "the Communists were more firmly embedded in government than I supposed." At the same time, he came to see the New Deal, not as a reform movement, but as a "genuine revolution" in which liberals were unwittingly being directed by Communists.

After a year on the run, Chambers resurfaced. Author Robert Cantwell, Chambers's friend, introduced the ex-Communist to *Time* editor T. S. Matthews, who, impressed with the short stories Chambers had written earlier for *The New Masses*, hired him as a book reviewer. *Time* editor Henry Luce first noticed Chambers when he reviewed the film version of John Steinbeck's *Grapes of Wrath*. Luce, who remained a conservative Republican amidst his largely liberal staff, was drawn to Chambers's criticism of the left-wing intellectuals. In 1942, he elevated Chambers to senior editor and put him in charge of books and features.

By this time, Chambers's political views and manner had swung full circle. Once a revolutionary Communist, he had become a counterrevolutionary anti-Communist, for whom even the New Deal was anathema. Living on a farm in Westminster, Maryland, he had abandoned the proletarian revolutionary's fascination with the working class for a romantic agrarianism.* He had adopted the Republicanism of his grandparents and the Quaker faith of his paternal grandmother. And by 1942, barely four years out of the Communist Party, Chambers had exchanged dialectical materialism for the Quaker's evangelical Protestantism. "The belief in God or belief in Man," he wrote Luce in a 1942 memo, is "the real line of cleavage in the modern world between conservative and revolutionary."

Chambers's sudden transformation was undoubtedly due to the surfeit of fear and guilt that he suffered—fear of Communist revenge and guilt from having served the Communist cause. But it also reflected a religious nature that craved absolutes, that wanted to believe in the grand design, that conceived of life and history in terms of moral polarities. In *Witness*, Chambers described his first hint of disillusionment with Communism as coming when he realized that theology provided a better explanation for the "delicate convolutions" of his daughter's ear than Communism. Sitting in his apartment one day, Chambers perceived that her ears "were not created by any chance coming together of atoms (the Communist view). They could have only been created by immense design."

Chambers's decision to break with Communism in 1938 coincided with his religious awakening. A voice had said to him, "If you will fight for freedom, all will be well with you." In *Witness*, Chambers also drew an analogy between the satisfaction he derived from Communism and that which he received from being a Quaker. "My need was to be a practicing Christian in the same sense that I had been a practicing Communist. I was seeking a community of worship in which a daily mysticism . . . would be disciplined and fortified by an orderly, and even practical, spirit and habit of life and the mind."

---

* "The land-owning farmer, big and little, is the conservative base of every healthy society, no matter how many miles of factories may be required to keep the average city dweller in a state of civilized neurosis," Chambers wrote in a 1944 book review in *The American Mercury*.

At *Time*, Chambers became part of a group of writers and editors, including future *National Review* editors Willi Schlamm and John Chamberlain, who held out doggedly for an anti-Soviet foreign policy during the period of wartime cooperation with the Soviet Union. In 1943, Luce and Matthews elevated Chambers to foreign news editor. In that position, Chambers made *Time* the voice of anti-Communism, warning of Tito in Yugoslavia and Mao in China. (When *Time*'s distinguished China correspondent Theodore White reported on Chiang Kai-shek's corruption, Chambers rewrote his story to warn of the fall of Chiang's "democratic forces" in China and their replacement by pro-Soviet Communists.) In March 1945, after the Yalta conference, Chambers published a parable in *Time*, "The Ghosts on the Roof," describing the Communist plan for world conquest and prophesying a struggle between "two faiths."

Luce, the son of Protestant missionaries, shared Chambers's conception of the Communist menace as spiritual as well as material; yet, as would become apparent, Chambers's view of the Soviet threat was far more expansive than Luce's. For Luce, Soviet Communism was an obstacle to the final realization of the American Century; for Chambers, the struggle against the Soviet Union was the be-all and end-all of existence. Luce was a nationalist; his views were a blend of realism and evangelism. Chambers bordered on being a religious mystic.

Even before Chambers's anti-Yalta parable, protests from Chambers's correspondents and fellow editors forced Luce to reduce Chambers's responsibilities. After Chambers suffered a heart attack, Luce shifted him off to special projects, where he wrote long features on the history of civilization for *Life*. Deprived of his influence on *Time*'s foreign coverage, Chambers was on the verge of resigning when HUAC summoned him to testify in August 1948. His revelation the next year that he had not merely been a Communist agent but a Soviet spy ended his career at *Time*.

After Hiss was found guilty, Chambers retired to his farm to write *Witness*. While he would later spend months toiling over a book review or a letter, he wrote the 800-page *Witness* quickly, propelled by his own rage and grief. It was in part a ponderous and pretentious book, marred by its author's inflated estimate of his own virtue and importance. As a whole, however, *Witness* succeeded in conveying not only its subject's agitated mental state but also the peculiar ambience of both the Communist underground and the postwar domestic Cold War. *Witness* was part of a tradition of Christian confessional literature and part of an entirely modern postwar genre that blended together journalism, autobiography, and political commentary.

When *Witness* appeared in 1952, it briefly topped the best-seller lists, but its tone and length proved too much for most readers. There was one group of readers, however, that found it both inspiring and enlightening: young right-wing intellectuals who were groping during the early 1950s for a way to develop a new conservative intellectual and political movement.

In the late 1940s and early 1950s there was, strictly speaking, no conservative movement in America. There were individuals and organizations identified with the right wing, from Gerald L. K. Smith to Ohio senator Robert Taft, but they often had nothing in common except an estrangement from the New Deal and American globalism. Intellectuals like traditionalist Russell Kirk, libertarian Frank Chodorov, and former leftist Frank Meyer, who wrote for journals like *Plain Talk, The Freeman,* and *The American Mercury,* often denounced each other more vociferously than they denounced the liberal enemy. Through the apocalyptic anti-Communism of *Witness,* Chambers helped to give these individuals a new focus.

Chambers portrayed the struggle between Western civilization and Communism as a struggle between "two rival faiths," between good and evil. Communism was the Antichrist, and the Cold War was Armageddon. But Communism was not simply the social system developed in the Soviet Union. According to Chambers, what distinguished Communism was the Communist's belief that human beings could achieve "order, abundance, security, peace" through politics—through a "purpose or plan"—without resort to God. Communism posed "the most revolutionary question in history: God or Man?" It answered: "Man."

In this sense, modern liberalism, socialism, and social democracy, which also aim to eliminate "age-old senseless suffering" with "a purpose or a plan," were mere variants of Communism. Chambers described socialism as "Communism with the claws removed." While the "focus of concentrated evil" in the world was the Communism embodied in the Soviet Union, the evil essence of Communism could be found unfocused in Roosevelt's New Deal or in the British Labour Party's program for the nationalization of industry.

Thus, Chambers synthesized the preoccupations of the right. Communism was not merely undesirable; it was evil. And it was present not merely in Moscow but in Washington, disguised in the form of economic planning, or Keynesianism. In a passage that Reagan quoted in his own autobiography, Chambers wrote:

> When I took up my little sling and aimed at Communism, I also hit something else. What I hit was the force of that great Socialist revolution which in the name of *liberalism*, spasmodically, incompletely, somewhat formlessly, but always in the same direction, has been inching its icecap over the nation for two decades.

Chambers's anti-Communist theology was based, however, on decidedly nontheological assumptions. Chambers's view of Communism was still shaped by his own experience in the party. While Chambers no longer believed that Communism was a desirable social system, he continued to accept Stalinism and official Marxist-Leninist ideology as a theory of history and an explanation of Soviet behavior. Chambers interpreted Soviet actions in the light of Soviet ideology, rather than subjecting its ideology to the test of its actions. Thus, Chambers ignored the extent to which Soviet Communism bore little resemblance to the Marxist paradigm but was instead a hybrid of Czarist authoritarianism and Marx's nightmare of the state as collective capitalist. Similarly, Chambers ignored the extent to which Soviet foreign policy was dictated by nationalism, great-power imperialism (another relic of Russia's past), and the experience of two world wars, rather than by proletarian internationalism. Chambers saw the Soviet Union as an entirely new kind of nation whose role was to create a world revolution after its own image.

Perhaps most important of all, Chambers, following Marxist-Leninist dicta, defined contemporary history as the last phase of the struggle between capitalism and Soviet-led Communism, in which Communism would probably prevail. As he confessed in *Witness*, Chambers continued to believe what he told his wife after leaving the Communist Party: "You know, we are leaving the winning world for the losing world." This made his vision of history fundamentally different from that of Luce, who viewed the Soviet Union as a temporary impediment in the grand succession from the British to the American world empire, and gave his conservatism the same apocalyptic cast as his prior Communism.

Chambers's view of American liberalism was shaped both by the wishful thinking of some Communists during the post-1935 Popular Front period who saw the New Deal, not as capitalist reform, but as the groundwork for socialism, and by the warnings of Friedrich von Hayek's influential 1944 book, *The Road to Serfdom*. Hayek warned that "mixed economies" like those of Britain and the United States risked evolving into economies like those of the Soviet Union and Nazi Germany, with their accompanying political forms. Hayek posed to the Western democracies a stark choice between individualism and collectivism, liberty and equality, with the New Deal being lumped together with Stalinism and Nazism. Chambers translated this into "God or Man?"

Chambers's views were, of course, not accepted by everyone who came to be called a conservative. Max Eastman, for instance, found no use for Chambers's theology. But Chambers showed the most active new conservatives how a militant anti-Communism could become the basis for the new movement.

In the 1950s, this movement grew rapidly. In 1953, Russell Kirk published his *Conservative Mind*, which gave the new movement its name. In 1955, William F. Buckley, Jr., with the assistance of Willi Schlamm, Burnham, and others, founded *National Review*. By the early 1960s, a conservative faction had formed within the Republican Party that in 1964 would help nominate Arizona senator Barry Goldwater for the presidency.

Chambers cast a watchful and sometimes supportive eye over these proceedings. When Kirk's book appeared, Chambers used his influence at *Time* to secure it a featured review. In 1954, he began a close friendship and correspondence with Buckley that culminated in his presence on *National Review*'s editorial board from 1957 to 1959. But Chambers kept his distance from the conservative movement that he had helped to inspire. He was held back from full participation by successive heart attacks, the last of which killed him. In addition, he could not fully reconcile himself to the new movement.

For one thing, Chambers sharply disagreed with the conservatives' choice of heroes. As Buckley had learned when he asked Chambers to write a blurb for his and Brent Bozell's 1954 book, *McCarthy and His Enemies*, Chambers despised McCarthy and didn't want to have anything to do with him. Chambers was convinced, he presciently wrote Buckley's publisher in February 1954, that McCarthy's "flair for the sensational, his inaccuracies and distortions, his tendency to sacrifice the greater objective for the momentary effect [would] lead him and us into trouble."*

Nor did Chambers know how to apply the worldview he articulated in *Witness* to the political issues of the 1950s. On the most abstract level, Chambers found himself wondering what it meant to be a conservative in a country like America, whose basic ideas reflected the liberal Enlightenment. Chambers concluded that the only solution was to compromise or, as he put it, "to maneuver." He wrote his friend and former *Time* colleague Duncan Taylor-Norton in 1954:

> Of course, it is the duty of the intellectuals of the West to preach reaction, and to keep pointing out why the Enlightenment and its fruits were a wrong turning in man's history. But it was a turning, and, within its terms, we must maneuver at the point where to maneuver is to live.

When Buckley and Schlamm approached Chambers in 1954 to become an editor of *National Review*, he was forced to confront the dilemma on a more specific basis. Programmatically, Buckley and Schlamm stood for the revocation of the New Deal and the welfare state; politically, they opposed the Eisenhower administration and Eisenhower's Vice President, Richard Nixon, whom Chambers had met and grown to admire during the Hiss case. In a series of letters, Chambers argued that Buckley and Schlamm's position was "reactionary" rather than "conservative." Chambers's conservative politics drew upon his version of Marxist dialectics and upon the example of British Conservative Party leader Benjamin Disraeli, Lord Beaconsfield, who convinced the Tories in 1867 to take the

---

* Chambers met McCarthy personally when the Wisconsin senator visited Westminster in March 1953 to consult with him on Eisenhower's nomination of Charles Bohlen to be Ambassador to the Soviet Union. Chambers, finding that McCarthy had no evidence of Communist sympathy or attachment against Bohlen, urged him to drop the battle against his nomination, but McCarthy attempted to use the visit to suggest that he had received from Chambers final confirmation of Bohlen's apostasy. Chambers, deeply offended at being used, issued a public statement rejecting any link between Bohlen and Communism.

leadership in extending the suffrage. "I remain a dialectician," Chambers wrote Buckley and Schlamm,

> and history tells me the rock-core of the Conservative Position, or any fragment of it, can be held realistically only if conservatism will accommodate itself to the needs and hopes of the masses . . . That is, of course, the Beaconsfield position.

In saying that he was still a dialectician, Chambers meant that he still believed that social and political change was determined by events outside the control or prescription of any individual—by the inevitable advance of technology under capitalism and by the evolving needs and sentiments of the majority of the people. The role of conservatives, Chambers argued, was not to try to block or revoke those changes, which was futile, but to shape them according to conservative ideals and principles.

Chambers tried to explain this point to Buckley and Schlamm with the example of the government price supports for agriculture that Henry Wallace had first initiated, which Chambers called "rural socialism." Such supports, Chambers contended, were the inevitable outcome of new agricultural technology, which produced a new abundance that would drive farmers' prices down to almost zero. The farmers had no choice but to demand price supports, the government no choice but to grant them. "The machine had made the economy socialistic," Chambers wrote. "The government has only enacted one aspect of the fact into law." A conservatism that opposed price supports, Chambers warned, would have to advise farmers to smash their machines, "but a conservatism that would say that is not a political force, or even a twitch: it has become a literary whimsy."

Writing to Schlamm, Chambers summed up in a memorable passage what the conservative position entailed:

Escapism is laudable, perhaps, the only truly honorable course for humane men—but only for them. Those who remain in the world, if they will not surrender on its terms, must maneuver within its terms. That is what conservatives must decide: how much to give in order to survive at all; how much to give in order not to give up basic principles. And of course that results in a dance along a precipice. Many will drop over, and always, the cliff dancers will hear the screaming curses of those who fall, or be numbed by the sullen silence of those, nobler souls perhaps, who will not join the dance.

In September 1955, after more than a year of correspondence and discussion, Chambers finally decided not to join *National Review*. Writing to Buckley, he explained that while he agreed with them that "socialism is death," he disagreed on "certain tactical, or, if you prefer, practical considerations." Buckley believed that these had to do with Chambers's support in the 1956 election for Eisenhower and Nixon. And Buckley was at least partially correct: after Eisenhower and Nixon's reelection, Chambers did agree to join the *National Review* editorial board. But more stood between Chambers and the new conservatives than simply a question of whom to support in 1956.

Chambers stayed on *National Review* for two years, but he never abandoned his own dissent from the direction that the right had taken. Instead, he spent much of his writing criticizing his fellow conservatives. Chambers's most outstanding and influential article was his 1957 panning of Ayn Rand's novel *Atlas Shrugged*. Rand, a Russian émigrée, used her novels to proselytize for what she called "objectivism"—a philosophy of economic individualism that extolled selfishness and rejected religion. Her movement's symbol was a dollar sign. Chambers condemned Rand's objectivism as a cousin of Marxism. "Randian man, like Marxian man, is made the center of a Godless world," Chambers wrote. But above all, he condemned Rand for trying to impose an abstract, bloodless philosophy on the complexities of human existence. "In this fiction, everything, everybody is either all good or all bad, without any of those intermediate shades which, in life, complicate reality and perplex the eye that seeks to probe it truly," Chambers the mature realist wrote.

In April 1959, Chambers astounded many conservatives by arguing in *National Review* that Hiss, who had been released from jail, should not be denied a passport. Chambers believed that the defense of civil liberties should be an essential part of the conservative position. Commenting on conservative opposition to a passport for Hiss, Chambers wrote Buckley:

> Liberals, by default, preempt the humane and intellectually sound positions, when it is precisely the Liberals who, in the name of freedom, are inviting the Total State. I think the Right is playing into their hands, and that the time has come for those who claim that general position for themselves to examine and define with a special scrupulousness the civil liberties field.

But the climax of Chambers's dissent came, ironically, over the conservative attitude toward the Soviet Union that he had helped spawn. In 1959, some of *National Review*'s editors were gearing up to oppose Richard Nixon's election in 1960. *National Review* was also leading a nationwide campaign to protest Soviet Premier Nikita Khrushchev's visit to the United States at the invitation of Eisenhower. Chambers protested the magazine's inability to distinguish Khrushchev from Stalin ("He is not a monster . . . in the sense that Stalin *was* a monster," Chambers wrote Buckley). More generally, Chambers argued that the magazine's opposition to any discussion with the Soviet Union amounted to a declaration of war, which Americans were simply not willing to accept. The conservatives were again defying the dialectic. With a touch of irony, Chambers wrote Buckley:

The logic of *National Review*'s policy . . . is: war. If gentle-
men hold that war is necessary, I, for one, wish they
should say so simply . . . It is not an easy position, it
should take courage to set it forth at all. But it would be
an intelligible position, and popular, I am told, with the
SAC [the Strategic Air Command], though I doubt that it
would be so with wider circles.

Chambers's view of the Cold War remained subtly different
from that of most conservatives—or liberals. Like George Kennan, Chambers saw the Cold War primarily, or even exclusively, as a battle for men's souls. He discounted warnings of
imminent nuclear war or of a "missile gap" between the two
countries that favored the Soviet Union. In February 1959, he
wrote in *National Review* that each side had achieved "approx-
imate destructive parity." To respond to the Soviets, Chambers
warned, Americans do not need more weapons, but "a basic
attitude toward mind."

By the late 1950s, an alienated Chambers was no longer
calling himself a "conservative," but a "man of the Right." He
set forth some of his reasons in a letter to Buckley in December
1958. Temperamentally, Chambers, the old individualist, felt
himself at odds with the trend toward political and religious
orthodoxy that he found among conservatives. "The temptation to orthodoxy is often strong, never more in an age like
this one, especially in a personal situation like mine," Chambers wrote Buckley. "But it is not a temptation to which I have
found it possible to yield."

But Chambers also came back to the more general problem
of American conservatism:

I am a man of the Right because I mean to uphold capitalism in its American version. But I claim that capitalism
is not, and by its essential nature cannot conceivably be,
conservative. This is particularly true of capitalism in the
United States, which knew no Middle Ages; which was

born, in so far as it was ideological, of the Enlightenment
... Capitalism, whenever it seeks to become conservative
in any quarter, at once settles into mere reaction ... Hence
the sense of unreality and pessimism on the Right, running
off into all manner of crackpotism.

Chambers was not, of course, repudiating the conservative
movement the way he repudiated the Communist Party when
he broke with it and the left in the late 1930s. He continued
to identify with the broader right, even as he became exas-
perated with the politics of the new conservative movement.
And he remained close to Buckley and Burnham to the end
of his life. But the strains that were emerging were not merely
tactical. And they affected Chambers's own ultimate assumptions.

The problem with the conservative movement that Chambers
sensed in the late 1950s was also a problem with Chambers's
own worldview as put forth in *Witness*. The conservative movement's most sectarian and crackpot tendencies were consistent
with the position that Chambers had propounded in *Witness*.
If Communism was the "focus of concentrated evil" in the
world, why should an American administration invite one of
its satanic representatives to visit its shores? If liberalism was
really socialism, which was really "Communism with the claws
removed," why should conservatives condone Social Security
or government price supports for agriculture? If an evil, and
not merely undesirable, policy is the issue, what room is there
for compromise or maneuver?

The problem can be restated in this way: Disraeli, Chambers's
model, revived the Tory Party in Britain not simply by teaching
it compromise but by challenging its antiquated social ideal,
which conceived of government as the province of the Crown
and landed estates. Similarly, Chambers sought to teach American conservatives the art of political compromise. In *Witness*,
however, he provided them with a worldview and an ideal

that brooked no compromise. His vision was ultimately religious, rather than political or historical.

In November 1959, Chambers once again resigned from *National Review*, partly for reasons of health, partly because he wanted to go back to college (Chambers enrolled at Western Maryland College to study science and classical Greek, among other things), but also because he found himself at odds with *National Review*'s conservatism.

Chambers spent the last two years of his life wrestling with the contradictions in his own and in the conservative outlook, but he never resolved them. His published writings of the 1950s, which were republished in 1989 in a collection, *Ghosts on the Roof*, and his letters to Buckley, which were published posthumously in *Odyssey of a Friend*, show a man impatient with political absolutes. But the Chambers of *Witness* also remained intact. Chambers's unpublished writings of the period, collected later in *Cold Friday*, largely reiterate, with considerably less grace, the apocalyptic themes of *Witness*. In one essay, "A Direct Glance," Chambers literally parodied himself. "If God exists, a man cannot be a Communist, which begins with the rejection of God," he wrote. "But if God does not exist, it follows that Communism, or some suitable variant of it, is right."

During the 1950s, American conservatives did not have to worry about the contradictions in Chambers's thinking. Their politics, from the John Birch Society's brand of paranoid anti-Communism to the more cosmopolitan anti-Eisenhower polemics of *National Review*, derived from *Witness* rather than from Chambers's reflections on Disraeli or Lenin. But in the 1960s, as conservatives began taking over the Republican Party, they found themselves faced with Chambers's dilemma: "how much to give in order to survive at all; how much to give in order not to give up basic principles."

Goldwater's landslide defeat in 1964 forced the more thoughtful conservatives to reassess their political strategy. In an October 1964 speech to members of New York's Conservative Party, William Buckley restated in his own terms Chambers's call for a realistic conservative politics:

A conservative is simultaneously concerned with two things, the first being the shape of the visionary or paradigmatic society towards which we should labor; the second, the speed with which it is thinkable to advance towards that ideal society, and the foreknowledge that any advance upon it is necessarily asymptotic, that is, that we cannot hope for ideological home runs and definitive victories; not, at least, until the successful completion of the work of the Society for the Abolition of Original Sin.

But neither Buckley nor the other conservatives who adopted a more realistic politics after 1964 abandoned Chambers's original anti-Communist worldview. Like Chambers, they tried to reconcile an otherworldly demarcation of politics into good and evil forces with the worldly imperatives of winning and retaining office. As a result, they did not create a strategy with which they could attain their goals of a world without evil, but instead developed a rationalization for proceeding as if it were possible to do so. They recognized the necessity of taking the Beaconsfield path at the same time as they denounced every step along that road as base opportunism. Like Chambers, conservatives were torn between a vision of Armageddon and the real world of politics and nations.

# 5

# *James Burnham*

## Cold War Machiavelli

> This is not a moral, but a strategic and geopolitical program. In fact, I would say that if morality enters in at all on this point, it is immoral for one nation not to try to coexist peacefully with every other—no matter what their regimes.
>
> —JAMES BURNHAM, 1957

In March 1947, the same week that Truman asked Congress for military aid to prevent Communists from seizing power in Greece, James Burnham published *The Struggle for the World*. The sheer coincidence, combined with the anti-Communist tenor of the book and the fact that the first half of it had originally been written for the Office of Strategic Services, the precursor of the Central Intelligence Agency, convinced more than one reviewer that the book was intended as a larger justification of the Truman Doctrine. Luce's *Life* printed a thirteen-page condensation, and the *Christian Century* declared, "It fits the 'stop Russia' policy of the Truman Doctrine so exactly that one can hardly read it without thinking, 'Here, whether they realize it or not, is what the senators and representatives who voted for the initial move under the new doctrine . . . were really approving as the foreign policy of the United States.' "

But anyone who read Burnham's book carefully could detect a significant difference between his position and that of the Truman administration. In its cryptic hints about the advisability of a preemptive nuclear strike against the Soviet Union, in its emphasis on "offensive" rather than "defensive" strategy, and in its apocalyptic view of the Soviet Union itself, it was the first statement of what Burnham himself later labeled the "liberation" or "rollback" doctrine. If Chambers provided the theology of the new conservative movement, Burnham, beginning with *The Struggle for the World*, provided its strategy. As historian George Nash wrote in his authoritative study, *The Conservative Intellectual Movement in America*: "More than any other single person, Burnham supplied the conservative intellectual movement with the theoretical formulation for victory in the Cold War."

Burnham, a quiet, urbane man of encyclopedic powers who died in Kent, Connecticut, in 1987 at the age of eighty-two, became a cult hero to many conservatives. Patrick Buchanan, the columnist who served as Nixon's speechwriter, reread Burnham's 1964 book, *The Suicide of the West*, as preparation for his post as Ronald Reagan's Director of Communications. Daniel Oliver, the chairman of the Federal Trade Commission under Reagan, kept a framed set of Burnham's favorite sayings near his office desk. Former Ambassador to France Evan Galbraith said of Burnham, "His *Suicide of the West* was the piece of work that said it all about what is happening in connection with the Soviets' effort to deceive the West, and the West's effort to deceive itself."

But Burnham's legacy was more complex than many of his followers cared to admit. The strategy and worldview that conservatives adopted from Burnham was based upon apocalyptic and highly abstract assumptions about the Soviet Union and the clash between East and West—assumptions consistent with Chambers's *Witness*. But beginning in 1955, when he joined *National Review*, his tactical advice to the right was almost unfailingly based upon concrete and realistic assessments of the American and world situation, framed in terms of what was historically possible rather than transcendentally ideal. Burnham constantly surprised and offended his right-wing followers—in his responses to the Soviet invasion of Hungary, the diplomatic recognition of China, and the Panama Canal treaty. And during one brief period, he seemed ready to abandon the very foundations of the conservative strategy and worldview that he had helped to develop.

Moreover, Burnham's political sensibility was radically different from that of many of the conservatives who believed that they were following in his footsteps. Except at the very end of his life, when he rejoined the Catholic Church of his youth, Burnham was not a religious man, and his underlying worldview was skeptical and even cynical. While he attributed a certain evil to the Soviet Union, he viewed both national and international conflict entirely within the framework of a struggle for power. Power, rather than good or evil, was Burnham's absolute. And he framed his proposals for an American offensive against Communism, not in terms of a quest for global democracy, but in terms of American national interest. His was a singularly brazen view of the American Century.

The key to understanding Burnham's political outlook was his evolution from Trotskyism to conservatism. Unlike Chambers, Burnham did not move quickly from left to right. He spent more than a decade trying to sort out what was valid and what was invalid in the assumptions that he had acquired during his years on the left. The two books that Burnham wrote while in transition during the early 1940s—*The Managerial Revolution* and *The Machiavellians*—are his best. And the political position that Burnham finally adopted bore deep traces and scars from his Trotskyist past.

Even though he was several years their junior, Burnham, who was born in 1905, can be most fruitfully grouped with Edmund Wilson, Max Eastman, John Dos Passos, Chambers, and other intellectuals who came of age in the 1920s and early 1930s rather than in the more conformist Popular Front days. Like them, Burnham was an individualist who saw the calling of the intellectual as being, in some sense, above politics. This meant that, unlike many intellectuals who matured politically in the late 1930s, Burnham never entirely allowed politics to dictate his allegiance to ideas. In the face of contrary evidence, he was willing to revise the grand theoretical schemes that were his passion and his vice, even if that meant threatening existing political loyalties.

As with other radical individualists, Burnham's model of worldly success was the artist rather than the political leader. Throughout his life, he remained detached from the struggle for supremacy within the organizations and institutions that he helped found. His most observable quality was his reserve. Yet he retained a curious fascination with social collectivity and political power. It was as if, having been denied by temperament the worldly struggle for power, it became his theoretical obsession. His life's work was fixed on describing what he himself could never have.

Born in Chicago, the son of a railroad executive, Burnham was educated at Princeton and Oxford, where he became a Marxist. In 1930, he was hired to teach in New York University's philosophy department. His colleague William Barrett said of him that he "bore the stamp of the gentleman in his bearing—so much so that in comparison with some of the more raucous types of the New York intellectual he appeared almost shy and diffident." But Burnham's calm, urbane exterior concealed an ardor for ideological politics.

From the start, Burnham was drawn toward the more skeptical and critical politics of the Trotskyist movement. In the 1930s, Trotskyism was the refuge of committed Marxists like Irving Howe and Dwight Macdonald who believed in political organization but insisted on retaining their intellectual individuality. It was a politics of total opposition, to both capitalist and existing socialist society, defined entirely by ideas rather than actual movements or countries. If American Communism's vice was lockstep sectarianism, Trotskyism's foible was schismatic individualism.

In 1934, Burnham joined the Workers' Party. The Workers' Party (later the Socialist Workers' Party) was an outgrowth of Leon Trotsky's attempt to promote world revolution in the Soviet Union as well as the capitalist countries. Trotsky believed that Stalin had "betrayed" the 1917 revolution. According to the creator of the Red Army and the most eloquent and literary of the Soviet leaders, Russia had become a "degenerated workers' state" and Soviet foreign policy had become an expression of narrow national interest. But it was still in "transition" to socialism—which distinguished it from the world's capitalist states and made it worthy of critical support against capitalist encirclement.

After the 1939 Nazi-Soviet nonaggression pact and the Soviet invasion of Finland in 1940, Burnham decided that the Soviet Union was no better than its capitalist adversaries. He resigned from the Workers' Party in May 1940. But Trotsky's political legacy remained central to Burnham—so much so that over the next six years, while World War II raged, Burnham remained preoccupied with defining the nature and possibility of socialism. Once Burnham had done so to his satisfaction, he then turned to devising a strategy to confront the Soviet Union, the leading socialist state.

In *The Managerial Revolution*, published in 1941, and *The Machiavellians*, published in 1943, Burnham rejected the Marxist and liberal view of the world as being divided between capitalism and socialism. Instead, he saw the main division being between managerial and capitalist states. He described the Soviet Union as being neither capitalist nor socialist, but as evolving, along with the United States, Germany, and Japan, toward a new form of managerial society, characterized by state bureaucratic rather than individual capitalist control of the economy. He portrayed Soviet socialism and internationalism as "ideologies" or "myths" whose "formal meaning" differed from their "real meaning." Socialism, for instance, was supposed to mean a democratic system, but in fact rationalized a dictatorship.

Burnham did not abandon the Marxist dialectic, but he jettisoned its precise view of the stages of history. Instead of socialism following capitalism, managerialism followed capitalism, and socialism became a distant and receding goal. The strength of *The Managerial Revolution* lay precisely in its novel characterization of the Soviet Union as neither capitalist nor socialist. The weakness was its inference that a worldwide managerial revolution was displacing capitalism itself.

Like Burnham's other books, *The Managerial Revolution* reflected a certain theoretical subservience to passing events—almost a faddishness. Its theory of contemporary history arose directly from the Nazi-Soviet pact of 1939, which, to Burnham, united the managerial states of the Soviet Union and Nazi Germany against the bulwark of entrepreneurial capitalism, Great Britain. Unlike Luce, Burnham saw Germany and the Soviet Union rather than the United States as equal heirs of the fall of British power. Burnham would have to revise the thesis of *The Managerial Revolution* after Germany attacked the Soviet Union, and then finally abandon it after the Allied victory over Germany and Japan.

In a perceptive essay, "James Burnham and the Managerial Revolution," George Orwell noted that while Burnham's theory of managerialism, shorn of its predictive pretensions, was an "extremely plausible . . . interpretation of what is happening," the world-historical framework of his theory reflected a continuing overestimation of transient trends, based on what Orwell described as Burnham's "power worship." Burnham tended to endow militaristic states like Nazi Germany and Stalin's Russia with magical capacities, based in part on his perception of their evil. By contrast, he constantly underestimated his own country.

In *The Machiavellians*, Burnham attempted to summarize the contribution that Machiavelli and his modern followers—a group in which Burnham lumped Gaetano Mosca, Vilfredo Pareto, and Robert Michels with Georges Sorel—made to explaining the nature of politics and of political science. Following their lead, Burnham maintained that all societies were divided into classes of the ruling and the ruled and that the ruling class or elite perpetuated its dominance through "force and fraud." The fraud need not, however, be conscious, but could consist rather in what Marx called "ideology," Sorel called "myth," and Mosca called the "political formula." Included in these myths were religion and the leading concepts of both Western capitalism and Soviet socialism.

The role of the political scientist was to discover "the laws of political life" by laying bare the relationship between political myth and the reality it was intended to sustain. To do this, the political scientist, guided by realism rather than utopian or Platonic idealism, had to study what human beings actually did rather than what they said they were doing. For instance, to understand what a political party really stands for, a political scientist would be better advised to study what its leading politicians did in office rather than the party's quadrennial political platform. Machiavelli, Burnham noted, was a republican who would have liked to rid Italy of princes and kings. But Machiavelli didn't let his own political ideals blind him to the fact that only a prince could unify Italy. Thus, he put aside his "utopian" longings for a republic and studied the steps by which a prince could unify the nation.

In *The Managerial Revolution*, Burnham had denied socialism any immediacy; but in *The Machiavellians*, he denied that a classless society was possible at all. Following Mosca, Michels, and Pareto, Burnham insisted that there would always be a ruling class and a ruled. Revolutions consisted in "very rapid shifts in the composition and structure of elites" rather than in the total destruction of elite rule. Thus, capitalism was being displaced by managerialism—rule of economic and bureaucratic elites—rather than by Marx's or Trotsky's "utopian" concept of socialism.

Beginning from a very different point, Burnham arrived at the same typology of political society as Lippmann did in *The Good Society*. For Burnham, the relevant distinction was not between class society and classless society, but between different kinds of elite rule. Burnham distinguished a "democratic" form of elite rule from a "totalitarian" one by "the right of opponents of the governing elite to express publicly their opposition view and to organize to implement those views." As a form of elite rule, socialism tended naturally toward totalitarianism. "It would seem to be true that, since economic power comprises in all so large a percentage of total social power, the full concentration of all economic power in a centralized state apparatus would necessarily destroy the foundations of liberty." Thus, Burnham not only denied the possibility of socialism but, like Lippmann, warned that the pursuit of the socialist goal led toward totalitarianism.

Burnham's critique of socialist politics was extremely telling. Along with Max Eastman and other newly minted critics of Marxism, Burnham understood the looming contradiction between political freedom and the expansion of state economic power. But unlike Eastman, he was not drawn to a laissez-faire paradise lost. Burnham regarded right-wing Republicans who idealized nineteenth-century laissez-faire capitalism as hopeless utopians whose proposals were irrelevant to contemporary reality. "It is in any case impossible to return to private [entrepreneurial] capitalism," Burnham wrote.

Burnham's position in *The Machiavellians* was an uncomfortable one—poised between the broken dreams of capitalism and socialism. He had adopted Marx's critique of politics in a class society, as updated by the Machiavellians, but rejected Marx's classless solution. His view of humanity was deeply cynical, conditioned by the failure of the Soviet experiment and two world wars. Burnham's position in *The Machiavellians* was similar to Lippmann's and the post-socialist liberalism of Arthur Schlesinger, Jr., and Reinhold Niebuhr. But while these three men would remain progressives, and both Lippmann and Niebuhr would resist the siren call of Cold War evangelism, Burnham was headed toward a new anti-Communist conservatism.

When he wrote *The Machiavellians* in 1943, Burnham still believed, consistent with the theory of the managerial revolution, that the three most advanced managerial states, the United States, Germany, and Japan, would emerge from World War II as the new loci of world power. He did not believe that the Soviet Union, which he regarded as a primitive managerial state, could defeat Nazi Germany. But when the Soviet Union triumphed, Burnham was forced to revise his theory of the principal conflict in the world.

Like a number of other prominent intellectuals who were too old to serve on the front, Burnham spent World War II in Washington in the Office of Strategic Services (OSS), the wartime intelligence service. Many Washington policymakers with whom Burnham talked during those years believed that the main postwar conflict would be between the United States and Britain over the disposition of Europe's former colonial possessions. But Burnham, chastened by his own errors, was among the first to realize that the Soviet Union would emerge as the United States' principal adversary. Britain, Burnham believed, would merely be a junior partner of the United States.

But just as he had once grossly underestimated Stalin's power, overestimating Hitler's, he now proceeded to endow the Soviet Union with an almost magical potency. Unlike Chambers in *Witness*, Burnham did not cast his vision of the Soviet Union in religious terms. He did not come to see the Cold War as Armageddon. Instead, his severe schematic formulations were highly influenced by Arnold Toynbee's neo-Spenglerian theory of history.

Burnham first revised his view of world history and the Soviet Union in a 1945 essay entitled "Lenin's Heir," published in *Partisan Review*. In that essay, Burnham became so admiring in his description of Stalin's successful exercise of dictatorial power ("His liquidation of the various oppositions . . . is classically molded. The Moscow trials have stood the test of action") that the usually perceptive Dwight Macdonald misread his essay as a "lefthanded apology for Stalinism."

Burnham's new judgment on Stalin was premised on turning the Marxist conception of socialism into a myth. According to Burnham, "Stalinism is communism." In "Lenin's Heir," Burnham also insisted that Stalin, through "an act of creative political imagination," had replaced Marx and Lenin's "abstract internationalism" with a new "multi-national Bolshevism" that allowed the different Communist parties to embrace rather than reject their own national heritage, while still pursuing world revolution.

Such an argument failed to answer Trotsky's contention that Stalin was not interested in foreign revolution except as it immediately advanced Soviet national objectives. As Trotsky pointed out, Stalin's "multi-national Bolshevism," embodied in the post-1935 Popular Front strategy, was merely a tactic designed to accomplish Soviet national objectives rather than a revision of the Marxist corpus. When it suited Stalin to abandon it, as it did at the onset of the Cold War, he did so.

But Burnham rested his case on metaphysical rather than historical grounds. If politics was the struggle for power, then international politics was the struggle for absolute power or world domination. Thus, it appeared to make sense to Burnham, even without empirical evidence, that "Bolshevism (communism) . . . is a conspiratorial movement for the conquest of a monopoly of power in the era of capitalist disintegration." And it made equal sense to posit a struggle to the death between the United States and the Soviet Union. This is precisely what Burnham did in *The Struggle for the World*.

In *The Struggle for the World*, Burnham announced that in April 1944, when Communist-led Greek sailors had revolted, "the Third World War had begun." This war, Burnham warned, would be even more dangerous than World War II because with the invention of nuclear weapons it could very well see the destruction of Western civilization. The only alternative to such an outcome was for either the United States or the Soviet Union to establish a "universal empire" based on a monopoly of nuclear weapons.

Burnham argued that in order to withstand the Soviet threat, the United States would have to establish a network of hegemonic alliances (similar to what later became NATO, SEATO, etc.) and colonial and neocolonial relationships. Burnham candidly acknowledged that such an American empire already existed in Latin America and the South Pacific. "The empire extends to wherever the imperial power is decisive, not for everything or nearly everything, but for the crucial issues upon which political survival depends," Burnham wrote.

To sustain the empire in the face of Soviet aggression, the United States would also have to maintain its monopoly of nuclear weapons. To do this, Burnham warned, it would have to be "willing to fight," presumably with those very weapons. Burnham never said so explicitly, but he appeared to be arguing in *The Struggle for the World* for a preemptive nuclear strike against the Soviet Union.

Burnham's strategic deliberations were based upon his view of the Soviet Union. Even more than in "Lenin's Heir," Burnham identified Soviet socialism as a frozen regime incapable of internal alteration. In *The Managerial Revolution*, Burnham had described totalitarianism as an early stage of the managerial revolution that would give way to a kind of managerial de-

mocracy in the same way that capitalist absolutism had predated capitalist democracy, but in *The Struggle for the World*,
Burnham insisted that "it should not be supposed that the
terror with which communism is linked is a transient phenom-
enon . . . Terror is proved by historical experience to be integral
to communism, to be in fact, the main instrument by which
its power is increased and sustained."

Burnham described the Soviet Union and Stalin's foreign
policy objectives as "a worldwide, conspiratorial movement for
the conquest of a monopoly of power in an era of capitalist
decline." He offered no evidence for this assertion in "Lenin's
Heir," but in *The Struggle for the World* he presented the kind
of superficial evidence that he had himself eloquently argued
against in *The Machiavellians*.

In *The Machiavellians*, Burnham had warned that "the laws
of political life cannot be discovered by an analysis which takes
men's words and beliefs, spoken or written, at their face value."
But in *The Struggle for the World*, Burnham resorted to quota-
tions from Stalin's writings, official Soviet documents, and even
the *Communist Manifesto* to prove his contention that the Soviet
Union was steadfastly pursuing, not a "great power imperialism," but the Marxist-Leninist goal of world revolution. The
only historical figures he cited on behalf of his thesis were
precisely those who would later contradict it—Yugoslavia's
Tito and China's Mao.

*The Struggle for the World* had its merits. Burnham was willing
to discuss an American imperial presence with a frankness that
was entirely absent in American policymakers of the period,
intent as they were on selling America's postwar foreign policy
as a neo-Wilsonian attempt to defend world democracy—the
"free world"—against the threat of totalitarian Communism.
But *The Struggle for the World* was also a deeply troubled, even
somewhat paranoid work, in which Burnham abandoned the
subtle framework of both *The Managerial Revolution* and *The*

*Machiavellians* for an apocalyptic—indeed mythic—view of world politics.

When Burnham published *The Struggle for the World*, he described himself (under the influence of his friend André Malraux) as being neither on the right nor on the left, but he was still part of liberal intellectual circles. He remained close to the anti-Communist liberals on *Partisan Review* and in the American Congress for Cultural Freedom. When the CIA, an institution identified with liberal anti-Communism, was formed in 1947, he resigned from NYU and became a CIA consultant. In the CIA, he briefed agents on world events and helped organize the International Congress for Cultural Freedom, of which the American Congress was a branch.

Working out of his Washington home, he maintained his detachment from the centers of power at the same time as he served them. E. Howard Hunt, a fledgling CIA agent in the late 1940s who later attained renown for his inglorious role in the Watergate scandal, recalled visiting Burnham:

> He was very quiet. He was professorial in the best sense of the word. He wore tweed jackets and British shoes and a nice foulard. I would pick up *The New York Times*, and I would say, "Do you have any idea of what is going on in Morocco?" That would be good for a minimum of a half hour because he knew the personalities involved. He had an encyclopedic acquaintanceship.

His books were denounced equally by the pro-Soviet left and the isolationist right. For instance, isolationist *Human Events* editor Felix Morley, reviewing *The Struggle for the World*, charged Burnham with using "the very real threat of Soviet Russia . . . to advocate the dissolution of the American republic" and "the establishment of an American empire in its place." But Burnham's overestimation of the Soviet threat eventually put him at odds with his liberal colleagues in the CIA and New York's intellectual circles.

Burnham most clearly broke with liberal anti-Communist strategy in a 1952 book, *Containment or Liberation?* Burnham focused his attack on former State Department official George Kennan's writings—not only his 1947 X article that defined the containment strategy, but a 1951 *Foreign Affairs* article, "America and the Russian Future," in which Kennan modified his earlier hard-line position in line with Lippmann's criticisms. But in rejecting Kennan, Burnham still went beyond not only the former diplomat's moderate realism but also the prevailing views of most Democrats and liberals.

In *Containment or Liberation?* Burnham charged that Kennan's containment policy was a classic balance-of-power strategy, based on understanding the Soviet Union as an "extension of Czarist imperialism." In contrast, Burnham contended that the Soviet Union was "an entirely new revolutionary power" that had "irrevocably set itself the objective of monolithic world domination." It could not be contained like the typical "post-Renaissance nation-state":

It is hard to see what it means to try to "contain" a universalistic militant secular religion, based on a vast land mass inhabited by 800 million humans, which irrevocably set itself the objective of monolithic world domination and which already exists and acts inside every nation in the world.

Burnham warned that if the containment strategy was followed, the United States was doomed. "If the Communists succeed in consolidating what they have already conquered," he wrote, "then their complete world victory is certain." He expressed his fear in terms of a metaphor that reveals a certain amount of sheer paranoia:

The development and consolidation of the present Soviet sphere as a strategic unit would in itself be intolerable from a strategic standpoint. How could a man sleep secure if he lived in the path of a rock big enough to crush his house to bits, and poised to drop at the shove of a surly neighbor?

In *Containment or Liberation?* Burnham recommended an "open policy of liberation toward the USSR and its satellites and captive nations." While he warned against encouraging "premature narrow uprisings," he insisted that the United States would have to be prepared for war, even in circumstances not of its own choosing:

What if in a captive nation a broad mass uprising against the regime began? Or what if one of the communist governments, supported by the majority of the people, decided against Moscow? And, in either case, what if help were then asked from the free world? . . . Would not passivity under such circumstances be a final proof of the irreversibility of communist world victory?

*Containment or Liberation?* was one of Burnham's least sophisticated works. Its argument was hysterical at times. Much of the evidence adduced by Burnham to make his case was later flatly disproved by events. (For instance, in arguing that containment had failed, Burnham ridiculously insisted that the Truman administration had failed to build a "situation of socio-economic strength" in Western Europe.) Yet the book exerted a great appeal among conservatives and fanatic anti-Communists who were looking for a seemingly authoritative and scientific study to sustain their theological understanding of the Cold War.

Along with Chambers's *Witness, Containment or Liberation?* quickly became a classic of modern conservative thought. Most conservative foreign policy writing since the 1950s has simply been a gloss on its argument. But Burnham himself, while adhering rhetorically to the strategy of *Containment or Liberation?*, surprised his followers by departing from it.

In the early 1950s, Burnham found himself at odds with his liberal colleagues not only over the extent of the Soviet external threat but also over the internal threat of subversion. Burnham refused to repudiate Senator Joseph McCarthy, even after the Wisconsin senator had targeted the CIA for one of his witch hunts. Because of his "neutrality" toward McCarthy, Burnham was asked to resign from *Partisan Review*'s advisory board in December 1953 and was more or less forced out of the American Congress for Cultural Freedom the next year. And he was fired and even blacklisted by the CIA. Buckley, whom Burnham recruited into the CIA in 1951, said of Burnham's expulsion, "I don't know as much as I should, but I have a feel for what happened. Jim was a principal organizer of the Congress for Cultural Freedom and disagreed with the governors on what the official position should be on McCarthy, he taking a hard line."

Burnham retired in 1954 to his prerevolutionary-era home in Kent, Connecticut, to write a book, *The Web of Subversion*, defending Congress's internal security investigations and calling for the outlawing of the American Communist Party.

Burnham's ostracism from the left, center, and isolationist right coincided, however, with the emergence of a new conservative movement. The older isolationist right expired with Senator Robert Taft's defeat in 1952 for the Republican presidential nomination. The new generation of Republican conservatives was largely internationalist in background—Arizona senator Barry Goldwater and *National Review* publisher William Rusher were both staunch Eisenhower backers in 1952. These new conservatives adopted Burnham and former Communists like Whittaker Chambers and Frank Meyer as their intellectual guides.

In the fall of 1954, Buckley visited Burnham in Kent to ask him to become an editor of the new right-wing weekly that he was planning. When *National Review* began publishing in November 1955, Burnham was joined by Willi Schlamm, Willmoore Kendall, Ralph de Toledano, Frank Meyer, and other former Communists and Trotskyists on the masthead.

Burnham began writing a regular column, aptly titled "World War III," and served as a foreign policy mentor to Buckley. But Burnham's first years on *National Review* were not entirely peaceful. Beginning in the spring of 1956, he became embroiled in a bitter political dispute with Schlamm and Meyer. This dispute was precisely over the application of his own doctrine to world events.

Schlamm and Meyer were both Burnham's opposites. They were excitable and emotional where he was cool and detached. While Burnham had assiduously avoided making a career of his political convictions (in the late 1930s he repeatedly turned down party requests that he become a full-time functionary), both Schlamm and Meyer had spent most of their lives as either professional Communists or professional anti-Communists. Schlamm had been the editor of an Austrian Communist newspaper and then a German anti-Stalinist journal before emigrating to the United States, where he became Henry Luce's house anti-Communist.* Meyer had been a functionary within the American Communist Party before trying to forge a career as an anti-Communist intellectual. He was as doggedly optimistic about the conservative future as he had been about the Communist future.

Both Schlamm and Meyer were brilliant, but, like other ex-

---

* In *Witness*, Chambers describes a dinner party that he and Schlamm (named "Smetana" in the book) attended at Luce's house in 1948 right after Chambers had appeared before HUAC. According to Chambers, Luce could not understand why his upper-class friends were trying to get him to fire Chambers. "You don't understand the class structure of American society," Schlamm said, "or you would not ask such a question. In the United States, the working class are Democrats. The middle class are Republicans. The upper class are Communists."

Communists, they had exchanged one romantic and quasi-religious ideology for another. Just as they had once believed in all things Soviet, they now believed in all things anti-Soviet. When events appeared to contradict their ideology, they denied the events rather than their ideology.

Burnham had changed sides, but he had retained the underlying skepticism and individualism that had led him to choose Trotskyism over Stalinism and then abandon Trotskyism. Burnham also had a more sophisticated understanding of politics than Meyer, Schlamm, and the other conservatives of the 1950s. Drawing upon his experience in the left, Burnham had developed in *The Machiavellians* a fundamental distinction between a "utopian" and a "scientific" politics. It was this distinction that informed his tactical understanding of the Cold War and separated Burnham from his right-wing brethren.

Two events shook Burnham to rethink both his strategy and the view of the Soviet Union upon which it was based. In February 1956, Soviet Premier Nikita Khrushchev gave a speech to the Twentieth Congress of the Soviet Communist Party denouncing Stalin's terror and his "cult of personality" and initiating a process of "de-Stalinization" that led to a significant relaxation in internal repression.

Khrushchev's speech and the subsequent "thaw" directly contradicted Burnham's assertion that the Stalinist terror was "integral to Communism" as well as his broader identification of Stalinism with Communism. Burnham was initially skeptical of the speech and its effects, but by August, faithful to the evidence, he gave in. " 'The thaw' is modest in degree," he wrote. "Nevertheless it is real."

Then, in October, Burnham's assumptions were more severely tested. Hungarian Communists and nationalists, inspired by the thaw, restored to power Imre Nagy, who had been previously ousted by the Soviets. When the Nagy government, spurred by anti-Soviet rioting, announced that it was withdrawing from the Warsaw Pact, the Soviet Union launched a major invasion, overthrowing Nagy and installing its own puppet regime. The Hungarians called upon the United States and the Western European powers to come to their aid, but Eisenhower refused to intervene.

The events in Hungary corresponded almost exactly to the scenario that Burnham had sketched out in *Containment or Liberation?*, where he had warned that the West's failure to intervene would signal "the irreversibility of Communist world victory." But Burnham refused to join other conservatives in pressing for American intervention. In fact, he actively defended the Eisenhower administration's unwillingness to intervene militarily. He explained that in refusing to risk war through an "ultimatum or any comparable move with military implications," Eisenhower was following "liberal humanitarian" axioms that "are part of the reality of our time." "The basic Eisenhower axiom is that the United States will not deliberately initiate the risk of all-out nuclear war," Burnham wrote. "This axiom is probably accepted by the leadership of all nations, at least until and unless one of them makes a decisive armament breakthrough. Therefore a policy proposal that contradicts this axiom is merely Platonic, and not serious in a strategic sense."

Burnham's use of the term "Platonic" to describe the proposal of the liberationists was particularly significant. Burnham was saying that those who called for military intervention were practicing a utopian rather than a scientific politics. They were refusing to recognize that society's historic values and traditions ("axioms" did not merely refer to passing currents of public opinion), expressed in the opinions of Western leaders, did not permit the enactment of the kind of foreign policy that conservatives—and Burnham himself!—had espoused.

In addition, while most conservatives saw the Hungarian invasion as an affirmation of Soviet power, Burnham perceptively saw it as a first sign of disintegration. In *National Review*, he argued that the Hungarian uprising was the "initial phase" in the "breakup of 'the Yalta pattern' according to which Eastern Europe has been organized as a satellite area of the Moscow-dictated Soviet empire." And he contended that Eastern Europe was kept within the Soviet camp not only by force of arms but also by fear of a rearmed, reunified Germany. In order to accelerate the breakup of the Soviet empire, the United States would have to find some way of allaying Eastern European fears of a rearmed Germany.

To accomplish this, Burnham advocated exactly what Lippmann had proposed in 1947 and Kennan a year later: the unification and neutralization of a disarmed Germany and the withdrawal of American troops from Western Europe and Soviet troops from Eastern Europe. Burnham called on the United States and West German Chancellor Konrad Adenauer to negotiate reunification and neutralization along the lines that had been followed in Austria in 1955, when both sides had agreed to withdraw in exchange for an Austrian guarantee of neutrality in the Cold War.

Burnham was proposing to negotiate with a power that he had formerly described as being irrevocably at war with the West. He defended his proposal by altering his view of the Soviet Union's relationship to Western Europe. In *Containment or Liberation?* Burnham had argued that by referring to the Soviet Union as "Russia," Kennan had revealed his mistaken conception of Soviet global intentions. Burnham now conceded that Soviet behavior could not be understood exclusively in terms of Communism. "The relative weight" of the Russian and Communist elements "shift from time to time, with now one and then the other predominant," he wrote. "The Soviet Union is Communist in its relation to the underdeveloped nations, but more and more Russian in its relation to Europe (including the captive nations of East Europe) and the West generally."

And Burnham rejected the charge—expressed in an earlier

*National Review* editorial by Buckley—that it was "immoral" to seek coexistence with the Soviet Union. "This is not a moral, but a strategic and geopolitical program. In fact, I would say that if morality enters in at all on this point, it is immoral for one nation not to try to coexist peacefully with every other— no matter what their regimes."

Burnham's articles predictably caused a furor on *National Review*'s editorial board as well as among the conservative public. In a series of rebuttals in *National Review*, Schlamm and Meyer accused Burnham of abandoning the doctrine he had conceived. Schlamm threatened to resign over the publication of Burnham's "Austrian solution," and his rift with Burnham played an important part in his resignation from *National Review* in August 1957.

For their part, Meyer and Schlamm refused even to acknowledge a change in the Soviet regime since Stalin's death. They insisted that the Soviet Union remained Stalinist to its core and that Khrushchev's speech and the "thaw" were an elaborate ruse. "The incorrigibly naive West does not understand that Stalinization was the prerequisite for any 'denial of Stalin,' " Schlamm wrote.

Meyer was particularly aghast at Burnham's defense of coexistence. "If the essential dynamic of the enemy is an ideology directed towards the destruction of religion, of freedom, of the very kind of moral being we regard man to be . . . ," Meyer wrote, "then it is immoral to base long-term policy on anything less than the destruction of that ideology by all means in our power."

Burnham's colleagues were correct about this much: his "Austrian solution" amounted to a de facto abdication and his "Russian" view of the Soviet Union a de jure abandonment of the liberation doctrine. Burnham's new position was in practice not all that different from George Kennan's and anticipated the strategy pursued by Henry Kissinger in the Nixon and Ford administrations. Hearing the rumble of Soviet tanks in Budapest, Burnham had discerned, not totalitarian power, but weakness. He sensed the possibility of ending the Cold War, and called upon the Eisenhower administration to hasten the process.

Burnham's about-face was testimony to his own lack of dogmatism—to his exercise of the realism that he admired in the Machiavellians. In the course of a year, faced with events that defied his prior analysis, Burnham had undertaken a revision of his views no less drastic than the revision he undertook in the year he left the Trotskyist movement.

During the two years he was fighting with Schlamm and Meyer, Burnham was writing a book about American government, which he called *Congress and the American Tradition*. In *The Struggle for the World*, Burnham had expressed doubt that American pluralism could stand up to the challenge of a cold war, but now he expressed a far more optimistic and generous view of the American system. Burnham's approach to American democracy, drawn from Madison and the Machiavellians, complemented what had become his realistic approach to foreign policy. Burnham contrasted a liberal with a conservative philosophy of government: liberals believed in the perfectibility of man; they sought to embody the democratic will in unmediated institutions. If socialism had tended toward totalitarianism, liberalism tended toward what Burnham called "Caesarism"—meaning, in America, the unchecked rule of the executive.

Burnham identified conservatism with the Federalists' skeptical view of human nature and with the constitutional theory of checks and balances. In American history, Burnham identified conservatism with the supremacy of Congress, and he saw in the diminution of Congress's role—a process that had begun during Theodore Roosevelt's presidency at the dawn of the American Century—the growing ascendancy of liberal political thought.

Burnham's view of government jibed with the prevailing conservative disenchantment with the New Deal and Court-ordered desegregation. But it also ran counter to a kind of right-wing authoritarianism that had sought political salvation in the rise of strong national leaders like General Douglas MacArthur and Senator Joseph McCarthy. It also appeared inconsistent with Burnham's call, in *The Struggle for the World* and his early Cold War books, for a centralized national leadership that could counter Communism's centralization. Burnham's philosophy of government, like his foreign policy in the wake of Hungary, bespoke caution and gradualism, containment rather than roll-back.

Burnham appeared to be on the verge of a new synthesis whose premises would be as different from those of *Containment or Liberation?* as Burnham's *The Managerial Revolution* had been from Trotsky's *The Revolution Betrayed.* The new philosophy would be termed conservative but in the tradition of Burke and Disraeli rather than of Buckley and McCarthy. It would be an evolutionary rather than counterrevolutionary conservatism that aimed to modify rather than overthrow existing society, which was liberal. Burnham failed, however, to draw the logical conclusions from his writings in *National Review* and *Congress and the American Tradition.* Having taken one step forward, he took one step backward, retreating to the verities of the 1950s right wing and his old Cold War books.

By 1957, Burnham may have wearied of factional quarrels and feared the consequences of a new revision. Ralph de Toledano, also a refugee from the left, believed that Burnham's "lance was broken" in the bitter quarrels of the 1940s and early 1950s.

Whatever the reason, Burnham did not go from the debate over his "Austrian solution" to a new conception of U.S. foreign policy. Instead, he reverted to the dreary paranoia of *Containment or Liberation?* By December 1957, he was urging in *National Review* that the United States "knock Albania out of the Soviet empire."

Burnham's discussion of the Vietnam War in *National Review* reflected both the best and the worst of *Containment or Liberation?* His assessment of American tactics was far more realistic than that of the Kennedy and Johnson administrations. From 1964 to 1972, he continually warned that *"la sale guerre"* could not be won on the scale on which the United States was fighting it. And he attacked the Wilsonian premises of American intervention. "If we have an excuse for being in Vietnam," Burnham wrote, "it can only be our own security." But as if the debate about the "Austrian solution" had never occurred, he blithely proposed that the United States consider nuclear, chemical, and biological weapons and an invasion of China. He also wildly overestimated the effect of an American defeat in Vietnam. It would, he warned in June 1965, mean "the foldback of our basic line of defense to our own Pacific coast." "Rollback" still obsessed him—this time in reverse.

In 1964, Burnham tried to sum up his reflections on liberalism and the Cold War in *The Suicide of the West*, but it simply reiterated the formulations of *Containment or Liberation?* It was as if he had learned nothing in the intervening decade. Gone was his recognition, stated clearly in the debate over Hungary, that the Soviet empire was not expanding but "breaking up," however long that process would take. Instead, Burnham reverted to the hysterical but comforting warnings of the early 1950s.

He defined his terms more crudely than ever. According to Burnham, the West (a term he identified with post–700 A.D. white Northern European Christian civilization) was "shrinking" because it had lost the "will to survive" in the face of the threat of Soviet Communism and the challenge from backward

Third World peoples. What had sapped the West's will was liberal ideology. "Liberalism is the ideology of Western suicide," Burnham wrote.

To prevent this suicide, Burnham argued,

> there would have to be reasserted the pre-liberal conviction that Western Civilization, this Western man, is both different from, and superior in quality to, other civilizations and non-civilizations . . . And there would have to be a renewed willingness, legitimized by that conviction, to use superior power and the threat of power to defend the West against all challenges and challengers.

In *The Struggle for the World*, Burnham had used Toynbee's theory of the rise and fall of empire—adapted from the British experience—to illuminate America's rise to world leadership and to spell out the responsibilities that had fallen to America and that few Americans at the time were willing to acknowledge. But in *The Suicide of the West*, Burnham merely used Toynbee to rationalize his pessimism and as a club with which to beat liberals. In Burnham's earlier works, he had been able, if facilely, to come to terms with the rapidly shifting world pyramid. But in the end Burnham was incapable of seeing past the evangelical polarizations of the Cold War.

*The Suicide of the West* was the product of an old man grousing about the world having gone downhill. At best, it was a work of imperial nostalgia. Just as the American Century was beginning to falter—the victim not of Soviet military aggression but of European and Japanese economic development—Burnham wanted the United States to mimic nineteenth-century Britain and to pick up the white man's burden of imperialism.

In the Nixon years, faced with an apparent threat to established order from the left, Burnham swung back to the authoritarianism of his Cold War books, calling for a "regime that will be authoritative and not liberal." But he was among the very first conservatives to recognize and denounce the threat to constitutional government posed by the Watergate scandal. In the mid-1970s, after the threat of the New Left had receded, Burnham appeared particularly open to new directions. He praised the Carter administration's initiatives toward China, the Panama Canal, and Israel and Egypt. "Our government," he wrote in a *National Review* column, "has been doing better than we have a right to expect."

Burnham took the lead in backing the Panama Canal treaty, helping to convince Buckley of the treaty's merits. In January 1978, Burnham assisted him when he debated Ronald Reagan on the treaty. But on the airplane back to New York, Burnham suffered the first symptoms of a debilitating illness that by the end of a year would deprive him of his memory. For the last nine years of his life, Burnham was incapable of recalling what happened from one day to the next.

On the right, Burnham has been remembered primarily for his apocalyptic Cold War strategy of rollback. In 1983, for instance, conservative foreign policy expert and self-described Burnham disciple Brian Crozier recommended in *National Review* that "American (and British) politicians in high places take time to read Burnham, or at the very least, the most succinct of the vital series, *Containment or Liberation?*" *The Suicide of the West*, probably his worst book, was reprinted and became a cult object among Reagan's speechwriting staff. Until the very end of the Cold War, conservatives remained trapped within the worldview and strategy that Chambers and Burnham provided.

# 6

# William Fulbright and Barry Goldwater
## The Realist and the Ideologue

Of all the changes in American life wrought by the Cold War, the most important by far, in my opinion, has been the massive diversion of energy and resources from the creative pursuits of civilized society to the conduct of a costly and interminable struggle for world power.

—WILLIAM FULBRIGHT, 1964

On June 29, 1961, speaking to an almost empty Senate chamber, J. William Fulbright offered what he called "reflections upon recent events and continuing problems." Self-effacing, scholarly in manner, and slightly stooped, the senator from Arkansas had become the chairman of the Senate Foreign Relations Committee in 1959 and had barely missed being selected as John Kennedy's Secretary of State. Now he offered his first tentative criticisms of the administration's foreign policy.

Fulbright warned that the United States should not allow itself to be drawn into "costly commitments of its resources to peripheral struggles in which the principal Communist powers are not themselves directly involved." In both Cuba and Laos, Fulbright noted, the United States was not facing a threat to its "national security," but it was "exaggerating their significance and not reacting to them judiciously . . . We often hear that the existence of a Communist regime in Cuba is intolerable to the United States. But is that really the case? I know it is embarrassing and annoying and potentially dangerous, but is it really intolerable?"

Fulbright's words—barely two months after the Kennedy administration's abortive Bay of Pigs invasion—bordered on heresy, and Senator Barry Goldwater of Arizona was quick to take him to task. Widely known for his best-selling 1960 book, *Conscience of a Conservative*, the square-jawed, silver-haired Arizona Republican had become the leader of the hard-line conservatives advocating the rollback of Communism, even if it entailed world war. Listening to Fulbright's speech, Goldwater said he found himself "becoming first surprised, then amazed, and finally alarmed." If the United States followed Fulbright's advice on Russia and China, then, Goldwater warned, "the world—all of it—is theirs for the taking." Goldwater called upon the Kennedy administration to make "total victory" over "the tyrannical forces of international communism" its "fundamental purpose."

Fulbright was not willing to let the junior senator have the last word. Ten days later, he took the Senate floor to answer Goldwater. "I must confess to some difficulty in understanding precisely what 'total victory' means in this age of ideological conflict and nuclear weapons," he remarked.

For the decade to come, Fulbright and Goldwater would define the alternatives in the debate over foreign policy. When the Kennedy administration signed a test-ban treaty with the Soviet Union, Fulbright enthusiastically championed it through Senate ratification and Goldwater led the opposition. And then, as the United States began sending troops to Vietnam, Fulbright called for negotiated withdrawal, while Goldwater advocated further military escalation.

On a deeper level, Fulbright's and Goldwater's words in the early 1960s—uttered as American power reached its zenith—set the terms of debate for the rest of the century. In Fulbright's warning about "costly commitments to peripheral struggles" was the dawning realization that in attempting to fight the Cold War and to redeem the promise of the American Century, the United States was overextending itself, eroding the foundations of its supremacy. And Goldwater's insistence upon "total victory" appealed to the dogged refusal of many—conservatives in particular—to accept a world in which U.S. power had limits.

Both Fulbright and Goldwater were politicians defined primarily by their ideas rather than by their service to party, constituents, or lobbyists. Both had a reputation for saying what they believed—sometimes to their own detriment. In November 1946, after the Democrats lost both the House and the Senate, freshman senator Fulbright deeply offended President Harry Truman by suggesting that the chief executive follow British precedent and resign. During his 1964 presidential campaign, Goldwater frightened many voters by his jocular threat to "lob a nuclear weapon into the men's room of the Kremlin."

The son of a wealthy farmer-businessman, Fulbright was raised in Fayetteville, the site of the University of Arkansas. After starring as a halfback on the Razorback football team, he went to Oxford on a Rhodes scholarship. At Oxford, Fulbright fell under the spell of political scientist R. B. McCallum, an admirer of Woodrow Wilson's internationalism. He also absorbed the British respect for government and politics as a principled vocation—a conviction that, in the context of American politics, placed him in the tradition of Croly, Wallace, and other progressives.

In 1939 Fulbright returned to Fayetteville to become the nation's youngest university president. He got the job partly through the influence of his mother, who after his father's death had become the editor and owner of the Fayetteville newspaper, but then was fired in 1941 after one of his mother's political enemies won the governorship. In 1942 Fulbright ran successfully for Congress, and in 1944 was elected to the Senate over the man who had fired him. Fulbright quickly made a mark for himself. In his maiden House speech, Fulbright defended Henry Wallace when first-term Republican House member Clare Boothe Luce termed Wallace's support for a United Nations "Globaloney." Fulbright, like Wallace, was flush with Wilsonian idealism. He favored a powerful international body that would have its own armed forces and in 1943 even got the House to pass a resolution approving "the creation of appropriate international machinery with power adequate to prevent future aggression and to maintain lasting peace." Then in Fulbright's first term in the Senate, he won acceptance of an international exchange program for scholars that still bears his name.

In Washington, Fulbright felt the influence of Walter Lippmann, who befriended the young senator. From Lippmann, Fulbright acquired a more realistic view of international relations. Fulbright fought for a strong UN, criticizing both Roosevelt and Truman for failing to put enough teeth into the organization. But when the organization emerged in final form, weakened by a great-power veto in the Security Council, Fulbright laid aside his hopes for world federalism and began to see the world and the emerging Cold War in classic balance-of-power terms. For the next twenty-five years, Fulbright saw the world through the lens of realism rather than Cold War evangelism.

Fulbright backed the Truman Doctrine, the Marshall Plan, NATO, and the Korean War, but dissented from the apocalyptic anti-Communist rhetoric with which Truman and Secretary of State Dean Acheson clothed their initiatives. As the historian Eugene Brown argues, Fulbright's support for the Cold War was based on a kind of "economic realpolitik," rather than on fear of a worldwide Communist conspiracy. He worried about the Soviet Union "shutting off the U.S. from the resources of the greater world." He was more concerned about an expansionist Soviet Union dominating Middle Eastern oil supplies than a Communist conspiracy taking over the State Department. In 1951, Fulbright told an interviewer that he "had not thought of our enemy as being Communism, I thought of it as primarily being an imperialist Russia." In the late 1940s, only a few policy experts like Burnham, Lippmann, and Kennan appreciated the subtlety of the distinction, but it would be an important basis for Fulbright's dissent during the 1960s.

Fulbright also made another distinction that would not appear critical until the 1960s. In 1956, he sharply criticized the Eisenhower administration for withdrawing a promised loan from Nasser's Egypt because Nasser had refused to align himself with the United States against the Soviet Union. Eisenhower's Secretary of State, John Foster Dulles, brooked no middle ground between the U.S.-led "free world" and the Soviet-led Communist bloc, but Fulbright argued that the United States should distinguish Third World nationalism from Communism even when they seemed sometimes to be combined in the same movements. "Egyptian nationalism was a powerful force which could, if recognized for what it was and carefully handled, be directed toward political freedom instead of Communism," Fulbright commented. This distinction would shape Fulbright's views of the Vietnam War.

Fulbright was a peculiar combination of Wilsonian liberal, Burkean conservative, and Southern Bourbon Democrat. He had an abiding skepticism about popular democracy. The dilemma of democratic thought, Fulbright said in a lecture in 1963, was "to reconcile the irrefutable evidences of human weakness and irrationality, which modern history has so abundantly provided, with a political philosophy whose very foundation is the assumption of human goodness and reason." The development of foreign policy is hampered, Fulbright continued, by "the durable myth of Jacksonian democracy, the view that any literate citizen can do almost any job and that a democracy can do without a highly trained administrative elite."

Fulbright despised Senator Joseph McCarthy not only because he wildly exaggerated the threat of Communism but also because he was a populist demagogue who betrayed the worthy vocation of politics. McCarthy's antics "offended" him, he later said. Indeed, Fulbright was the only senator in February 1954 to vote against appropriating funds for McCarthy's Government Operations Committee and later that year he wrote and got Vermont Republican Ralph Flanders to sponsor the censure resolution that eventually destroyed McCarthy's career.

Fulbright's views on civil rights unashamedly reflected the conventional views of the Southern politician of his day. He defended the South's use of a poll tax and voted against every major civil rights bill of the 1950s and 1960s. In 1957, he signed Senator Richard Russell's infamous Southern Manifesto urging states to resist the Supreme Court's 1954 decision desegregating schools. Fulbright explained his opposition to civil rights as the price he had to pay to be able to hew to an independent line on foreign policy. In a 1946 speech at the University of Chicago, he said, "The average legislator early on in his career discovers that there are certain interests, or prejudices, of his constituents that are dangerous to trifle with. Some of these prejudices may not be of fundamental importance to the welfare of the nation, in which case he is justified in humoring them even though he may disapprove."

Fulbright probably would not have been reelected in 1962 had he defied his state's white majority, but he and the country eventually paid for his opposition to civil rights. In December 1960, Kennedy decided not to nominate Fulbright as his Secretary of State largely because of pressure from civil rights organizations. Instead, Kennedy chose the dour, unoriginal Dean Rusk, who helped lead the United States into the Vietnam quagmire.

Barry Goldwater was the first major political leader of the new conservative movement that first emerged among intellectuals in the mid-1950s. He exemplified much of what was new about that conservatism: its spread from the Midwest to the Sunbelt and its abandonment of isolationism and anti-Semitism. Goldwater's paternal grandparents were Polish Jews who emigrated to the United States during the gold rush. "Big Mike" Goldwater started a combination bordello-saloon in Sonora, California. Mike and Sarah's children eventually made their way to Arizona, where Goldwater's uncle Morris became the mayor of Prescott and Goldwater's father, Baron, became the owner and manager of a Phoenix department store. Baron married a Midwestern Episcopalian who had come to Phoenix for her health. Barry, born in 1909, was raised as an Episcopalian. He was sent to Staunton, a socially prestigious military school in Virginia that accepted Jewish students. He wanted to go to West Point, but had to return to Arizona and attend the University of Arizona because of his father's ill health. When his father died in his sophomore year, he dropped out to join the family business. For the rest of his life, Goldwater would regret not having pursued a career in the military.

Much of Goldwater's conservatism was simply that of the Western small businessman. He was antilabor, antigovernment, and suspicious of big corporations and New York banks. Conservatives who hated Eastern establishment Republicans would take delight in quoting Goldwater's request to give him a saw and he would cut off the Eastern seaboard and let it float out to the Atlantic. But the quip had nothing to do with Goldwater's distrust of New York's Council on Foreign Relations. It originated in his experience in New York City in the 1930s when the banks would not honor his out-of-state checks.

If Goldwater harbored irrational resentments, he did not share the isolationism, nativism, and anti-Semitism of the Republican conservatives of the 1930s. In his first autobiography, *With No Apologies*, which appeared in 1976, Goldwater said that he came to fear Hitler well before war broke out because he recalled how his ancestors had been driven from Poland by anti-Semitism. While the Republican right was organizing in 1940–41 against American entry into the war and some right-wing intellectuals were blaming Jewish influence for the Roosevelt administration's eagerness to intervene, Goldwater was volunteering for the Arizona Air Corps and cheering on Roosevelt's efforts at rearmament. After the war, when Goldwater became active in Arizona Republican politics, he continued to back the party's internationalist wing, supporting Eisenhower against Senator Robert Taft in the great nomination battle of 1952. (In fact, many of the new conservatives of the 1950s like Burnham and *National Review* publisher William Rusher backed the internationalist Eisenhower against Taft. They were far more concerned with the threat of Communism than the danger of "entangling alliances.")

As he campaigned for Eisenhower, Goldwater ran for the Senate. On the coattails of Eisenhower, he upset the Democratic incumbent. In his campaign, Goldwater had focused on economic issues rather than foreign policy, and in his first term he was far more concerned with fighting big government and big labor than Communism. As a member of the Labor and Human Resources Committee, Goldwater insisted that United Auto Workers' Walter Reuther was a greater menace to freedom than the Teamsters' Jimmy Hoffa or the Soviet-led world Communist conspiracy. "I would rather have Hoffa stealing my money than Reuther stealing my freedom," Goldwater said. "Reuther is more dangerous than the sputniks or anything Russia might do." When Goldwater broke with the Eisenhower administration, it was not over foreign policy, but over government spending, and he denounced the administration's 1957 budget as a "Dime Store New Deal." At the Western Republican Conference in 1959, Goldwater referred entirely to domestic issues in distinguishing his own views from those of New York governor Nelson Rockefeller. "My kind of Republican Party is committed to a free state, limited central power, a reduction in bureaucracy, and a balanced budget," Goldwater declared.

Goldwater's foreign policy was based on a simpleminded analogy between the Nazis and the Soviets and between World War II and the Cold War. He did not begin to draw sharp distinctions between his foreign policy views and those of other

Republicans until the late 1950s—probably under the influence of *National Review* and of *National Review* senior editor Brent Bozell, who became an aide to Goldwater. In 1957, Bozell had joined Frank Meyer in the magazine's pages in attacking James Burnham for favoring the neutralization of Eastern Europe; but privately Bozell went even beyond Meyer—advocating not only the "rollback" of Soviet Communism but also a preemptive nuclear strike against Moscow. In 1959, Goldwater delegated Bozell to write *Conscience of a Conservative*, which was then brought out under Goldwater's name by Victor, an obscure publishing house in Kentucky.

Goldwater's book was based on the apocalyptic worldview of Chambers's *Witness* and Burnham's *Containment or Liberation?* Missing from it was any recognition of the Soviet turn from Stalinism or the growing divisions within the Communist camp. Goldwater portrayed the Soviet Union as the leader of a monolithic movement that had grown increasingly more powerful and was on the verge of dominating the world. "We are confronted by a revolutionary world movement that possesses not only the will to dominate every inch of the globe, but increasingly the capacity to do so," Goldwater wrote. If the United States did not want to be defeated, "our only hope is to proclaim victory as our aim and then to press boldly and unremittingly on all fronts—always prepared to fight and making sure the Communists always know we are prepared to fight."

Goldwater was not consistently dogmatic—he could change his opinions of people if presented with contrary evidence—but he did not read seriously and did not subject his views to any serious reflection. Whereas Fulbright liked to spend his spare time reading history, Goldwater liked to go down to the Senate machine shop and tinker. As a result, Goldwater's simple views, as articulated by Bozell in 1960, never really changed.

At the 1960 Republican convention Goldwater became a national figure when he denounced the "Park Avenue Compact" between nominee Richard Nixon and Rockefeller that committed the Republicans to civil rights—Goldwater called it a "Republican Munich." As a protest candidate, Goldwater was nominated for President and received support from delegations from South Carolina, Louisiana, and Arizona. By 1962, his supporters were organizing a draft Goldwater effort for 1964, and Goldwater himself had become the party's chief critic of the Kennedy administration's foreign policy.

Goldwater's criticisms of Kennedy's policies were summed up in the title of his 1962 book, *Why Not Victory?* Goldwater backed an invasion of Cuba; he opposed Kennedy's willingness to make Laos neutral; he accused Kennedy of acquiescing in the construction of the Berlin Wall; he opposed any arms treaties with the Soviet Union, charging that they prevented the United States from maintaining its supremacy. Goldwater even denigrated Kennedy's success in October 1962 in forcing the Soviet Union to remove its missiles from Cuba, because the President had promised not to invade Cuba. The United States either had to fight or be defeated.

When Goldwater attacked Fulbright, he conflated Fulbright's positions with those of the Kennedy administration. It was typical of Goldwater's failure to make distinctions. Fulbright's relationship to Kennedy, who had been a junior member of the Foreign Relations Committee, was quite complicated. President Kennedy had considerable respect for Fulbright and, unlike President Johnson, tolerated dissent on the part of congressional leaders. Fulbright, for his part, did not hesitate to state his opinions, even when they diverged from the administration's.

Fulbright was critical early on. He had advised Kennedy not to go ahead with the Bay of Pigs. "The Castro regime is a thorn in the flesh; but it is not a dagger in the heart," he wrote the

President in a private memo. Fulbright also warned Kennedy against trying to achieve a military solution in Laos, where a Communist insurgency was on the verge of taking over the country. And he remained contemptuous of the space program, which he regarded as a waste of money. But he applauded the administration's Alliance for Progress and its other efforts to deter Communism through economic development rather than through military alliance.

By the administration's third and last year, however, Fulbright had become more enthusiastic. He backed the plan to neutralize Laos. He had paid little attention to what was going on in Vietnam, but believed the United States was following a prudent course backing the Diem regime against an attack from North Vietnam. He applauded Kennedy's blockade of Cuba —the Soviet missiles constituted a direct provocation, he believed—and he saw an opportunity for Soviet-American détente emerging from the blockade's success. In May 1963, Fulbright expressed his optimism at the Fletcher School of Law and Diplomacy at Tufts University, where he delivered a series of lectures on international relations.

In these lectures, subsequently published in a short book, *Prospects for the West*, Fulbright spelled out a new direction for American foreign policy—one that not only repudiated Goldwater's "rollback" strategy but went considerably beyond Kennedy's tentative efforts at achieving stability in the Cold War. Fulbright easily dismissed Goldwater's view that America had to fight or risk inevitable defeat by an increasingly powerful Communist bloc. Fulbright argued that the United States and its allies had become steadily more powerful than the Soviet Union and its allies. He noted that while Western Europe had fully recovered from the war and become an economic power in its own right, the Soviet bloc was splintering. "No longer the single monolithic center in the Communist bloc, as it was in Stalin's time, Moscow is now confronted with independent centers of power in Peking and, to a much lesser extent, in certain of the less subservient European satellites."

Fulbright rejected out of hand the common view of the Soviet Union as bent inexorably on world domination. Instead, he argued that whatever its domestic practices, the Soviet Union had become less revolutionary in its foreign policy. "The evolution of Soviet policy," Fulbright said, "has largely reflected the intrusion of traditional nationalist attitudes upon an internationalist ideology with universal aims." He renounced the prevailing understanding of the Cold War as a life-or-death struggle between capitalism and Communism. "The issue between the Soviet Union and the West is not 'Communism versus capitalism,' but the universal and unlimited aims of Soviet policy."

Fulbright disavowed any idea of changing Soviet society. The West should make it clear "that it is not Communism which is at issue between the Soviet Union and the West but Communist *imperialism*, and that the Soviet Union, in so far as it renounces expansionist and subversive ambitions, can enjoy a safe and honorable national life without threat or danger from the West." Even more significant, Fulbright rejected any concept of winning or losing the Cold War. Rather than being concerned about the preponderance of Soviet power, Fulbright was worried that overwhelming American and European military and economic power would drive the Soviet Union into a corner. He suggested that the United States model its policy on the balance-of-power strategy that Britain pursued after the defeat of Napoleon in 1815. The United States, like Britain with France, should be careful not to become so superior to the Soviet Union that it might provoke "an act of desperation on the part of a powerful adversary who has become convinced that he must either strike or go under."

Fulbright's analysis now seems prescient, but at the time it was shared by no other politicians and by only a few maverick policy experts, realists like Lippmann, George Kennan, and Hans Morgenthau. Not only Goldwater Republicans but also Secretary of State Dean Rusk still referred to a monolithic "Sino-Soviet bloc" that threatened the imminent destruction of the United States. And even Kennedy's most liberal advisers would not have accepted Fulbright's classical balance-of-power analysis of America's role. Most policymakers continued to believe that the United States was fighting a version of World War II. Yet Fulbright's words did have some influence on the Kennedy administration.

In Kennedy's pathbreaking speech at American University on June 10, 1963, he declared his willingness to achieve peace with the Soviet Union. Much of his prescription for peace echoed Fulbright's advice. "We must conduct our affairs in such a way that it becomes in the Communists' interest to agree on a genuine peace," Kennedy said. "Let each nation choose its own future, so long as that choice does not interfere with the choices of others." Following that speech, Kennedy won agreement from Khrushchev to a limited test ban, and Fulbright accompanied Kennedy to Moscow in August to sign the treaty. It looked to Fulbright and the administration as if U.S.-Soviet relations were on the verge of being transformed.

Kennedy's assassination in November by no means quelled Fulbright's optimism. He had had a long-standing friendship with Lyndon Johnson, who referred to him fondly as "my Secretary of State," and who had made it possible for him to assume the chairmanship of the Foreign Relations Committee in 1959 by convincing the aging chairman, Theodore Green, to step down. Fulbright was the first legislator with whom Johnson conferred after being sworn in as President. And Fulbright enthusiastically predicted that under Johnson the United States was on "the verge of a golden age."

In March 1964, Fulbright expressed his hope for a new future in a speech on the Senate floor. Later published in a book, *Old Myths and New Realities*, it was perhaps the most impressive statement by a senator since World War II and one of the few that could rival the speeches of Clay, Calhoun, and Webster. Ironically, it was given during a Southern filibuster against the Civil Rights Act of 1964.

Fulbright's theme was similar to that of *Prospects for the West*, but he now argued it more aggressively. He labeled as "myth" the quasi-religious Cold War conception of the Soviet Union as the embodiment of evil. "We are used to looking at the world and indeed at ourselves in moralistic rather than empirical terms," Fulbright explained. "We are predisposed to regard any conflict as a clash between good and evil rather than as simply a clash between conflicting interests."

Fulbright insisted upon looking beyond the labels of "Communist" and "capitalist" to the diverse reality that they denoted. "I believe that the Communist world is indeed hostile to the free world in its general and long-term intentions, but that the existence of this animosity in principle is far less important for our foreign policy than the great variations in its intensity and character both in time and among the individual members of the Communist bloc," Fulbright said. "The Soviet Union, though still a most formidable adversary, has ceased to be totally and implacably hostile to the West. It has therefore became possible to divert some of our energies from the prosecution of the Cold War to the relaxation of the Cold War and to deal with the Soviet Union, for certain purposes, as a normal state with normal and traditional interests."

Fulbright also sounded a theme that would become more important to him in the years ahead: how the Cold War had "inverted America's priorities." "Of all the changes in American life wrought by the Cold War," Fulbright said, "the most important by far, in my opinion, has been the massive diversion of energy and resources from the creative pursuits of civilized society to the conduct of a costly and interminable struggle for world power." He was particularly critical of America's diversion of resources to the space project. "The issue between freedom and dictatorship is a great deal more than a competition in technological stunts," Fulbright said. "We must reassess the priorities of our public policy, with a view to redressing the disproportion between our military and space efforts on the one hand, and our education and human welfare programs on the other."

Fulbright reiterated his doubts about the American obsession with Castro. "We have flattered a noisy but minor demagogue by treating him as if he were a Napoleonic menace," he said. But he backed Kennedy and Johnson's support for the Diem government, which he believed was under attack from an aggressive China and North Vietnam. "Our purpose is to uphold and strengthen the Geneva agreements of 1954 and 1962—that is to say, to establish viable independent states in Indochina and elsewhere in Southeast Asia, which will be free of and secure from the domination of Communist China and Communist North Vietnam." In seeing China through the lens of Vietnam, Fulbright showed that even his vision was clouded by Cold War myth.

Fulbright's colleagues on both sides of the aisle assumed that his speech was not merely an expression of his own opinion but a statement of the Johnson administration's priorities. That winter, Johnson launched his Great Society program—the most ambitious set of social welfare measures since Roosevelt's New Deal—and he continually rejected Republican calls to escalate American involvement in the war in Vietnam. In the 1964 presidential election against Goldwater, Johnson appeared to be posing the alternatives in exactly the terms that Fulbright had used in his "Old Myths and New Realities" speech. But Fulbright and much of the country soon learned otherwise.

By the beginning of 1964, the draft Goldwater committee, organized by Clifton White and William Rusher, had almost gotten enough commitments from delegates to win the nomination for Goldwater. But Goldwater was not enthusiastic about running for President against Johnson. He tried to back out in December, but was finally persuaded to change his mind by conservative senators who raised the specter of a Rockefeller takeover of the Republican Party.

As a presidential candidate, Goldwater was doomed from the start. His staff was inexperienced, and he was unwilling to disguise his extremist views. Goldwater's naïveté destroyed his own candidacy. He insisted on attacking tobacco subsidies in North Carolina and the TVA in Tennessee. He suggested giving NATO field commanders the right to use nuclear weapons. He refused to deliver scripted speeches and didn't like to say the same thing twice. Reporters always succeeded in goading him into what his campaign staff began to call "Goldwaterisms."

Goldwater opposed the Civil Rights Act of 1964, and was not above telling white audiences that "minority groups are running the country," but he did resist some of the more unseemly racial appeals pushed on him by his right-wing supporters. When black riots swept through Northern cities in the summer of 1964, Goldwater initiated an agreement with Johnson not to make the riots an issue in the fall election. In the campaign's last month, Goldwater also vetoed the broadcast of a film, *Choice*, that Clifton White and Rus Walton (later a minor figure on the Christian right) had produced for the campaign. The film, under the banner of "Mothers for a Moral America," featured a montage of black rioters, beatniks, and bare-breasted women. It was precisely the kind of demagogic appeal that Nixon would make in his "law and order" campaigns and that George Bush would stress in the 1988 campaign. But Goldwater wanted no part of it.

Johnson, meanwhile, successfully portrayed Goldwater as a warmonger who would precipitate a nuclear war. In the most famous commercial of the campaign, viewers saw a little girl picking petals from a flower followed by a nuclear explosion. And Johnson unequivocally rejected Goldwater's call to escalate the war in Vietnam by bombing the North. "I have had advice to load our planes with bombs and to drop them on certain areas that I think would enlarge the war and escalate the war, and result in our committing a good many American boys to fighting a war that I think ought to be fought by the boys of Asia to help protect their own land," Johnson said in a speech on August 29. "We have tried very carefully to restrain ourselves and not to enlarge the war."

In the end, Goldwater was obliterated. He won his home

state of Arizona and five states in the Deep South, largely because of his opposition to the Civil Rights Act. Goldwater returned to Arizona and never actively participated in presidential politics again. In 1968, he supported Richard Nixon, who had backed him in 1964, for President, and he ran successfully for the Senate seat vacated by retiring Carl Hayden. His simpleminded foreign policy views flourished in the Republican Party, revived in 1976 by Ronald Reagan's primary challenge against Gerald Ford and then triumphant in 1980 when Reagan won the presidency.

In 1964, Fulbright enthusiastically campaigned for Johnson, helping him win Arkansas in spite of popular opposition to the Texan's civil rights views. Fulbright liked Goldwater personally—they had belonged to the same college fraternity, Sigma Chi, and would jokingly give each other the secret fraternity handshake every time they met. But Fulbright thought the Arizonan was stupid and, if elected, would be a genuine menace. On the eve of the election, Fulbright wrote in *Saturday Review*, "It is possible—just possible—that the nation could withstand the domestic effects of a Goldwater presidency, but there seems little possibility that the nation could escape disaster under a Republican administration committed to the kind of foreign policy proposed by Senator Goldwater."

In part out of fear of Goldwater's challenge, Fulbright played a crucial role in backing Johnson's conduct of the war in Vietnam. At the beginning of August, the administration reported that North Vietnamese PT boats had attacked the U.S. destroyer *Maddox*, on an intelligence-gathering mission in the Gulf of Tonkin. Johnson responded with bombing raids against North Vietnam, claiming that the United States had done nothing to provoke the attacks. Johnson got Fulbright to introduce a resolution in the Senate authorizing the President to "take all necessary measures to repel any armed attack against the forces of the United States and to prevent further aggression."

However, Fulbright had already begun to have doubts about the war. In May 1964, he had sent a private note to Secretary of Defense Robert McNamara: "I have been gravely concerned over the situation even without reports of torture and indiscriminate bombing. We should cut our losses and withdraw." But convinced by Johnson that the attack was unprovoked and wishing to defend Johnson against Republican charges of appeasement, Fulbright steered the Tonkin Gulf resolution through Congress, brushing aside questions about who had fired first and whether the resolution gave the administration carte blanche to pursue the war in Vietnam. Later, he would see his role in winning support for the resolution as the greatest mistake of his career. As Johnson sharply escalated the war, Fulbright's assessment of Vietnam and the administration would change dramatically, as would his understanding of America's place in the world. He would come to see Vietnam as a watershed event in the country's postwar history.

Vietnam had been a French colony before World War II, when it was occupied by the Japanese. In accordance with America's anticolonial tradition, the Roosevelt administration planned to support UN trusteeship of Vietnam after the war, but the French insisted on recolonization. Eager for French cooperation in Europe, the United States acquiesced. When the French reinstalled Emperor Bao Dai, the Communist leader Ho Chi Minh organized a nationalist movement and raised a formidable guerrilla army.

Ho Chi Minh exemplified the ambiguities of the Communist as nationalist. Trained and sheltered by the Soviet and Chinese Communists, he was nonetheless a Vietnamese patriot brought up to suspect the great power to the north as much as the

French colonizers. He modeled Vietnam's first constitution on the American Declaration of Independence, and in 1946 addressed eight letters to Truman pleading with him to aid Vietnam's independence. But the French portrayed the colonial war as a Cold War battle, and after Communists seized control of China, the United States was determined to aid the French. By 1954, when Ho's forces defeated the French at Dienbienphu, the United States was paying 78 percent of France's military bill.

At Geneva in 1954, the French, British, Vietnamese, Soviets, and Chinese signed an agreement ending French rule and setting elections for a unified Vietnam for 1956. Foreign military presence was strictly limited. The United States did not participate in the Geneva accords, but publicly stated afterward that it would agree to their terms. The Eisenhower administration had no intention, however, of doing so. It sent in military advisers to strengthen the anti-Communist Ngo Dinh Diem, who in 1955 seized power in the South by deposing Emperor Bao Dai, who had appointed him Prime Minister. The United States was happy to back Diem in rejecting the North's pleas to hold elections in 1956. But as Diem began assassinating Communists in the South, a resistance began. North Vietnam initially discouraged a military response, but by 1959 assumed control of what had become a civil war in the South.

Under Kennedy, U.S. military involvement steadily increased—from 1,000 men in 1960 to about 16,000 by the end of 1963. As the Diem regime lost support, Kennedy decided to cooperate in his overthrow, but Diem's assassination in November 1963 only increased instability. By 1964, when Johnson took over the war, the South Vietnamese were on the verge of being defeated by the Communist-led National Liberation Front. Rather than negotiate his way out, Johnson had secretly decided that spring to escalate the war and had begun looking for a pretext to do so. The United States started sending the South Vietnamese on commando raids against the North and flying bombing runs over North Vietnam in unmarked planes from Laos. As Fulbright learned to his distress three years later, North Vietnam's attack against the *Maddox* was not unprovoked, but had been in response to the U.S.-sponsored South Vietnamese commando raids against nearby islands in the Gulf of Tonkin.

Fulbright's break with Johnson, however, did not first occur over Vietnam. In April 1965, the administration invaded the Dominican Republic—an action that spelled the end of the Alliance for Progress. In 1962, after the notorious dictator Rafael Trujillo was assassinated, democratic reformer Juan Bosch had been elected President, but Bosch was overthrown by a military coup ten months later. In April 1965, Bosch was on the verge of regaining power from the military when the Johnson administration, claiming Communists were behind Bosch's effort, intervened on the side of the military. After conducting hearings, Fulbright concluded that Communists played a minimal role in Bosch's movement. In a speech on the Senate floor in September, Fulbright said, "The United States turned its back on social revolution in Santo Domingo and associated itself with a corrupt and reactionary oligarchy." Angered by Fulbright's rebuff, Johnson cut him off, ending forever their close relationship. "Goldwater was able to maintain a personal relationship even if he disagreed with someone politically," Fulbright later recalled, "but Johnson demanded that you were either with him 100 percent or against him."

In January 1966, Fulbright took a much more serious step in opposition to the administration. Instead of holding cursory hearings to back the administration's request for foreign aid, Fulbright convened major hearings to examine the administration's conduct of the Vietnam War, and invited highly respected dissenters like Kennan and General James Gavin. The hearings were nationally televised, and succeeded in legiti-

mating opposition to the war, which previously had been con-
fined to radicals on a few college campuses. The hearings made
Fulbright a figure with a national constituency.

Fulbright's awakening on the war had come partly because
of the administration's escalation and because he had begun
to read widely about the war, including studies by French historian Jean Lacouture. He and his aide Seth Tillman had also
invited Vietnam expert Bernard Fall, who was then lecturing
at Howard University, to counsel them. Fall and Lacouture
convinced Fulbright of what the Pentagon Papers would later
establish: that the United States—not North Vietnam—had
originally violated the Geneva accords and that the rebellion
against the Diem regime had begun in the South rather than
in the North. Fulbright began to see the war in Vietnam, not
as an American effort to defend a sovereign nation against
Communist aggression, but as American intervention in a civil
war on the side of a corrupt client regime fighting forces that
stood for nationalism and against colonialism. Luce's *Time* was
not amused. Commenting on Fulbright's conduct of the hearings, the magazine wrote that the senator suffered from "a
blind spot" and "an emotional and intellectual reluctance to
believe that communism is a monolithic doctrine of belliger-
ence based on a fanatical dream of world domination."

After the hearings concluded, Fulbright gave a series of lectures at Johns Hopkins University, which were published at
the end of the year in a book entitled *The Arrogance of Power*.
Fulbright's lectures reflected how much the Dominican invasion and the escalation of war had transformed his own view
of America. In *Prospects for the West*, he had urged America to
model itself on the Britain that had emerged triumphant from
the Battle of Waterloo. America, in Fulbright's eyes, was a rising
rather than declining imperial great nation that must come to
terms with its almost unlimited power.

Now Fulbright compared the United States to late-
nineteenth-century Britain and to imperial Rome—nations

that had reached the apex of world power but in overreaching had declined. Like Britain and Rome, the United States had arrogantly identified its own power with the spread of virtue. "A great nation is peculiarly susceptible to the idea that its power is a sign of God's favor," Fulbright said. "Other great nations, reaching this critical juncture, have aspired to too much, and by overextension of effort have declined and then fallen."

In the Dominican Republic and South Vietnam, Fulbright saw the beginning of overextension. The United States, he said, "may be drifting into commitments which . . . are so far-reaching as to exceed even America's great capacities." Fulbright ascribed two different kinds of motives to America's will to intervene. One was the benevolent but misguided attempt to spread "the gospel of democracy." The other was a kind of imperial arrogance. "Despite its dangerous and unproductive consequences, the idea of being responsible for the whole world seems to be flattering to Americans and I am afraid it is turning our heads, just as the sense of universal responsibility turned the heads of ancient Romans and 19th century British."

In Vietnam, the United States had made the same mistake it made in Egypt in 1956, failing to give the drive toward nationalism priority over the threat of Communism. He described the Vietnam War as "an Asian civil war that has been expanded into a conflict between the United States and Asian communism . . . In Asia, as in Latin America, we have given our opposition to communism priority over our sympathy for nationalism because we have regarded communism as a kind of absolute evil."

Fulbright's foreign policy prescriptions in *The Arrogance of Power* were as farseeing as they were controversial. He urged the United States to seek the neutralization of Vietnam along the lines proposed by French President Charles de Gaulle. (Privately, he had advised Johnson in April 1965 that a Communist

Vietnam, wary of Chinese imperialism, might be more useful to American interests than a crippled client state in the South.) Fulbright also pressed for the normalization of relations with China. American hostility "is probably prolonging the extremist phase of the Chinese revolution," he argued.

Fulbright urged Americans to spend more time thinking about improving their democracy at home and less about exporting it overseas. "An excessive preoccupation with foreign relations over a long period of time is more than a manifestation of arrogance," Fulbright warned. "It is a drain on the power that gave rise to it, because it diverts a nation from the sources of its strength, which are in its domestic life."

The antiwar movement in the meantime was beginning to mass thousands in street demonstrations. *The Arrogance of Power* was quoted at protest rallies, and the aristocratic Foreign Relations Committee became identified with the fledgling forces of the New Left. But, as Fulbright noted in this book, the doctrines he was proposing were anything but liberal or left-wing. They were the kind of foreign policy measures espoused by European traditionalists like Burke, Castlereagh, and Metternich and were based upon nineteenth-century conceptions of diplomacy. "The kind of foreign policy I have been talking about is, in the true sense of the term, a *conservative* policy," Fulbright concluded. "It is an approach that accepts the world as it is, with all its existing nations and ideologies, with all its existing qualities and shortcomings."

Burnham and Chambers would have understood this use of the term "conservative," even if they did not agree with Fulbright's specific prescriptions. In the late 1950s, both men had seen themselves as representing older traditions of conservatism against the kind of mindless radical reaction that was so characteristic of 1950s conservatives. But Goldwater, temporarily in retirement in Phoenix, failed utterly to fathom what Fulbright was talking about. To Goldwater, the Arkansas senator was now verging on treason. "No American has the right or the justification to level such charges against his country,"

Goldwater said of Fulbright's lectures. Johnson himself called Fulbright a "nervous Nellie."

Fulbright survived Johnson's scorn and Goldwater's obloquy. In March 1968, Johnson, under siege from demonstrators and abandoned by the foreign policy establishment, partially halted the bombing, called for negotiations, and declared that he would not seek reelection. But Johnson's Vice President, Hubert Humphrey, was defeated in November by Richard Nixon, and the incoming President shelved Johnson's peace plans.

Fulbright had little influence over Nixon and Nixon's National Security Adviser and later Secretary of State, Henry Kissinger. While he adamantly opposed their continuation of the war in Vietnam, Fulbright applauded Nixon and Kissinger's détente policy with the Soviet Union and their normalization of relations with China. When some of Fulbright's Democratic colleagues complained that he was being too friendly to Kissinger, Fulbright replied, "What am I supposed to do? They are doing what I proposed for years." Writing in 1972, Fulbright noted the irony of Nixon having adopted his recommendations. "It is ironic that the shift from ideological crusade to classical power politics should have taken place—in so far as it has taken place—under the leadership of a president who was recently in the vanguard of that crusade."

Fulbright generously praised the arms-control treaties that the administration signed with the Soviet Union at a summit in May 1972. "The great importance of the Moscow summit was the acknowledgement by the two 'superpowers' of mutual vulnerability to each other's devastating nuclear power; the acceptance by the United States of the Soviet Union as an equal 'legitimate' great power; the acceptance by the Soviet Union of a stabilized non-revolutionary status quo; and reciprocal acknowledgement of each other's 'spheres of influence'—that term being a euphemism for zones of domination." In 1974, when Kissinger came under attack for wiretapping members of the National Security Council, Fulbright protected him from being swept up in the Watergate scandal. "What good does it do to have another scalp on the shelf?" he remarked.

But just as Nixon and Kissinger were embracing the conservative framework he had recommended in *The Arrogance of Power*, Fulbright was returning to the Wilsonian preoccupations of his youth. He had embraced power politics when his hopes for the UN foundered and he remained convinced that these politics were far preferable to the "ideological crusade" that Truman and Acheson had initiated. But once it appeared that Americans were about to abandon Cold War ideology for Metternichian realism, Fulbright himself felt obliged to move on to the next step and reassert the importance of international organization.

In *The Crippled Giant*, which was published in 1972, Fulbright, echoing arguments that Croly and Wilson had made in 1916, argued that the balance of power was at best only a temporary solution for the world's problems. "The fundamental defect of the balance of power system is that it is hardly more durable than the men who control it. As long as it is manipulated by intelligent or agile statesmen, like Metternich or Bismarck in the nineteenth century, the system is likely to hold up. But clever men pass from the scene, leaving their juggling acts to clumsy or pedestrian successors, who soon enough start dropping balls." Fulbright's solution was a strengthened UN that could genuinely mediate international disputes and play the role of "world policeman" that the United States had assigned to itself. "In international as in domestic affairs, we are in need of a system of laws rather than of men, a system that does not depend upon the cleverness or benevolence of the men who run it," Fulbright concluded. "If our lives are to be made secure, there is no alternative to an international community which is capable of making and enforcing civilized rules of international conduct, enforceable upon great nations as well as small ones." Fulbright, like Wilson, was advocating a "community of power" as an alternative to the balance of power. In *The Crippled Giant*, he even reintroduced Wallace's scheme for a UN-controlled armed force.

Fulbright also tried to solve the greater moral problem posed by U.S.-Soviet détente and the American Century. Harshly critical of nostalgic appeals to an all-powerful America, Fulbright urged his countrymen to turn their attention to making a better society. "There must something more substantial for a nation to seek, something more durable and rewarding, than the primacy of its power," Fulbright wrote. "The alternative that seems so obvious, so desirable and yet so elusive is the pursuit of public happiness."

But if Fulbright was trying to be a step ahead of Nixon and Kissinger's realpolitik, the President and his National Security Adviser had left much of their own party and many Democrats behind. By the mid-1970s, conservative Republicans, allied with Democratic hawks, had sabotaged their balance-of-power strategy. Fulbright's internationalism and appeals to the pursuit of public happiness appeared a fantasy. American politics turned decisively away from Fulbright and back toward Goldwater's dreams of total victory over Communism.

Goldwater benefited from the change. With Reagan's victory in 1980, Goldwater became chairman of the Armed Services Committee and a kind of senior statesman. But on the Armed Services Committee, his simplicity and sentimentality were easily manipulated by the ranking minority member, Senator Sam Nunn of Georgia. In fact, Goldwater became a figurehead behind which operated a much more cunning man who shared none of his apocalyptic visions.

Goldwater had his greatest influence during the Reagan years as an antagonist of the religious right. He despised the Reverend Jerry Falwell and his Moral Majority, seeing their holy crusade as a threat to personal liberties. In 1988, Goldwater also gave short shrift to George Bush's demagogic use of right-wing social issues such as the Pledge of Allegiance. When Dan Quayle, who had grown up in Arizona and whose family had been instrumental in promoting Goldwater through *The Arizona Republic* and *The Phoenix Gazette,* came to receive the old man's blessing, Goldwater dismissively told him to tell Bush to stop exploiting phony themes. Quayle, the heir to the Goldwater wing, was stunned.

Fulbright left the Senate years before Goldwater. In becoming the Senate's leading expert on foreign policy, Fulbright had long neglected his Arkansas constituents. He would return in election years to pose as the shirt-sleeved "Bill Fulbright" and talk about hog prices. And he would pay proper obeisance to the racial prejudice of Arkansas's white majority, but he had gotten a reputation of being aloof from and indifferent to the state. Some Arkansas voters, noting his continuing dissent on Vietnam, had begun to question his patriotism.

Under the impact of the 1965 Voting Rights Act, the state was also changing. In 1970, Arkansas elected to the governorship an affable forty-five-year-old lawyer, Dale Bumpers. Unlike Fulbright, Bumpers backed civil rights and dramatically increased the number of black state employees. In 1974, Bumpers challenged Fulbright in the Democratic primary, charging that Fulbright was out of touch with Arkansas voters. Bumpers easily won with 63 percent of the vote.

Fulbright, sixty-nine, took the path of many other defeated politicians: he became a Washington lawyer and lobbyist, representing, among other clients, the government of Saudi Arabia. Bumpers had a pleasantly liberal but undistinguished record. And Fulbright's wisdom was not drawn upon by the politicians who came to dominate the debate over foreign policy in the early 1980s.

# 7

# Richard Nixon and Henry Kissinger

## The Long View and the Short One

> The nemesis of the statesman is that equilibrium, though it may be the condition of stability, does not supply its own motivation.
>
> —HENRY KISSINGER, 1968

As Richard Nixon and his new National Security Adviser, Henry Kissinger, took office at the beginning of 1969, America stood at the end of one era and the beginning of another. For the first time, the country was on the verge of losing a war—to a small undeveloped country in Asia. Foreign bankers, who had learned to hold the dollar instead of gold, were threatening to exchange their dollars for marks or yen. America's trade balance—once impregnable—began to slip as goods from Western Europe and Japan poured into the domestic market. Former Western colonies in the Middle East, Asia, and Latin America, emboldened by Vietnam's defiance of the United States, began to assert their own independence. Humiliated by John Kennedy in the 1962 Cuban Missile Crisis, the Soviet Union had built a nuclear arsenal that could easily destroy the world. Henry Luce's American Century was drawing to a close.

To complicate matters, even as the war in Vietnam raged, the Cold War was ebbing. Under Aleksei Kosygin and Leonid Brezhnev, who succeeded Nikita Khrushchev in a coup in 1964, the Soviet Union had halted domestic reform, but was receptive to reducing tensions with the United States. The once monolithic Soviet bloc, in fact, was falling apart. The Soviet Union had had to send troops into Czechoslovakia in 1968, and war between the Soviet Union and China would break out the next year.

Few people seemed less equipped to deal with the challenges of this new era than Nixon and Kissinger. Before their collaboration in 1969, they had the reputation of being hard-line Cold Warriors who would stop at nothing to destroy world Communism. As a fledgling member of the House Un-American Activities Committee, Nixon had championed Whittaker Chambers against his detractors, and in his public statements on Communism gave voice to the same kind of apocalyptic sentiments about Communism. Writing in *The Saturday Evening Post* in October 1963, he framed the issue in stark terms: "The communist goal is to impose slavery on the free world. Our goal must be nothing less than to bring freedom to the communist world."

Kissinger had a reputation as a cool nuclear strategist, but like Paul Nitze, he had put his dispassionate objectivity in the service of an evangelical foreign policy. Kissinger made his mark with a 1957 book, *Nuclear Weapons and Foreign Policy*, in which he advocated that the United States contemplate limited nuclear war against the Soviet Union and ruled out any arms negotiations between the two powers. "It is hardly realistic to expect sovereign nations, whose failure to agree on issues of much less importance has brought about the arms race, to be able to agree on giving up their superiority," Kissinger wrote. Both Nixon and Kissinger, it was feared, would be unable to transcend their past obsession with the Cold War between the United States and the Soviet Union.

Yet once in office, Nixon and Kissinger—seemingly so inflexible in their overall views—sought to move beyond the Cold War and to challenge Americans' conception of their own mission. By 1971, they had laid aside the Cold War vision of a world divided between the godly West and the satanic East and were describing the world in classic balance-of-power terms—divided into the five power blocs of the United States, the Soviet Union, China, Japan, and Western Europe, no one of which was predominant. They openly advocated "détente" with the Soviet Union and lauded the contribution that the Soviet Union and China might make to a new "structure of peace." By Nixon's second term, the former witch hunter and the former nuclear theologian were on the verge of a new post-Cold War synthesis.

At the top of his popularity, Nixon won his second term in a landslide, and Kissinger, elevated to Secretary of State, was touted as a great statesman in the tradition of Dean Acheson and John Hay. But then everything crumbled. Barely three years after the 1972 landslide, Nixon was ousted from office, Kissinger became a pariah in the Republican Party, and their ideas fell into disrepute. By 1980, Nixon and Kissinger were desperately trying to restore their reputations by repudiating their own forward-looking ideas.

In their backgrounds and outward appearance, Richard Nixon and Henry Kissinger could not have been less alike. Nixon, born in 1913, was a small-town California Quaker whose father owned a grocery store in Whittier. Armed with the parochial beliefs of his class and region, but with an unquenchable ambition, Nixon went to Whittier College and Duke Law School. After a hitch in the Navy during World War II, he returned home to run for Congress as an anti-Communist, antilabor Republican. Boyishly handsome in his early years, with an ingratiating grin that would only later become a scowl, Nixon seemed prototypically American. During his first year in Congress, the Associated Press—impressed by Nixon's wholesome image—sent out a photo of Nixon and wife riding a bicycle along the Potomac at cherry blossom time with their elder daughter, Tricia, perched demurely in the basket on Nixon's handlebars.

Kissinger was a Jewish émigré from Nazi Germany—fifteen years old when his parents fled in 1938—many of whose relatives were murdered in the Holocaust. His father was a high school teacher in Germany (the equivalent in status of an American college professor) until he lost his job when the Nazis took power. When the family arrived in New York, he had to become a bookkeeper. Henry Kissinger briefly attended the City College of New York, but while he was in the Army, he fell under the spell of an erudite German émigré who convinced him that a "gentleman" should attend Harvard. Kissinger graduated summa cum laude in 1950 and after earning a Ph.D. in 1954 was made a member of the faculty. He retained a strong German accent, and his views and interests remained strongly European. He saw himself as a conservative, but a European rather than an American one. His models were Burke, Disraeli, and Bismarck. "I thought of myself as a historical conservative," Kissinger explained. "Most American conservatives were Manchester liberals or populists."

Despite these obvious differences between the two men, there were certain underlying similarities that made them successful collaborators. Above all, both saw themselves as outsiders: they had an ambivalent attitude toward the political establishment to which they belonged but from which they still felt somewhat excluded.

Nixon's feelings of estrangement went back to his childhood. Nixon's father, Frank, had run away from home at fourteen, finishing only the fourth grade. When he was twenty-five, he journeyed west from Ohio to rural Southern California and married Almira Milhous, the daughter of a prosperous, well-educated Quaker family in Whittier. Frank felt slighted and snubbed by the Milhouses, upon whom he initially had to depend for financial support. Richard, born in 1913, grew up with the same kind of exaggerated sensitivity about his social status. Even though he was successful in school and respected by his classmates, Nixon, mimicking his father, later complained about "the laughs and slights and snubs" that he claimed to have endured as a child.

Nixon seemed naturally to blend resentment with envy. He always wanted to be part of the elite, but felt excluded. Instead of accepting his fate, however, Nixon fought back. For instance, when he was a student at Whittier College, he was not invited to join the Franklins, the elite social club, even though he was class president. In retaliation, Nixon organized his own club, the Orthogonians, composed primarily of athletes and commuters from town.

As a Republican politician, Nixon repeatedly displayed the same ambivalence toward the Eastern political establishment. Nixon's enmity toward former State Department employee Alger Hiss was based as much on Hiss's social bearing as on the Harvard law graduate's alleged links to world Communism—Hiss was "condescending" toward him, Nixon later complained in *Six Crises*. Yet, as the case was playing itself out before the House Un-American Activities Committee, Nixon kept in constant touch with the establishmentarian par excellence, John Foster Dulles. Dulles had been Hiss's boss at the Carnegie Endowment for International Peace and was then serving as Republican presidential candidate Thomas Dewey's foreign policy adviser. Nixon showered Dulles with evidence showing that the charges against Hiss were merited and tried to ingratiate himself with the Dewey campaign by providing memos about how the candidate should address the issue of Communists in government.

Undoubtedly, what embittered Nixon most toward the Eastern establishment was his experience in 1952 as Dwight Eisenhower's running mate. In that campaign, *New York Herald Tribune* publisher John Hay Whitney and the other Eastern Republicans who had urged Eisenhower to choose the Californian suddenly turned on Nixon and called for his resignation. The reason was a story printed in the *New York Post* about a secret millionaire's fund set up for Nixon. Nixon rescued himself through his "Checkers" speech, but the experience deepened his feelings of being an outsider. In 1956, some of the same Republicans again tried to force him off the ticket.

By the time Nixon became President, he had acquired a contempt for the Eastern establishment—lumping under the same rubric the management of *The Washington Post* and *The New York Times*, the Rockefellers, and the Kennedys as well as "wise men" like Clark Clifford and McGeorge Bundy. He still relied upon the Eastern Republicans, but in private he railed against them. "The American leader class has really had it in terms of their ability to lead," Nixon wrote in his diary in 1969. "It's really sickening to have to receive them in the White House as I often do to hear them whine and whimper."

Kissinger shared some of Nixon's animus toward the establishment, but he took a different journey to these sentiments. Unlike Nixon, whose initial feelings were largely based on identification with his father, Kissinger was a genuine outsider, a European with a strong German accent among Americans and a stocky Jew with thick curly hair among upper-class WASPs. Kissinger wrote in his memoirs of how McGeorge Bundy treated him when Bundy was the dean of arts and sciences and he was a junior professor:

> Bundy tended to treat me with the combination of politeness and self-conscious condescension that upper class Bostonians reserve for people of, by New England standards, exotic background and excessively intense personal style.

In spite of his considerable accomplishments, Kissinger's academic career was stalled at Harvard. The university granted him tenure only after Kissinger wrote the best-selling *Nuclear*

*Weapons and Foreign Policy* under the sponsorship of the Council on Foreign Relations.

In 1961, when the "best and brightest" of Harvard's government department went to Washington to join the Kennedy administration, Kissinger, a Republican and Disraeli conservative, served briefly as a consultant to the National Security Council, resigning after several spats over policy and after feeling out of place in Kennedy's upper-class circle. Meanwhile, as New York governor Nelson Rockefeller's foreign policy adviser, Kissinger fared no better within the increasingly right-wing Republican Party, which nominated Senator Barry Goldwater for President in 1964 and loudly booed Rockefeller when he addressed the convention.

By the time Nixon—grateful for Kissinger's assistance during the campaign—summoned the Harvard professor to the Pierre Hotel in New York in December 1968 to assess his foreign policy views, Kissinger had come to share Nixon's ambivalence toward, though not his dark hatred of, the political establishment. While the two men did not necessarily agree on the iniquity of *The New York Times*, they did agree that the administration would have to insulate itself from establishment pressure and influence, concentrated traditionally in the State Department bureaucracy. Even before Nixon was inaugurated, they reached agreement on a method of making foreign policy—to vest power in the White House and remove it from established channels.

The two men had also come to share an underlying perspective. Nixon, the arch anti-Communist, and Kissinger, the strategist of limited nuclear war, had both embraced a dispassionate, almost amoral view of international relations, in which they viewed nations as contesting for power rather than goodness. Nixon acquired this view by applying to international relations the same method that he used to analyze domestic politics; Kissinger brought to bear a European balance-of-power perspective, informed by his experiences as an émigré from Nazi Germany.

Nixon's understanding of politics bore the imprint of his father, a Midwestern Republican, who loved nothing better than political argument. Frank Nixon was even willing to lose grocery store customers to score a point. His son became a fierce political debater for whom winning was everything. According to one contemporary, Nixon "offended some of his Quaker teachers by his willingness to justify bad means by the end. They said he cared too much about winning school contests." Indeed, Nixon craved the sheer contest, and he probably chose politics as a career because it afforded the kind of clear-cut victories that other endeavors did not. Throughout his life, he would describe his most important moments as "battles" won or lost in "the warfare of politics."

Nixon's political beliefs were conventionally Republican, but they played a merely supporting role in his political campaigns. Nixon stressed the issues that would bring him victory, regardless of merit. Unlike Goldwater, he was utterly ruthless. His first campaign against incumbent Democratic congressman Jerry Voorhis established a pattern he followed in every campaign except the 1960 presidential race, when he was still operating under the shadow of Eisenhower, an intimidating father figure. Voorhis was a strongly anti-Communist liberal Democrat who in 1940 had sponsored a bill requiring political groups tied to a foreign power to register with the federal government; yet in the 1946 campaign Nixon unashamedly painted him as a tool of the Communist Party. Afterward, Nixon privately admitted that Voorhis was not a Communist, but he told an aide who questioned his tactics, "I had to win. That's the thing you don't understand. The important thing is to win."

Throughout his career, Nixon gauged issues by their political weight. In the mid-1950s, believing that the black vote was going to be critical for Republican successes in the North, he became a crusader for civil rights, befriending Martin Luther King, Jr., and leading an antifilibuster move in the Senate aimed at segregationist Southern Democrats. He explained to one close political adviser in 1956, "From a vote-getting standpoint, the South appears lost, whereas the large Negro voting groups in states with heavy electoral votes can be most important."

Then, as it became apparent to Nixon during the mid-1960s that the black vote was going Democratic and that Republicans stood a good chance of winning white backlash votes in the South and in Northern cities, he shamelessly changed his tack, waging in 1968 an implicitly antiblack campaign that stressed "law and order." That year, he told a Philadelphia Republican who urged him to back civil rights, "I am not going to campaign for the black vote at the risk of alienating the suburban vote." What was Nixon's real position on civil rights? It remains unclear; what is clear is that his public position varied according to his calculations.

Nixon inadvertently revealed his modus operandi in *Six Crises*, written after his 1960 defeat. Asked by Doubleday to write his memoirs, Nixon chose instead to focus on his "crises," his "battles." The book contains very little about Nixon's political philosophy. It is a blow-by-blow guidebook to political survival under stress, the key to which, according to Nixon, is "selflessness." By this term, Nixon did not mean altruism, but rather the ability to calculate means and ends without regard to one's own immediate values, emotions, prejudices, and preoccupations. This was Nixon's political method, and as President he applied it to foreign relations.

In his foreign policy views, Congressman Nixon initially aligned himself with the internationalist wing of the Republican Party, backing both the Marshall Plan and NATO. He defied his advisers in Southern California, who were Old Guard isolationists, but conformed to the other Republicans of his generation— New York's Kenneth Keating and Kentucky's Thruston Morton, for instance—who entered Congress in 1946. But within this framework, Nixon pitched to the right. During the Korean War, Senator Nixon favored General Douglas MacArthur's disastrous plan to advance to the Yalu River. In 1954, Vice President Nixon advocated sending troops to Vietnam to rescue the French and, if necessary, even using nuclear weapons. In 1957, he urged the Eisenhower administration to back the French in Algeria. During the Vietnam War, campaigner Nixon criticized President Lyndon Johnson for not sending enough troops or dropping enough bombs. He unequivocally opposed diplomatic recognition of China and called for the United States to maintain its nuclear superiority over the Soviet Union.

Yet sometime in the mid-1960s, while he was practicing law in New York and campaigning for Republican candidates, Nixon began to look more dispassionately on international relations—what he called "taking the long view." It was possible for him to do so because of his distance from political decision making, which allowed him to view the world outside the immediate framework of domestic anti-Communism and missionary moralism.* In his method of observing international relations, Nixon was influenced by his favorite among world leaders, French President Charles de Gaulle, who had graciously received Nixon at the Elysée Palace during his years out of power. Nixon, who later described de Gaulle in *Leaders* as "a man of enormous ego and yet at the same time enormous selflessness," was struck by his ability to look at the world without immediate preconceptions. De Gaulle had granted independence to Algeria, distanced France from the United States, and taken the first steps toward what he called "détente" with the Soviet Union. As France prospered, Nixon saw in the French statesman the rewards of "selflessness" and unconventionality in international relations.

---

* Nixon's method of viewing foreign relations can be compared to what philosopher Edmund Husserl called a "phenomenological reduction." This occurs when an observer views phenomena without regard to their actual existence, the idea being to discover the underlying structure of appearance. By analogy, Nixon performed a similar phenomenological reduction, observing the world of nations while "bracketing" his own moralism and anti-Communism.

During the mid-1960s, Nixon periodically invited newspaper columnists, businessmen, and influential Republicans to his New York apartment, where he took them on a *tour d'horizon* to demonstrate his expertise. In July 1967, Nixon displayed his method in an off-the-record speech that he gave at the Bohemian Grove, an annual gathering of the country's business and media elite in Northern California. He warned his audience that he would not dwell "on current issues like Vietnam and the Mideast," but would instead "take the long view."

Nixon's talk was almost iconoclastic in tone. He informed his audience that "the UN, NATO, foreign aid, USIA [U.S. Information Agency]" have become "obsolete and inadequate." He noted that the Communist world was no longer "monolithic," but warned that by 1970 the Soviet Union would have achieved strategic parity with the United States. He predicted that the success of capitalism in Japan, Korea, Taiwan, Malaysia, and Thailand would doom Communism in Southeast Asia. And he warned against insisting on exporting an American model of democracy to Third World countries.

The first public result of Nixon's new look at the world was an essay in the fall 1967 *Foreign Affairs*, "Asia after Vietnam." In it, Nixon tried to imagine what Asia would be like in the 1970s and what the U.S. response should be. While much of the essay contained warmed-over analyses from the Eisenhower-Dulles era, it included two passages that showed Nixon was laying aside his own preconceptions. The difficulty that the United States had encountered in Vietnam, he wrote, proved that "the role of the United States as world policeman is likely to be limited in the future"—a dawning acknowledgment on Nixon's part that the American Century was drawing to a close. Instead of relying solely on its own military power, the United States should encourage "a collective effort by the nations of the region to contain the threat themselves"—what came to be known during his administration as the Nixon Doctrine. This partly reflected advice de Gaulle had given Nixon during his visits in 1965 and 1967.

De Gaulle had also strongly urged Nixon to follow his lead in normalizing relations with China, and de Gaulle's advice clearly had an effect. "Taking the long view," Nixon wrote, "we simply cannot afford to leave China forever outside the family of nations, there to nurture its fantasies, cherish its hates, and threaten its neighbors." The statement was deliberately ambiguous. Most contemporary readers believed that Nixon was simply urging the United States to apply more pressure on China to change, but it became clear four years later that Nixon was really arguing that in order to pressure China to change, the United States had to bring it into "the family of nations."

Nixon gave other hints before January 1969 that his view of foreign relations was changing—at the Republican convention in August 1968 he urged that the "era of confrontation" be replaced by the "era of negotiation"—but these statements were discounted because, during most of his campaign, Nixon, obsessed with being outflanked on his right as he had been by Kennedy in 1960, reiterated his former hard-line views of the Cold War. (In the 1960 campaign, Kennedy openly favored overthrowing Cuba's Castro, while Nixon, mindful of a planned invasion, responsibly refused to take a clear position.) As late as October 24, Nixon was warning of a "security gap" with the Soviet Union and calling on the United States to maintain a "clear-cut military superiority" over the Soviet Union. It would become apparent only later that Nixon had radically altered his view of international relations.

Kissinger came to virtually the same conclusions as Nixon from an entirely different approach. Kissinger brought to foreign policy a distinctly European rather than American cast of mind, far more concerned with achieving order and equilibrium than securing freedom and democracy. Throughout his academic and political career, Kissinger would never display the slightest interest in domestic policy; it concerned him only insofar as certain social systems generated international instability.

Kissinger's view reflected his European upbringing, and especially his deeply unsettling experience in Nazi Germany, which contributed to his dread of revolution and his quest for order and stability. He told ABC interviewer Ted Koppel in a 1974 interview, "I think the deepest impact it [the rise of National Socialism] made on me was that twice, once in 1933 when the Nazis came to power, then in 1938 when I came to the United States, all the things that had seemed secure and stable collapsed and many of the people that one had considered the steady examples suddenly were thrown into enormous turmoil themselves and into fantastic insecurities."

In his academic work, Kissinger was concerned above all with international stability. His first book, *A World Restored*, published in 1957, was an analysis of the Congress of Vienna in 1815, which ended the Napoleonic wars and created a balance of power in Europe that lasted a century. Next to his *Memoirs*, it is still Kissinger's most impressive work and contains the germ of all his later ideas.

During the 1950s, when Kissinger was writing *A World Restored*, political scientists had drawn a sharp line between the world before and after 1945, but in his study of the Congress of Vienna, Kissinger developed a framework that showed the continuity between 1815 and 1955. According to Kissinger, what Austria's Metternich and Britain's Castlereagh did was to replace Napoleon's "revolutionary order," sustained by force, with a "legitimate order" based upon a balance of power and the recognition of competing sovereign nations. Kissinger applied this same distinction to the Cold War, stressing that the statesman's task was to thwart the Soviet bloc's revolutionary aims and to replace the revolutionary order of nations with a legitimate order. Kissinger's concept of international order did not entail democracy or pluralism; it could exist among monarchies and dictatorships as well as democracies. It was a de-

racinated realism—based on a rejection of both American evangelism and the American democratic tradition.

Until the eve of his joining Nixon, Kissinger's actual policy
recommendations contributed to the growing nuclear tensions
between the United States and the Soviet Union. In *Nuclear
Weapons and Foreign Policy*, Kissinger had urged that the only
way to repel the Soviet challenge was to incorporate tactical
nuclear weapons into America's arsenal. "The enormity of
modern weapons makes the thought of war repugnant," Kissinger wrote, "but the refusal to run any risks would amount
to giving the Soviet leaders a blank check."

Yet Kissinger's tactics were designed to achieve what would
have struck both liberals and conservatives as a modest result:
the transformation of the Soviet Union from a "revolutionary"
into a "status quo power." Unlike Burnham and Goldwater,
Kissinger had no interest in rolling back Communism or lib-
erating the Soviet people. Unlike contemporary liberals, he had
no particular interest in using the Cold War to export American
ideals of democracy. He had an inherently skeptical view of
American omnipotence and of the American Century, commenting in a 1966 hearing before Fulbright's Senate Foreign
Relations Committee that the United States should not play
God "in every part of the globe." While Fulbright and Kissinger
differed in their policies during the 1950s and early 1960s, they
shared an underlying worldview.

Kissinger himself ascribed the greatest moral purpose to the
goal of international stability, but once that goal was accepted
as a premise, his method, like Nixon's, was to screen out personal and moral considerations from the realm of policymaking. Kissinger admired Metternich, he wrote, because he was
"a 'scientist' of politics, coolly and unemotionally arranging
his combinations in an age that increasingly conducted policy
by 'causes.' " He respected Germany's Bismarck for the same
reason, describing his foreign policy as one that "depended on
calculation, not emotion." And both he and Nixon were fans

of de Gaulle, whom Kissinger had defended when he consulted for Kennedy's National Security Council.

After his unhappy experience in the Kennedy administration, Kissinger returned to full-time teaching at Harvard. Except for participating briefly in back-channel negotiations with the French and North Vietnamese during the Johnson administration, Kissinger was exiled from politics and policymaking during the mid-1960s, the same time Nixon was practicing law in New York. When Kissinger emerged in 1968 to write Nelson Rockefeller's speeches and position papers on foreign policy, he was thinking along the same lines as Nixon. Kissinger had been slow to recognize the enmity between the Soviet Union and China; once he did, however, he moved toward the conclusion that the United States should use traditional balance-of-power diplomacy to maintain international stability. America's unsuccessful experience in Vietnam was convincing him that the United States had to redefine its identity as a world power.

The speeches that Kissinger wrote for Rockefeller in 1968 were a better preview of Nixon's foreign policy than the candidate's campaign speeches and white papers. Kissinger had Rockefeller call for the United States to open negotiations with both China and the Soviet Union. "In a subtle triangle with Communist China and the Soviet Union, we can ultimately improve our relations with *each*—as we test the will for peace of *both*," Kissinger wrote on Rockefeller's behalf. Kissinger also had Rockefeller advocate ending the "Americanization" of the Vietnam War, shifting increased responsibility to the South Vietnamese government, while beginning negotiations with the North.

After Rockefeller's effort to win the nomination failed, Kissinger returned to Cambridge and expanded the ideas he had developed during the campaign. In an essay written for the Brookings Institution, Kissinger edged toward rejecting the bipolar Cold War analysis. "The age of the Superpowers is now drawing to an end," Kissinger wrote. "Military bipolarity has not only failed to prevent, it has actually encouraged political multipolarity." Amidst this growing diversity, what was now needed, Kissinger argued, "is an agreed concept of order."

During Nixon's first term, he and Kissinger would devote considerable energy to defining their concept of order, which they first described as "the era of negotiations," then as the new "structure of peace," and then—borrowing de Gaulle's term—as "détente."

Even before he was inaugurated, Nixon took steps to transform American foreign policy. In November, he told the Johnson administration that he wanted to resume the general diplomatic talks in Warsaw with the Chinese that Johnson had broken off. In December, Nixon and Kissinger laid the groundwork for shifting the making of foreign policy from the State Department to the White House and the National Security Council—a move that Kissinger aide and Nixon biographer Roger Morris called a "coup d'état." Concentrating policymaking in the White House made it easier for Nixon and Kissinger to initiate dramatic changes, but it also set in motion a dynamic of stealth and secrecy that helped to undermine Nixon's presidency. And as former administration official Raymond Garthoff argued in *Détente and Confrontation*, the bitter conflict between the NSC and the Cabinet departments allowed the Soviets to play the NSC off against the State Department in SALT negotiations.

Once in office, Nixon moved rapidly. In his inaugural address, he reiterated his call for moving toward an "era of negotiations," and in his first press conference, he rejected a goal of nuclear superiority over the Soviet Union in favor of "sufficiency"—in effect acknowledging that the United States no longer possessed strategic superiority and implying that it really didn't matter. In his first budget, he reduced defense spending by $6 billion—from 45 to 37 percent of the budget

—the first cut in the 1960s. In 1970, Nixon rejected pleas from establishment leaders John McCloy, Lucius Clay, and Dean Acheson that he oppose West German Chancellor Willy Brandt's policy of détente (*Ostpolitik*) with the Soviet Union. (Nixon understood that with East Germans in contact with Western prosperity and democracy, Brandt's policies would threaten the Soviet Union in East Germany far more than they would aid it in West Germany.) Nixon resumed arms-control negotiations with the Soviet Union, and in June 1972 signed a SALT and antiballistic missile (ABM) treaty.

Nixon tried to draw the Soviets and the Chinese into what Kissinger had described as a "triangular" relationship with respect to Vietnam—soliciting their aid in pressuring the North Vietnamese in exchange for American economic and diplomatic concessions. The President initially expected that by "linking" Vietnam to the improvement of relations with the Soviet Union and China, he could secure "peace with honor" in Vietnam in a year. Right after he took office, Nixon invited Fulbright to his office and told him he was going to get the country out. "I assume we'll have everything under control in six months," the President told him.

Nixon soon began withdrawing troops from Vietnam and shifting the responsibility for the ground war to the South Vietnamese forces—what Nixon's Secretary of Defense, Melvin Laird, called "Vietnamization." In an April 1969 column in *National Review*, Burnham, fearing betrayal, perceptively accused Nixon of being a "Gaullist." Burnham warned that an American withdrawal from Vietnam would have far greater consequences than a French withdrawal from Algeria. "It is not a junior, but No. 1 who is entangled in Vietnam. It is the strength and will of No. 1—therefore, of the non-Communist world quite generally—that is being tested in Vietnam."

Nixon, in the meantime, faced a difficult challenge in his economic policy. War-induced inflation was already at 5 percent when he took office—higher than at any time since the Korean War—and steadily increased over the next two years. As the Federal Reserve raised interest rates to dampen the money supply, industry began to slump. By 1970, the United States was suffering for the first time from "stagflation"—the combination of rising unemployment and inflation. Business blamed the persistence of inflation on wage pressure from unions, which they claimed threatened profits and was forcing them to increase prices.

At the same time, the United States was facing the early stage of the economic challenge from Japan and Western Europe. While American exports grew by 67 percent during the 1960s, West German exports jumped 109 percent and those of Japan 333 percent. Japan's growth was directly related to American orders during the Vietnam War. From 1965 to 1967, Japan's trade with the United States grew 100 percent, and American war purchases directly accounted for 10 percent of Japan's total exports. By 1971, the American trade balance was expected to show a $2 billion loss—the first deficit since 1893. This deficit in turn threatened the value of the dollar, which had been fixed at $35 an ounce of gold at the Bretton Woods conference. America's trade deficit showed that foreigners holding dollars were increasingly reluctant to exchange them for American goods.

Just as in foreign policy, Nixon showed boldness. In January 1970 and 1971, he submitted budgets to Congress with deficits. Eager to end the recession, Nixon had adopted a Keynesian strategy for stimulating the economy, heresy for a Republican. In a January 1971 press conference, he announced, "I am now a Keynesian in economics." In August, Nixon took still more dramatic measures—abandoning the Bretton Woods gold standard, slapping a tariff on imports, and instituting wage-price controls. Nixon's strategy was to force other countries (in particular Japan) to raise the value of their currencies in relation to the dollar—making American exports cheaper—while at the same time holding down wages and prices.

Nixon's aggressive trade strategy—which critics labeled the "Nixon shocks"—was backed by many businessmen and labor leaders, but adamantly opposed by the establishment policy experts and investment bankers clustered around the Council on Foreign Relations and other elite institutions. They saw Nixon's moves as a betrayal of the post-World War II commitment to free trade and open markets and warned that they could precipitate a trade war and another Great Depression. What they failed to understand—and what Nixon grasped pragmatically—was that a rigid commitment to free trade was appropriate only to nations enjoying the kind of absolute economic supremacy that the United States had after World War II or that Britain had for part of the nineteenth century. A rigid commitment became self-defeating once a nation was faced with strong competitors who did not adhere to the same ideals.

Nixon's trade strategy did temporarily reverse the decline in America's manufacturing trade balance. His overall strategy eventually foundered on the OPEC oil boycott of 1974, which caused prices to spiral, but it was still a significant break with postwar economic policy. Nixon, the presumed conservative, clearly had little practical use for laissez-faire mythology. Surveying Nixon's achievements in foreign and economic policy at the beginning of his second term, Walter Lippmann told *The Washington Post*:

His role has been that of a man who had to liquidate, defuse, deflate the exaggerations of the romantic period of American imperialism and American inflation. Inflation of promises, inflation of hopes, the Great Society, American supremacy—all that had to be deflated because it was all beyond our power.

Reading the column in his daily briefing, Nixon penciled in the margin: "wise observation."

As Nixon took these different measures, he attempted to put them in a framework of a new global understanding. Nixon made the first major statement of his new direction in an address on July 6, 1971, to Midwestern News Media Executives in Kansas City. This speech, in hindsight, is among the most significant of his presidency. Certainly, it was the most forward-looking. Nixon took sole responsibility for the speech, writing out four detailed outlines beforehand. Neither his staff nor his speechwriters knew what he was going to say. The press ignored it at the time—and it was not even included in a collection of Nixon speeches on foreign policy that was published the next year. Only Chinese leader Zhou Enlai and a few foreign policy experts, in particular James Chace, the managing editor of *Foreign Affairs*, recognized its importance. Yet viewed in retrospect, it represented the most significant recasting of American foreign policy since Kennedy's American University speech, in which he had called for a new "strategy for peace."

Nixon's speech could not have occurred at a more auspicious moment. As he spoke, Kissinger was secretly en route to Beijing to complete plans for Nixon's visit the next year, while Nixon's economic advisers were working on the response to the dollar crisis. Now Nixon synthesized the realms of economics and geopolitics. He looked past the Cold War to a time when economics would displace military competition and when America's supremacy would be severely tested.

The news executives had come to Kansas City to hear a routine briefing on domestic policy, and they got some of that from Nixon's Secretary of Health, Education, and Welfare, Elliot Richardson, and the director of the Environmental Protection Agency, William Ruckelshaus, but Nixon surprised his audience by conducting a grand tour of world politics. "What is the world going to look like as Vietnam moves from vision, or at least recedes from it, and what will be America's role in the world at that time?" the President began.

Nixon's analysis went well beyond the tentative forays of his *Foreign Affairs* essay and challenged the basic assumptions of American foreign policy. His presentation boiled down to five basic propositions that (recalling Burnham on Eisenhower) could be called the "Nixon axioms."

I. *The Cold War was drawing to a close.* For twenty-five years, Americans had seen the world riven by a military and moral conflict pitting the United States and its allies against the Soviet Union and its allies, including China. Now the possibility of military confrontation would be drastically reduced through following "a policy of negotiations rather than confrontations."

II. *International relations would be driven by economic rather than military competition.* With the eclipse of the Cold War, the relations among major powers would largely be determined by their economic strength and rivalry over markets, and trade balances would replace rivalry over nuclear throw weights. "Economic power will be the key to other kinds of power . . . in the last third of this century," Nixon said.

III. *America had lost its predominance in the world.* The Soviet Union had matched America's military might, and Japan and Western Europe were now competing vigorously with U.S. firms for markets. "When we see the world in which we are about to move, the United States no longer is in the position of complete preeminence or predominance," Nixon said.

IV. *Instead of international relations being driven by bipolar military conflict, they would be driven by pentagonal economic conflict.* "Instead of America being number one in the world from an economic standpoint, the preeminent world power, and instead of there being just two superpowers, when we think in economic terms and economic potentialities, there are five great power centers in the world today." These are, Nixon noted, the United States, Western Europe, Japan, the Soviet Union, and China. But Nixon recognized that in the near future U.S. economic competition would be primarily with Western Europe and Japan.

V. *In the future, as economic competition began to predominate, American relations with its Cold War allies could become fractious.* The United States would remain "friends" and "allies" with Western Europe and Japan, but they would be "competing and competing very hard with us throughout the world for economic leadership."

Nixon saw beneath the appearance of Cold War conflict to the multipolar reality that would only become fully visible two decades later. Of course, certain details eluded him. As American experts would continue to do until Gorbachev told them otherwise, he wildly overestimated the strength of the Soviet economy. But the outline of the future was clearly there. Even two decades later, Nixon's Kansas City speech has remained the most advanced exposition by an American President of the late-twentieth-century world.

Nixon also saw the perils that lay ahead for Americans who had based their own expectations of life on the American Century and the Cold War. For the first half of the century, Americans had looked toward America's becoming the most powerful nation on earth, believing that it would bring prosperity; then for a quarter century, they had believed that they had to defend their power and prosperity against the menace of Soviet Communism. Now Nixon was taking away both the promise of the American Century and the menace of Communism, leaving a world divided by mundane economic rivalries in which America could no longer readily dictate outcomes.

But, to the extent that Nixon understood the problem of late-twentieth-century America, he was incapable of resolving it. He had set aside the triumphalism of Luce and the apocalyptic moralism of the Cold War, but he was not able to replace them with new guideposts. In Kansas City, he made a feeble attempt to provide new goals for Americans but fell back on contemporary clichés about becoming "a healthy nation not simply with a healthy government and a healthy environment and a healthy physical system insofar as we personally are concerned, but healthy in terms of moral strength." Nixon created the ultimate mixed metaphor: a Whole Earth Catalog invocation of physical well-being combined with the Calvinist morality of his ancestors.

Kissinger also contributed to the new global synthesis—both in the annual reports on foreign policy that he wrote for Nixon and, when he became Secretary of State in 1973, in his own press conferences and speeches. (Nixon did not allow Kissinger to give a speech or hold an on-the-record press conference until October 27, 1971.) Kissinger stated unequivocally that the United States had discarded the strategy of containment and was moving beyond the Cold War itself. "Our alliances are no longer addressed primarily to the containment of the Soviet Union and China behind an American shield," Kissinger wrote in Nixon's annual statement in February 1972. "They are instead addressed to the creation with those powers of a stable world peace."

In the policy studies he had conducted during the 1950s and 1960s, Kissinger had always portrayed the United States as trying to blunt the Soviet and Chinese threat. By definition, these states could not be brought into a legitimate order. "The Sino-Soviet bloc," Kissinger wrote in *Nuclear Weapons and Foreign Policy*, "is determined to prevent the establishment of all equilibrium and is organized to exploit all hopes and dissatisfactions for its own ends." Now Kissinger became concerned with how the United States, working with these same powers, could build a legitimate order. The administration's "great task," he told an end-of-the-year press conference in December 1973, was "to construct an international system based on a sense of justice so that its participants would have a stake in maintaining it, with a sufficient balance of power so that no nation or group of nations would be dependent entirely on the good will of its neighbors, and based on a sense of participation so that all nations could share in the positive aspirations."

Not since Truman and Acheson had an administration attempted such a dramatic shift in policy or attempted such an ambitious reconceptualization of American aims. Yet by the end of what would have been Nixon's second term, the grand design was already beginning to crumble, and by 1980, it was in ruins. Why?

Among Nixon's many foreign policy triumphs in his first term, one abysmal failure stood out—not getting the United States out of Vietnam. By allowing the war to drag on another four years—as long as World War II—Nixon crippled the economy and politically polarized the nation. And in seeking to suppress his antiwar opposition, he was driven to actions that led eventually to the Watergate scandal, which ended his presidency.

Nixon failed to end the war because he insisted until mid-1972 that North Vietnam's army withdraw from the South after the United States left. Nixon wanted a settlement along the same lines as the settlement that Eisenhower had worked out in Korea in 1953, though in Korea the United States had driven the Communist forces out of the South. A more realistic Nixon, "taking the long view," might have seen the difference, but he was blinded by misconceptions.

Nixon and Kissinger believed that they could get the Soviet Union and China to force North Vietnam out of the South. At times, Nixon believed that he could win a military victory over the North Vietnamese. During the summer of 1969, Nixon developed a plan, he revealed in his *Memoirs*, to "go for broke—to end the war one way or another—either by negotiated agreement or by an increased use of force." The plan was wrongheaded, but it took Nixon and Kissinger four years to recognize this.

Nixon and Kissinger were afraid that if the United States pulled out without the appearance of victory, the United States, as Nixon said in defending the invasion of Cambodia, would be reduced to a "pitiful helpless giant." Nixon and Kissinger's fears were exaggerated, but had some basis. The Cambodian Khmer Rouge, the Iranian Mujahideen, and the Nicaraguan Sandinistas were inspired by North Vietnam's success. But the problem, as Kissinger seemed to recognize in 1968, was that the alternative to withdrawal—a protracted war that would tear the United States apart and perhaps lead to a wider war in Asia—was even less desirable.

And not least important, Nixon was obsessed with the political repercussions of losing Vietnam. As Nixon explained in an interview with historian Herbert Parmet, he was as worried about the threat from George Wallace on the right as he was the challenge from the left. Kennedy had defeated him in 1960 by running to his right on foreign policy, and Wallace had almost succeeded in throwing the 1968 election into the House of Representatives, where Hubert Humphrey would have won. Nixon knew from having built his career on labeling Democrats soft on Communism how damaging such accusations might prove. He had charged that the Democrats were cowardly appeasers who lost Eastern Europe and China. Nixon did not want such charges hurled at him about Vietnam. In his diaries, he approvingly cited Alexander Haig's concern that he handle the Vietnam negotiations "in a way that I can survive in office."

The Watergate scandal began with Nixon's attempts to suppress the antiwar opposition. He and Kissinger ordered the FBI to wiretap Kissinger's NSC staff in 1969 after *The New York Times* revealed the secret escalation of the air war. After the Cambodia demonstrations the next year, Nixon approved the Huston plan for establishing a White House police unit aimed at quashing dissent. Only FBI Director J. Edgar Hoover's jealousy prevented the plan's realization. After the unsuccessful foray into Laos in February 1971 and the publication of the Pentagon Papers in June, Nixon and his aide Charles Colson set up the "plumbers" to attempt to discredit the Pentagon Papers' leaker, Daniel Ellsberg, and to carry out surreptitious operations against Nixon political targets, including the Brookings Institution and establishment antiwar figures like former Secretary of Defense Clark Clifford.

If Nixon had cut his losses in Vietnam as de Gaulle had urged—if he had been able to get out during 1970 as he initially hoped—then he might not have been tempted to take the actions that eventually undermined his presidency. He and Kissinger might have solidified their foreign policy achievements instead of finding themselves at the mercy of their opponents in Congress. But Nixon was unwilling to get out of Vietnam until the very end of his first term, when he had little choice.

The theory and practice of détente also had weaknesses that both the right and the left were able to exploit. The most important had to do with the concept of linkage. In Nixon's and Kissinger's speeches, the new structure of peace was presented as transcending the bipolar conflicts of the Cold War. But linkage implied that almost every conflict or potential conflict could be *linked* to U.S.-Soviet relations. Nixon's pentagonal concept of foreign relations and Kissinger's balance-of-power view looked toward a more complex multitiered, multipowered international order, yet the theory of linkage suggested that all conflicts could be resolved through a U.S.-Soviet condominium.

In practice, Nixon and Kissinger—and Carter's National Security Adviser, Zbigniew Brzezinski, a Kissinger manqué—opted to apply linkage to any conflict they deemed significant, sometimes with disastrous results. Nixon and Kissinger prolonged the Vietnam War by erroneously assuming that it could be ended by linking it to U.S.-Soviet and U.S.-Chinese relations. They then clumsily linked the 1971 India-Pakistan War to U.S.-Soviet rivalries. And they created a martyr of elected Chilean President Salvador Allende by linking the need for his overthrow to U.S.-Soviet relations in Latin America. By the same token, Nixon and Kissinger oversold the new structure of peace, in particular détente with the Soviet Union, suggesting that conflict would fade away. As former arms controller Garthoff argued, Nixon and Kissinger allowed the public to confuse "détente" (a French word meaning reduction of tensions) with "entente" (meaning alliance).

At the same time, Nixon and Kissinger were unable to provide a compelling moral dimension to their policies. Neither replaced the Lucean understanding of America's purpose with one of their own. Nixon repeatedly acknowledged that something had to replace the battle against Communism. The onset of peace through détente, Nixon warned in an August 1971 speech before the Veterans of Foreign Wars, "poses the deep question of whether a nation, without some external threat to unite and motivate it, can find a higher inspiration to lift us all above the mire of softness and stagnation and division and decay." Yet Nixon himself could not answer the question.

Kissinger, too, understood that his and Nixon's new vision lacked a compelling moral dimension. While he craved stability, Kissinger knew that the American public sought more than this to justify its foreign policy. Since the 1940s, American policy had been based on defending the "free world" against the threat of Communism. Now Kissinger and Nixon asked Americans to ignore whether a country was democratic or not unless it threatened the global balance of power. In one of the papers that he wrote in the fall of 1968 after working for Rock-efeller's campaign, Kissinger spelled out the difficulty that any-one trying to reform American foreign policy would face:

> The nemesis of the statesman is that equilibrium, though it may be the condition of stability, does not supply its own motivation.

It was ironic that before assuming power Kissinger had written his own and Nixon's epitaph.

By denying the relevance of America's democratic tradition, Kissinger and Nixon opened themselves up to criticism for cul-tivating autocrats like the Shah of Iran, who had become the Persian Gulf representative of the Nixon Doctrine. Kissinger and Nixon also virtually invited criticism for ignoring the plight of oppressed minorities and dissidents within the Soviet bloc. And in the summer of 1975, President Gerald Ford provoked a storm of protest when, on Kissinger's advice, he refused to welcome exiled Soviet novelist Aleksander Solzhenitsyn at the White House—out of fear of offending Brezhnev.

They also failed to achieve the objectives of their own realism. As Lippmann had recognized in *U.S. War Aims,* the spread of democratic reform could contribute to global stability. By throwing U.S. power on the side of unpopular autocracies, Nixon and Kissinger laid the basis for what they most feared: anti-American revolutionary nationalism.

Nixon and Kissinger's policy aroused two powerful enemies that stood poised to take advantage of any weakness in their new approach. In the Democratic Party, a split had occurred in 1972 between the antiwar faction, led by presidential nom-inee Senator George McGovern, and a prowar Cold War faction led by Senator Henry Jackson of Washington, who had been trounced in his presidential nomination bid but was planning to run again in 1976. After the election, the Jackson forces regrouped as the Coalition for a Democratic Majority. While nominally favoring New Deal economic and social policies, the CDM Democrats, whose most prominent figures, such as Jeane Kirkpatrick, would later cross the political aisle, favored restoring the Cold War of the late 1940s in the mid-1970s. They adamantly opposed détente and its consequences, especially any reductions in military spending. These Democrats lacked Nixon's vision.

Within the Republican Party, the conservatives who had backed Goldwater in 1964 organized to recapture the party. Led in Congress by new militants like Senator Jesse Helms of North Carolina, they were also bitterly opposed to détente and military reductions. Some of them demonized Kissinger as an evil foreigner corrupting American policy, reflecting traces of America First isolationism and even anti-Semitism. Kissinger fought two engagements against the combined forces of Cold War nostalgia and lost both.

The first battle was over Jewish emigration from the Soviet Union. In 1973, Jackson introduced a bill tying the grant of most-favored-nation trading status for the Soviet Union to agreement to unrestricted Jewish emigration. (Without MFN, the Soviet Union would be subject to the confiscatory tariffs of the infamous Smoot-Hawley Act.) Jackson was genuinely concerned about the ability of Soviet Jews, who had been restricted by an "exit tax," to emigrate to Israel. But he and his aide Richard Perle, who later became the Reagan administration's chief operator against arms control, also opposed Nixon and Kissinger's policy of détente with the Soviet Union, and Jackson was looking for a way to dramatize his presidential candidacy in 1976.

Speaking in 1973 before the Senate Foreign Relations Committee, with Fulbright's wholehearted support, Kissinger denounced the act as "an ex post facto form of linkage" that "casts doubt on our reliability as a negotiating partner." The

Soviets and Kissinger tried to work out a private arrangement to forestall the Jackson-Vanik Act, but Jackson was determined to keep the issue alive. He developed a formidable coalition in the Senate of liberal Democrats concerned about Soviet human rights and conservative Republicans opposed to détente. His bill overwhelmingly passed the Senate, and the Soviets announced that they would not abide by its provisions. Kissinger was humiliated.

Then, in 1976, Ronald Reagan, running as the candidate of the Goldwater right, decided to challenge incumbent Gerald Ford. When Reagan initially focused his campaign on cutting the federal budget, Ford effectively responded by questioning his commitment to Social Security. In desperation, Reagan changed his campaign theme. Now he took direct aim at the Ford-Kissinger-Nixon foreign policies, charging that they had allowed the United States to become number two in the world. "Henry Kissinger's stewardship of U.S. foreign policy has coincided precisely with the loss of U.S. military supremacy," Reagan declared in Orlando in March 1976. "Under Messrs. Kissinger and Ford this nation has become number two in military power in a world where it is dangerous—if not fatal —to be second best . . . There is little doubt in my mind that the Soviet Union will not stop taking advantage of détente until it sees that the American people have elected a new President and appointed a new Secretary of State."

From that moment, Reagan's campaign gathered support, particularly in the South. In the end, Reagan failed to get the nomination, but he politically discredited the Nixon foreign policy within the GOP. Ford even stopped using the word "détente" in public statements; negotiations for a new SALT treaty lagged; and Ford banished Kissinger from the Republican convention and the campaign.

During the Carter administration, the Jackson Democrats and Reagan Republicans—organized through Paul Nitze's Committee on the Present Danger—finished off the job that they had begun in 1973 against Nixon and Kissinger. Carter, a neophyte in Washington ways, was sympathetic to détente, but was too hesitant and politically inept to maneuver successfully against the rising right wing. Carter's two main foreign policy advisers, National Security Adviser Brzezinski and Secretary of State Cyrus Vance, never agreed on the meaning of détente and did not adopt a common front against Nitze's powerful committee. Their division encouraged Carter's enemies.

Ironically, the event that brought about the final collapse of Carter's presidency was traceable directly to Nixon and Kissinger's policies. Carter had continued Nixon's policy of using the Shah of Iran as America's surrogate in the Persian Gulf, and when the Shah was toppled by Muslim fundamentalists, Carter incurred their wrath against the Nixon Doctrine. Kissinger, in turn, intervened with the Carter administration to get the United States to provide refuge for the Shah, who was seeking medical treatment. Iranian militants reacted by seizing hostages at the U.S. embassy, crippling Carter.

In the 1980 campaign, Reagan's attack on Carter was a resumption of the themes he had used against Ford—an attack on the Nixon-Kissinger foreign policy. Reagan's victory dealt it a final blow. The experiment was over. It had not yielded a new synthesis, but rather the restoration of old illusions.

Under fire within their own party, Nixon and Kissinger gradually abandoned their own policies and returned to the tired verities of the early Cold War. Short-range expediency finally got the better of their long-range insight. Kissinger's abdication came in 1978, when he joined Nitze, Jackson, and Reagan in attacking Carter's SALT II negotiations, even though the agreement being negotiated was almost identical to the one Kissinger had worked out with the Soviets at Vladivostok in 1976.

At the SALT II ratification hearings in 1979, Kissinger stopped short of calling for the treaty's defeat, but he advised the Senate not to ratify until the administration had agreed to a major arms buildup. When Senate Democrats asked Kissinger about his contention in 1976 that "military superiority has no practical significance under circumstances where both sides have the capability to annihilate each other," Kissinger said that the statement had been made at a time of "fatigue and exasperation." His defense was that he hadn't really known what he was talking about.

Nixon, for his part, initially remained obsessed with defending himself over Watergate. He devoted the second volume of his two-volume memoirs to answering charges from the scandal. But in 1980 he returned to the foreign policy fray with a dismal screed titled *The Real War*. In it Nixon recapitulated the theme that had thrust him onto the stage in the late 1940s—the imminent Soviet takeover of the world. "The Soviet Union today is the most powerful armed expansionist nation the world has known, and its arms buildup continues at a pace nearly twice that of the United States," he wrote. "The Kremlin leaders do not want war, but they do want the world. And they are rapidly moving into position to get what they want." Nixon clearly had no sense of the Soviets' growing weakness. He was recycling the neoconservative rhetoric that had been used against his own policies.

Nixon still retained his bilious hatred of the political establishment, which he now blamed for losing Vietnam and undermining his presidency. In the latest version of his memoirs, published in 1990, *In the Arena*, he even blamed America's "leadership class" for the infusion of drugs into the society. "The leadership class is made up of highly educated and influential people in the arts, the media, the academic community, the government bureaucracies, and even business," Nixon wrote. "They are characterized by intellectual arrogance, an obsession with style, fashion, and class, and a permissive attitude on drugs. In the drug war, they simply went over to the other side." Nixon had reverted to his crude us vs. them demagogy. The latest "new Nixon" was the oldest Nixon of all.

Kissinger, although not as filled with hatred and bitterness as Nixon, laid much of the blame for his and Nixon's failures at the foot of the same establishment. In his *Memoirs*, he argued that the United States had to retreat from Vietnam because "the internationalist Establishment, which had been responsible for the real achievements of our foreign policy, collapsed before the onslaught of its children who questioned all its values." They were soft on Communism because they were soft on their kids—this was the reductio ad absurdum of the Nixon formula.

Over the years, Nixon and Kissinger had little to do with each other, but in 1987 they decided to collaborate once more. The occasion was the Reagan administration's negotiations with the Soviet Union over an intermediate nuclear forces (INF) agreement. In many ways, the agreement represented a resumption of their own détente policies after a hiatus of nearly eight years. But instead of greeting the treaty as a vindication, Nixon and Kissinger denounced it. "If we eliminate American medium- and short-range forces in Europe without redressing the conventional imbalance," they warned in *National Review*, "the Soviet nuclear threat to Europe will remain, and the gap in deterrence of conventional attack will be reopened." The treaty, they cautioned, "could create the most profound crisis of the NATO alliance in its 40-year history." They were right: NATO was thrown into crisis, but not as they envisioned. With the end of the Cold War, NATO lost its purpose.

Nixon and Kissinger arrived at this historic moment blinded by political defeat. They had been among the first to prophesy the end of the Cold War and had taken significant steps toward this goal, but they were unable to recognize the culmination of the process they had spurred. They viewed the rise of Soviet President Mikhail Gorbachev warily and skeptically. Once they had seen through the bipolar conflict to its end. Now, when it was really ending, they mistrusted the appearance of harmony, regarding it as a ruse. The two visionaries had lost their sight. Belatedly, of course, Nixon and Kissinger came to their senses

# 8

# Ronald Reagan
## The Good Vibrations of Decline

How we've let that get away from us I'll never know.

—RONALD REAGAN, 1980

The spirit of the 1980s was best captured in a series of movies based on the premise that the present could be amended by returning to the past. These movies included *Back to the Future* (which had three parts), *Peggy Sue Got Married*, *Field of Dreams*, *Weird Science*, and *Bill & Ted's Excellent Adventure*. In *Back to the Future*, released in 1985, the beginning of Ronald Reagan's second term, the hero returns in a time machine to the early 1950s, where he finds himself a high school contemporary of his parents. He alters the past so that his best friend, the mad scientist, is saved from attack in the future by foreign terrorists. Along the way, he transforms his father from a struggling nerd into a rich and acclaimed science fiction writer and businessman.

These movies expressed the dominant political theme of the 1980s: the attempt by Americans to redeem the present by regression—to preserve the American Century by returning to those ideas they hazily remembered from its emergence. No one articulated this spirit better than Ronald Reagan, the former movie actor turned politician.

In 1980, Reagan ran for President on a promise to restore the American Century by ridding Washington of doubters and detractors. In announcing his candidacy, he declared, "There are those in our land who would have us believe that the United States, like other great civilizations of the past, has reached the zenith of its power. I don't believe that. I don't agree that our nation must resign itself to inevitable decline, yielding its proud position to other lands." In accepting the nomination in Detroit in July, Reagan pledged to restore America's "day in the sun."

Both Reagan's imagery and his programs were looted from the past. When Reagan told Americans they had a "rendezvous with destiny," he was plagiarizing the most memorable line from Franklin Roosevelt's 1936 inaugural address. When he denied that the nation was fated to decline, he mimicked Herbert Hoover's major campaign speech in the 1932 election. "I challenge the whole idea that we have ended the advance of America, that this country has reached the zenith of its power, the height of its development," Hoover proclaimed on October 31 at Madison Square Garden. Reagan's economic message recalled that of President Calvin Coolidge, the dour New Englander who had been President when Reagan was in high school and whose portrait Reagan hung in the White House Cabinet room in place of Harry Truman's. When Reagan talked about the Soviet Union, he echoed Whittaker Chambers, from whom he would appropriate his characterization of the Soviet Union as the "evil empire" and the "focus of evil in the modern world."

But there are no time machines in politics, only the rhetorical power of nostalgia. Reagan's efforts to re-create the past ended in an unfamiliar future. In attempting to restore the American Century, he produced results that brought the country far from the past he dreamed of. In trying to resuscitate the American economy, Reagan actually accelerated America's decline as a world economic power. Under Reagan, America's national debt tripled and its trade deficit quadrupled. In trying to revive the Cold War crusade against the Soviet Union, Reagan stumbled upon the end of the Cold War. To the chagrin of his conservative supporters, Reagan ended up abandoning the unwavering anti-Communism that had been his trademark. In trying to create a conservative Republican realignment that would accomplish for Republicans what the New Deal had accomplished for Democrats, Reagan instead laid the groundwork for the demise of the conservative right. By the time Reagan left office, the movement that had championed his nomination was in a shambles.

Reagan did not return America to the lighthearted prosperity of the 1920s or to the 1950s, when the United States stood imperiously at the forefront of a free world alliance fighting Communism. Instead, Reagan inadvertently laid the basis for the multipolar world that Nixon had predicted in 1971. But Reagan could not provide Americans with even an inkling of understanding to guide them in that new world. While he plunged America into unfamiliar terrain, his gaze remained firmly fixed on the past that never was.

Reagan was one of the strangest men ever to become President. He had very little interest in, or knowledge of, the mechanics of government. He followed debates over economic and foreign policy fitfully, sometimes dozing off during Cabinet discussions of technicalities. His ideas were a hodgepodge of New Deal idealism, pre-1960s conservatism, and millenarian religion. He presided blithely and complacently over the most scandal-ridden administration since Warren Harding's. Yet throughout this time, and during his prior eight years as governor of California, he retained the devotion of the electorate.

Reagan's political success rested in part on his unusual blend of ideological fervor and personal geniality. He leavened his fiery denunciations of Washington bureaucrats and Soviet commissars with wit and self-deprecating humor. It was said that Goldwater could make middle-of-the-road ideas sound extreme while Reagan could make the most extreme proposals sound middle-of-the-road. But the paradox went beyond Reagan's personal qualities. Reagan had a penchant for dogma, but at the same time an abiding belief that what was most important was the interaction between people. He could denounce the Soviet Union as an "evil empire," but still believe that through personal negotiations and a helicopter trip over suburbia, he could win over Soviet leaders.

Ronald Reagan was born in Tampico, a small town in northern Illinois, in 1911. His father, Jack, was a first-generation Irish Catholic who worked as a shoe salesman and then, during the Great Depression, ran the local office of the Works Progress Administration (WPA). Reagan described his father as a "black Irishman" with a cynical view of life. Reagan's mother, Nelle, known for her optimism and charity, was a Protestant of Scotch descent, active in the Disciples of Christ, an evangelical sect that during the time Reagan was growing up was preoccupied with the struggle for Prohibition. Reagan inherited his father's gift for storytelling and his mother's uplifting disposition.

Recounting his childhood in his first autobiography, *Where's the Rest of Me?*, written in 1964 in Hollywood, Reagan gave special prominence to his discovery that his father was an alcoholic. When he was eleven, he wrote, he returned home one evening to find his father "flat on his back on the front porch." Reagan says the incident marked his "first moment of accepting responsibility." For the young Reagan, a devout member of his mother's church, it must have created an enduring conflict between his sense of sin and his obligation to forgive the sinner. Reagan writes that his mother told him and his brother "over and over that we should love and help our father and never condemn him for something that was beyond his control."

This conflict between sin and forgiveness underlay Reagan's view of the world. For his first inaugural address in 1981, Reagan chose a biblical verse from 2 Chronicles that evoked the conflict in God's name:

If my people, which are called by my name, shall humble themselves, and pray, and seek my face, and turn from their wicked ways; then will I hear from heaven, and will forgive their sin, and will heal their land.

Translated into politics, condemning and then forgiving became denouncing and then compromising and negotiating. If the great theme of Reagan's public life was the crusade against the evils of Communism and bureaucracy, the abiding refrain of his private politics was compromise and negotiation. Just as he had done when he was a child, Reagan was always ready to deal with those he otherwise condemned. This made him an effective labor negotiator when he was president of the Screen Actors Guild (SAG), and it held him in good stead as a politician. In California, Reagan confounded his liberal critics and conservative supporters by working out a welfare-reform bill with the Democratic-controlled legislature. As President, he shocked his right-wing supporters by reaching arms-control agreements with Soviet President Mikhail Gorbachev.

In his political style, Reagan was almost the opposite of his predecessor as President, Jimmy Carter. Carter was strong on detail but vague on general political philosophy, whereas Reagan had little interest in detail but was the most ideological President since Wilson. He was also the only President who had undergone a political transformation as an adult.

Reagan was originally a New Deal Democrat like his father. In Hollywood, Reagan belonged to numerous liberal organizations, and he regularly campaigned for liberal Democrats. In 1948, for instance, he went to Minnesota to help Hubert Humphrey in his first Senate race. (Humphrey was a founder of the Americans for Democratic Action and at the 1948 convention had led the fight for the strong civil rights plank that had resulted in a Dixiecrat walkout.) In 1950, Reagan stumped for Helen Gahagan Douglas against Richard Nixon in their vitriolic campaign for the Senate.

But Reagan drew a very sharp line between liberals and Communists or pro-Communists. He helped convince the Screen Actors Guild to cross the picket lines of a union strike that he believed was Communist-led. He quit both the American Veterans Committee and the Hollywood Independent Citizens Committee of the Arts, Sciences, and Professions when they voted down anti-Communist statements; in 1947, he agreed to become an informant for the FBI; and in 1948, when HUAC came to Hollywood, he appeared as a friendly witness. But this was still true of other Democrats—Nixon's 1944 opponent, Jerry Voorhis, had, after all, authored legislation requiring Communists to register with the government.

By 1964, if not earlier, Reagan had gone so far to the right that Goldwater's handlers resisted allowing him to speak on the candidate's behalf. Reagan's conservatism was that of William F. Buckley, Jr.'s *National Review*, to which he had been an early subscriber. A speech he gave in Phoenix in 1961 was fairly typical. In it, Reagan warned that Communists were on the verge of taking over the world. "The inescapable truth is that we are at war, and we are losing that war because we don't, or won't, realize that we are in it," he said.

Like the members of the John Birch Society, Reagan believed that Communists were trying to take over the United States by enacting reforms that would eventually result in a socialist America. They were getting the United States, he explained in Phoenix, to "adopt emergency 'temporary' totalitarian measures until one day we'll awaken to find we have grown so much like the enemy that we no longer have any cause for conflict." These measures included Medicare, Social Security, and the income tax. "We have received this progressive tax directly from Karl Marx, who designed it as the prime essential of a socialist state," Reagan declared.

Reagan's vision was shaped by American evangelism. Americans had to lead the struggle against Communism and socialism because "in this land occurred the only true revolution in man's history. All other revolutions simply exchanged one set of rulers for another." But if America failed, Reagan saw its fate in millenarian terms:

There can only be one end to the war we are in . . . Wars end in victory or defeat. One of the foremost authorities on Communism in the world today has said we have ten years. Not ten years to make up our minds, but ten years to win or lose—by 1970 the world will be all slave or all free.

Neither Reagan nor his biographers have adequately explained how he underwent such a dramatic political conversion. In *Where's the Rest of Me?* and in his presidential memoirs, published in 1990, Reagan emphasized his struggles as president of the Screen Actors Guild in the late 1940s with Communist subversion in Hollywood. In his memoirs, Reagan wrote that he learned "from firsthand experience how Communists used lies, deceit, violence, or any other tactic that suited them to advance the cause of Soviet expansionism. I knew from the experience of hand-to-hand combat that America faced no more insidious or evil threat than that of Communism."

But Reagan wildly exaggerated his own experiences in Hollywood by portraying them through the prism of his later anti-Communism. Reagan did not abandon his support for Democrats or evince a fanatic anti-Communism until a decade after these events. In a 1947 interview, Reagan told columnist Hedda Hopper that the way to fight Communism was to create a better life for Americans—a standard liberal answer. "The Reds know that if we can make America a decent living place for all of our people, their cause is lost here," Reagan said.

Reagan's able biographer Lou Cannon portrays Reagan as having leaned in the late 1940s toward economic conservatism. After World War II, Reagan became annoyed with the high marginal tax rates that made it unprofitable for him to make more than four films a year. As the president of SAG in 1948, Reagan lobbied in Washington for a "human depreciation allowance" to benefit artists, actors, and writers who concentrated their income within a short period of time. Then, in the 1950s, Cannon argues, Reagan's propensity for economic conservatism was reinforced when he became a spokesman for General Electric. Reagan introduced the company's television show and gave speeches to management and to business groups on its behalf. Reagan's audiences were generally pro-business Republicans who welcomed attacks against "big government."

But Reagan was discharged in 1962 after his right-wing views—including his opposition to the Tennessee Valley Authority, one of GE's biggest customers—became an embarrassment to the company. By then, Reagan was not simply a conventional pro-business Republican with whom GE would have felt comfortable, but a member of what was called the "radical right."

Clearly, both Reagan's skirmishes against Hollywood Communists and his work for GE played some role in making him a conservative. So undoubtedly did the influence of his right-wing father-in-law, Dr. Loyal Davis, an early supporter of Barry Goldwater. But more important was Reagan's own search for a comprehensive ideology. Reagan had always been a highly political person—his first marriage had ended, Jane Wyman complained, because she got sick of his absorption in politics. And he sought in politics what he had found as a child in religion—a commanding worldview that could provide complete answers to the great questions of the day. Reagan fit the profile of the "true believer." In the 1940s, he had turned to the left, but finding it dormant and discredited, had moved to the only other comprehensive philosophy that was available —that of the new radical conservatism.

Whittaker Chambers and *Witness* appear to have had a particular influence on Reagan. Chambers was the only political thinker, and the only conservative, that Reagan quoted in his first autobiography, and thirty years after reading Chambers, he still regaled his White House speechwriter Tony Dolan with passages he had memorized from *Witness*. Chambers had an impact on Reagan because he expressed his political views through telling his own story. Reagan's subsequent revision of his own history in Hollywood—presenting himself as the last bulwark against a takeover by the "men in the Kremlin"— reflected his trying to draw an analogy between his own experience and that of Chambers.

For Reagan, Chambers explained the connection between opposition to Communism and opposition to the New Deal, big government, and liberalism. In *Where's the Rest of Me?* Reagan wrote that he was "too optimistic" to agree with Chambers's statement that in abandoning Communism, he was "leaving the winning side," but that he recognized "the bitter truth" that Chambers described about the connection between Communism and liberalism. Reagan quoted from the passage where Chambers took aim at Communism and hit "that great Socialist revolution which in the name of *liberalism*, spasmodically, incompletely, somewhat formlessly, but always in the same direction, has been inching its icecap over the nation for two decades."

But most important, Chambers appealed to Reagan because he couched his view of the world in religious terms. Chambers, who had rediscovered his own evangelical faith after leaving the Communist Party, portrayed the conflict between capitalism and Communism in terms of God and godlessness, good and evil. Reagan didn't even mention his own religious beliefs in *Where's the Rest of Me?* but his religious impulse had been transferred to politics, finding fulfillment in the view of Communism as what Chambers called "the focus of concentrated evil."

Indeed, after Reagan became governor of California in 1967, he would rediscover the evangelical religion of his youth. In that year, Reagan relates in his memoirs, he cured an ulcer through "the power of prayer." Then in 1970, singer Pat Boone brought three evangelical ministers to visit Reagan in Sacramento. Reagan and the ministers had an intense religious experience, and Reagan emerged from the meeting with an interest in the theory of Armageddon. By the time he came to the White House, Lou Cannon reports, he was convinced that he had to prevent an imminent nuclear holocaust between the United States and the Soviet Union.

Shorn of his geniality and removed from political consultants, Reagan represented the far extreme of American politics and religion. His view of the Soviet Union applied at best to the fantasies of a few Bolsheviks (principally allied with Leon Trotsky) after the revolution; his view of economics and social programs—Social Security as an "emergency 'temporary' totalitarian measure"—had been discredited by the Crash of 1929; and his global cosmology was derived from the millennial hysteria of the 1830s. Yet this man of bizarre beliefs succeeded in building political majorities for himself.

When Reagan ran for governor in 1966, few political experts in the state initially gave him a chance. The far right was strong in Southern California, but not in the state as a whole. In 1962, after he had left GE, Reagan chaired the Senate campaign of Loyd Wright, an ultraconservative who was challenging the moderate Republican incumbent, Thomas Kuchel. Wright got only 15 percent of the vote. In the 1964 Republican primary, a late-starting Nelson Rockefeller had almost defeated Goldwater, and Johnson won California against Goldwater with 60 percent of the vote. Reagan entered the primary as an underdog against moderate San Francisco mayor George Christopher. But the former actor defied the experts.

Reagan's secret as a politician was only partly his geniality and his skill as "the great communicator." Reagan also knew how to frame his own beliefs in terms that could appeal to an electoral majority. He did not abandon his principles, but he did not flaunt them in such a way as to allow voters to identify him with unpopular causes. Reagan showed conservatives how they could perform what Chambers had called the "dance along the precipice." His 1966 gubernatorial election became a model for Nixon's 1972 landslide and for the "new right" of the late 1970s.

Reagan understood the political problem that conservatives faced: their core beliefs—their opposition to the New Deal and their support for the aggressive rollback of the Soviet empire—were unpopular with most voters. While some conservatives deluded themselves into believing that they could win office by attracting conservative nonvoters, the more realistic recognized that to win they would have to attract erstwhile Democrats who backed Social Security and were worried about nuclear war.

Goldwater's defeat provided a clue. Goldwater had lost throughout the North, but he had attracted Southern Democrats who were opposed to civil rights. For Goldwater, opposition to federal civil rights laws was at best a secondary cause; but Reagan recognized that for conservatives to win, they would have to elevate what was secondary to them but primary to the voters. This is what Reagan did in the 1966 election.

Reagan hired Stuart Spencer, who had run Rockefeller's campaign, to manage his own. In the primary, he was able to count on Republican conservatives to carry him to an easy victory over the bumbling Christopher. But in the general election against Pat Brown he aimed his message much more clearly at discontented Democrats. He asked Goldwater to stay out of California during the fall election, and he carefully omitted opposition to Social Security. Instead, he focused on those social issues that appealed to middle-class and working-class Democrats whose support he needed to defeat the Democratic incumbent, Pat Brown. While reminding voters that he had been a union president, Reagan ran against the Berkeley radicals, accused them of drug and sex orgies "so vile I cannot describe them to you." Working-class Democrats applauded Reagan's attacks against student "elitists."

But more important, Reagan cultivated the growing backlash against civil rights. He opposed both the 1964 and 1965 Civil Rights Acts, criticized Brown for his handling of the Watts riot, and called for repealing California's Fair Housing Law. As he would do in every election, Reagan grew indignant at any hint that he was bigoted. Challenged about his opposition to the 1964 Civil Rights Act by black Republicans, Reagan uncharacteristically blew up. "I resent the implication that there is any bigotry in my nature," Reagan yelled. His insistence on his purity of heart only made him more attractive to voters who wanted to oppose civil rights legislation but did not imagine themselves to be prejudiced. Reagan could succeed precisely where an outright segregationist like George Wallace failed.

Reagan invented the tactic, which became a hallmark of the new right, of targeting the white working class by campaigning against the civil rights, antiwar, and countercultural movements of the 1960s. Even in 1966, Reagan was already running against the present on behalf of the past. The gambit paid off admirably in the election against Brown. While Reagan did much worse among blacks and upper-middle-class Northern California voters than Nixon had in his 1962 race against Brown, he easily outdid Nixon and Brown in white working-class districts. In one Southern California area dominated by a General Motors plant, Brown had defeated Nixon by eight to seven in 1962 but lost to Reagan by two to one in 1966.

In 1980, Reagan employed a similar strategy against Carter. He opened his campaign at the Neshoba County Fair in Philadelphia, Mississippi, where three civil rights workers had been slain in 1963. He told the all-white crowd that he "believed in states' rights"—an unmistakable signal that he would tilt the government away from black concerns; and as in 1966, Reagan became indignant when his opponent accused him of seeking the racist vote. Reagan also cultivated other constituencies alienated by the movements of the 1960s—working-class Catholic families threatened by feminist rhetoric, gun owners angry with demands for gun control, and veterans who believed that Vietnam was a "noble cause."

But Reagan faced far more formidable obstacles running for President than he had faced when running for governor in 1966. As a gubernatorial candidate, he could sidestep questions about national and international policy, but as a presidential candidate, he had to say what he thought about Social Security and the Soviet Union. Reagan again managed, however, to adapt his views to the exigencies of winning a majority.

In developing an economic policy, Reagan was aided by neoconservative intellectuals who, like Reagan, had formerly been Democrats. These intellectuals included Irving Kristol, the editor of *The Public Interest*, Jude Wanniski of *The Wall Street Journal* editorial page, Norman Podhoretz, the editor of *Commentary*, and academic Jeane Kirkpatrick. Working through these publications, through friendly columnists like Rowland Evans and Robert Novak, through think tanks like the American Enterprise Institute, and through receptive politicians like Buffalo congressman Jack Kemp, these intellectuals championed in the last half of the 1970s two kinds of ideas that would be crucial to Reagan in 1980. First, they drew a sharp distinction between the New Deal and Johnson's Great Society. They described such New Deal programs as Social Security as a "social safety net," while they condemned the Great Society programs, which were aimed primarily at minorities and the poor, for supposedly demoralizing and marginalizing the people they were supposed to help. Reagan followed this neoconservative approach.

Kemp and the neoconservatives also promoted the ideas of

maverick economists Arthur Laffer and Robert Mundell, who argued that lower tax rates would lead not only to economic growth but also to an increase in tax revenues. This miracle doctrine, called "supply-side economics," appeared to solve the dilemma that conservatives like Reagan had always faced: how to cut taxes without increasing the federal deficit. In the 1980 campaign, Reagan backed the Kemp-Roth tax-cut plan, which would cut tax rates by 30 percent across the board. While such a program had no appeal to the poor, who feared that it would result in budget reductions, it appealed to the middle- and upper-class voters who had joined the statewide tax revolts in 1978.

The new approach was epitomized by a campaign commercial first used in New Hampshire in February 1980 and then replayed through the campaign. In it, Reagan said:

> If there's one thing we've seen enough of, it's this idea that for one American to gain, another American has to suffer. When the economy is weak, as it has been in recent years, everybody suffers, especially those who have the least. If we reduce paperwork and unnecessary regulations, if we cut tax rates deeply and permanently, we'll be removing many of the barriers that hold everyone back. Those who have the least will gain the most. If we put incentives back into society, everyone will gain.

When critics, including independent presidential candidate John Anderson, charged that Reagan's economics were founded on "blue smoke and mirrors," he assembled a group of economists, including Alan Greenspan, who produced a report showing that with tax cuts *and* military spending increases, Reagan would still balance the budget by the end of his first term.

Like much of Reagan's campaign, his attacks on the Great Society were based on historical sleights of hand. He blamed the Great Society for enormous increases in the federal bureaucracy and federal spending that had in fact occurred in the Nixon administration, not during Johnson's tenure. Indeed, many of the Great Society programs were aimed at decentralizing the administration of welfare. Reagan's budget plan was also utter nonsense, as experience would show, but Greenspan's endorsement and the continuing disarray in the Carter administration prevented the Reagan budget from becoming a major issue in the campaign.

The great fear of the Reagan camp was that Carter would paint him as a warmonger. Reagan, a charter member of Nitze's Committee on the Present Danger, had opposed Carter's SALT II arms treaty with the Soviet Union, and the Republican convention had endorsed the goal of achieving nuclear superiority over the Soviet Union—a goal, policy experts warned, that if achieved could destabilize the arms race and could precipitate a war. Reagan also had a long history of bellicose rhetoric against the Soviet Union that suggested that, if he was elected, he would not hesitate to go to war.

Reagan insisted that even though he opposed all past treaties, he was willing to negotiate a new "SALT III." In his debate with Carter, he repeated the word "peace" in almost every other sentence. Reagan's sentiment was genuine—reflecting his fear of Armageddon and belief in his powers of personal persuasion—but was in conflict with his negative view of arms control. When Reagan said that what was needed was an arms race, not arms control, the Carter campaign believed it had an issue, but the press, to its dismay, collectively decided that this question wasn't worth any extended coverage.

Reagan tried to counter Democratic charges of warmongering by claiming that he merely wanted to parry a growing Soviet threat. The Soviet buildup, Reagan asserted, was the "greatest in the history of mankind" and had created a "window of vulnerability" through which the Soviets, with their land-based missiles, could launch a first strike against American forces. Reagan got his analysis of the Soviet threat from the Committee on the Present Danger. The committee had an exoteric and an

esoteric version of the window. In the exoteric version, meant
for the less educated public, the Soviets were developing a first-
strike capability. One widely cited article by committee member
Richard Pipes—later Reagan's National Security Adviser on the
Soviet Union—captured the point best. It was entitled "Why
the Soviet Union Thinks It Could Fight and Win a Nuclear
War."

In the esoteric version, meant for the more sophisticated, the
Soviets were not interested in fighting a war but intended to
use their newfound nuclear superiority to intimidate the United
States and its allies. In *The Present Danger*, Podhoretz, another
charter member of the committee, hysterically warned against
the "Finlandization of America" through the Soviet advantage.
Neither analysis had any merit. The Soviets had built up their
forces during the 1970s, but they had not changed their purpose
from deterrence; and as Kissinger had eloquently argued in
1976, nuclear superiority was a meaningless concept. Still Reagan was able to use the committee's analysis to stampede a
frightened public.

More important, Reagan used the Soviet threat, the Iranian
hostage crisis, and the flagging economy—at election time,
unemployment was 7.1 percent and inflation 12.5 percent—
to address voters' growing concern about the end of the American Century. At every turn in the campaign, contrasting past
and present, Reagan deplored the decline of American power.
Attacking Carter's handling of the hostage crisis, Reagan said
in New Hampshire in February 1980:

Some of us are old enough to remember back a few years
before World War II when Americans could be anywhere
in the world, in a banana republic revolution, in a war
. . . and all he would have to do is pin a little American
flag on his lapel and he could walk through that war and
no one would dare lay a finger on him because they knew
that the United States would go to the rescue of any of

its citizens wherever they might be. How we've let that get away from us I'll never know.

But Reagan also sent another message: that the U.S. decline was really a fiction created by the Carter administration. He called the United States "second to none" and said Americans were tired of leaders who told them "why we can't compete with the Japanese and Germans and why we cannot contain the Russians." Reagan took umbrage at a speech Carter gave in July 1979 in which he said that Americans were suffering from a "crisis of confidence." Even though Carter had not used the term "malaise," the speech became identified with the term. During the campaign, Reagan continually accused Carter of creating the crisis in confidence and perpetuating the malaise. In Reagan's concluding televised speech, he contrasted the dismal present with images of Pilgrims landing in New England and astronauts landing on the moon. "Does history have a place for America, for her great ideals?" he asked. "There are some who answer no, that our energy is spent, our days of greatness at an end, that a great national malaise is upon us. I find no national malaise."

Eight years later, political pundits, bemoaning the lack of substance in the contest between George Bush and Michael Dukakis, would look back upon the 1980 election as one of the more principled and straightforward campaigns in American history, yet it was anything but that. In the campaign, Reagan clearly voiced Americans' anxiety about the country's decline, but on every issue he touched—from civil rights to the Soviet threat—Reagan's approach was based upon misdirected bluster, misinformation, and in the case of his supply-side panacea, sheer nonsense.

As Reagan took office in January 1981, he faced daunting economic problems well beyond high unemployment and inflation. During the 1970s, the American economy had begun to slow down—growth averaged 4.8 percent between 1960 and 1973, but fell to 2.35 percent between 1974 and 1981. Productivity had risen only 1.4 percent a year from 1973 to 1980 compared with 4 percent for Western Europe and 6.9 percent for Japan. American firms had begun to lose out in key industries: in motor vehicles, the American share of the world market declined from 22.6 percent in 1962 to 17.5 percent in 1970 and then to 13.9 percent in 1979. In 1965, the United States exported five times as many machine tools as it imported. By 1980, it was importing twice as many as it was exporting.

The causes of decline lay partly in the fact that America's competitors, as they recovered from devastation after World War II, had built new, highly productive factories where they employed workers at lower wages than American workers received. In 1979, for instance, 50 percent of Japanese steel was being produced using the latest continuous-casting technology compared with 11 percent of American steel.

America's competitors also employed trade and industrial strategies to aid their companies. In both West Germany and Japan, close relations existed among business, finance, government, and labor that allowed companies to undertake long-term strategies, eschew short-term profits, and aim at winning world market shares. In Japan, the government heavily subsidized technological development and kept out foreign competitors until Japanese firms had established their superiority. Some Japanese electronics firms used cutthroat trade tactics, dumping television sets below cost on the American market in order to drive American firms out of business. Meanwhile, American firms made investment decisions according to quarterly balance sheets, while the U.S. government winked at its Cold War allies' protectionist trade practices.

During the Nixon, Ford, and Carter administrations, business and government leaders edged toward developing an industrial plan to halt the decline. Nixon broke with Bretton Woods and instituted wage-price controls, Carter established a Department of Energy and proposed a plan for more efficient use of resources and began to protect American industries from destructive trade practices. But the rise of Reagan definitively halted these experiments. Instead of moving forward to compete with the industrial planning used by Japan and Western Europe, the United States decided to go backward—to seek solutions for present ills by restoring the laissez-faire past.

Why did America retreat? One reason is that Americans had never really gone forward. Even during the height of the New Deal, Americans still retained an underlying commitment to the premises of what historian Louis Hartz called "Lockean liberalism." They saw society as a self-regulating realm and government as an alien institution—as a necessary evil. The only American President who waged a concerted campaign against this attitude was Theodore Roosevelt. Woodrow Wilson, Franklin Roosevelt, and John Kennedy mounted fleeting challenges, but retreated quickly under fire. Yet since the beginning of the century, with the exception of the 1920s, the government had actually practiced Theodore Roosevelt's philosophy of using the state as a means of correcting the inequities and imbalances of corporate capitalism.

During the 1970s, Reagan and other conservatives exploited this lingering contradiction between "operational liberalism" and "ideological conservatism," using the ideology to blame the practice for the decline of the American economy. And because the ideology had persisted, they were remarkably successful in stigmatizing "big government." In 1964, for instance, only 42 percent of Americans agreed when the Gallup Poll asked whether "the government has gone too far in regulating business and interfering with the free enterprise system." In 1978, 55 percent agreed, and in November 1980, 65 percent. Even AFL-CIO members turned against government economic intervention. A summer 1980 poll found that 66 percent of union members thought there was too much regulation of business.

But Reagan and the conservatives were also part of a historical pattern that was leading Americans to look backward rather than forward for solutions. It had happened to the prior great power on its way downward. In the 1920s, British Tories, backed by public opinion, restored the gold standard—ignoring the warning of John Maynard Keynes that doing so could price British goods out of foreign markets and set off a recession. That is exactly what happened, but the British of the 1920s were in the grips of an imperial nostalgia that seems to strike nations as they fall from world leadership. Like the British Tories, American conservatives of the 1980s set out to save the present by restoring the past. They, too, ignored the obvious: warnings that tax cuts combined with increases in military spending would precipitate massive deficits; warnings that revaluing the dollar would price American goods out of foreign markets; warnings that rising trade and budget deficits would mortgage America's future to foreign banks and bondholders. Indeed, it took almost a decade for Americans to recognize the disaster that had taken place, though even then they seemed paralyzed.

As Reagan took office, he also faced the specter of decay in the cities, concentrated among blacks and Hispanics. In 1969, unemployment among blacks and Hispanics was 6.4 percent, compared with 3.2 percent among whites; by 1981, it was 14.2 percent, compared with 6.7 percent among whites. In 1979, when the general unemployment rate was 5.8 percent, the rate among black male teenagers was 34.1 percent. As affluent whites moved to the suburbs, cities like Chicago, Detroit, and New York became poorer and blacker, with declining resources.

Urban blacks, the sociologist William Julius Wilson argued,

were being victimized by changes in the economy. During the 1970s, many manufacturing firms in cities either went out of business or moved to the suburbs or overseas. Cities were becoming service centers dependent upon highly educated labor. In New York, for instance, jobs requiring less than a high school diploma declined by over 400 percent during the 1970s, while jobs requiring a college education—primarily in the service sector—increased by 200 percent.

As central cities became poorer, they also became more violent. Family life began to disintegrate, and a vicious cycle of neglect was established, in which the cities' need for social services increased in proportion to their growing inability to pay for them. And as the middle class fled, the bonds between suburb and city, middle-class white and lower-class black were sundered—creating a politics of moral evasion, resentment, and chaotic violence. Politicians now appealed to racial fears without directly mentioning race, raising symbols of social unease and division such as welfare and crime.

At the beginning of the century, Herbert Croly and the progressives had feared that the society was disintegrating as the unregulated market created greater disparities in wealth and power. Croly's and Theodore Roosevelt's solution was to use the power of government to reduce inequities and to restore the social bond between the classes. Liberals in this tradition called in the 1970s for increasing federal welfare and job expenditures, but Reagan and the conservative Republicans argued that the real causes of urban decay were cultural and not economic: minorities were suffering from a culture of poverty fostered by the welfare state that destroyed the incentive to work. Accordingly, the right argued that the best remedy was to remove the government by reducing social spending.

The right-wing theory was merely a rehash of the contention of early-twentieth-century conservatives like William Graham Sumner that the ills of the poor were the result of "all the tinkering, muddling, and blundering of social doctors in the past." Current studies from the Urban Institute and elsewhere demonstrated that what sustained minority poverty was an absence of jobs paying higher than welfare.

Yet many white Americans backed Reagan's plan to dismantle the Great Society. The reason was not difficult to fathom. The white middle class blamed its steadily declining real income partly on taxes paid for growing state and federal welfare expenditures. Federal welfare spending had gone from $235 billion in 1970 to $434.6 billion in 1980. Both federal and state taxes had risen sharply. In California, for instance, the state collected 9.3 percent of its residents' income in 1957 and 15.5 percent in 1977.

While liberal Democrats were left to appeal to the middle class's generosity, Reagan could appeal to its narrow self-interest, as well as its prejudice. In 1980, Reagan easily won an argument that was not even joined by the divided Democrats and a faltering Carter in the fall campaign.

Reagan spelled out his conservative vision of government in his January 1980 inaugural address. He saw government as an alien intruder disrupting the magic of the market. "Government is not the solution to our problems; it is the problem," he said. Reagan's solution to stagflation and poverty was to withdraw government—cutting taxes, slashing social programs and regulations—while his solution to what he claimed to be a looming Soviet threat was wildly to increase Pentagon expenditures without any strategic focus.

Reagan largely succeeded in getting what he wanted from Congress. In 1981, Congress passed a bill that cut tax rates across the board by 30 percent. Subsequent tax bills would not alter the regressive thrust of the first Kemp-Roth bill. Over eight years, Congress reduced discretionary social programs targeted at the poor by 55 percent. Spending on employment and employment training programs were cut 70 percent. Meanwhile, military spending astronomically shot up 56 percent between 1981 and 1986.

The Reagan administration took aim at the regulatory apparatus that had sprouted during the Nixon administration. Where Reagan could not gut regulations, he appointed regulators drawn from the ranks of those they were supposed to regulate—for instance, a vice president of E. F. Hutton to head the Securities and Exchange Commission and a savings and loan executive to head the Federal Home Loan Bank Board. Anti-union conservatives filled the National Labor Relations Board. And so on. James Watt, who after a disastrous reign at Interior became enmeshed in the scandal at the Department of Housing and Urban Development, was hardly the exception to the rule. The results of these economic policies were almost uniformly disastrous—and scandalous.

Reagan's proudest claim when he left office was that the "misery index," the sum of inflation and unemployment, had dropped from when he took office. But the decline in inflation and unemployment was at best an unforeseen consequence—not even of Reagan's policies at that, but Federal Reserve chairman Paul Volcker's. The Fed's draconian policies, enacted by the Carter appointee, helped bury Carter and make the out-of-touch Reagan appear a prophet.

When Reagan took office, he adopted a strategy that was first proposed by *Wall Street Journal* editorial writer and supply-side publicist Jude Wanniski in a 1975 essay in *The Public Interest*. Summarizing the work of Mundell and Laffer, Wanniski argued that "monetary and fiscal policies are totally distinct policy instruments that can be employed for separate purposes and even utilized in opposite directions." Wanniski suggested that the best way to attack stagflation was to tighten the money supply, which would curb inflation, while simultaneously stimulating growth through tax cuts. The monetary notion was redundant with Volcker's policy already in place and the fiscal theory was make-believe.

Reagan adopted this so-called revolutionary strategy in 1981, promoting tax cuts while encouraging the Federal Reserve to continue tightening the money supply. But contrary to supply-siders' prediction of low-inflation growth, the Fed's actions canceled out the tax cuts, producing the worst recession since the 1930s. Inflation finally eased, but only because of the recession. And employment began to rise only after the business cycle had bottomed out. Over the entire period of the Reagan presidency, growth rates lagged behind those during the stagnant 1970s. The nation's wealth, for instance, grew 8 percent from the Reagan upturn of 1983 to 1988, whereas it had grown by 31 percent between 1975 and 1980. Meanwhile, budget deficits—financed through foreign lending—surged over $200 billion. In the last Carter budget, interest payments on the national debt amounted to 10 percent of the budget; in the 1989 budget, they amounted to 15 percent.

To no one's surprise (except doctrinaire conservatives), Reagan's policies also drastically worsened the ills of America's cities and underclass. His tax policies widened the gulf between rich and poor. From 1979 to 1989, real family income of the lowest fifth of the population declined by 1.9 percent, while income of the top fifth rose by 18.6 percent. The percentage of Americans living in poverty climbed from 11.4 percent in 1978 to 13.4 percent in 1987. By 1985, 32.1 percent of blacks and 49.4 percent of Puerto Ricans living in cities were below the poverty line.

During the Reagan years, the same trends that had been marginalizing urban blacks in the 1970s accelerated due to two seemingly contradictory developments—the sharp recession of the early 1980s and the increase in manufacturing productivity that came largely from computer automation. In both cases, the result was a net loss of manufacturing jobs—two million as a whole in the 1980s—most concentrated in cities and many held by blacks.

During the recession of 1981–83, for instance, Milwaukee lost 60,000 manufacturing jobs—a fourth of its total. After 1983, it gained back only 9,000 while adding thousands of new salaried jobs in white-collar services. "The result," reported Isabel Wilkerson in *The New York Times*, "is a city of 628,000 people where black men stand idle on street corners just blocks from the breweries and factories that used to employ them, while well-dressed white-collar workers sell insurance or computers out of some of those same factories, now converted into office parks." In Chicago, a very similar process took place. From 1972 to 1988, 60 percent of the new jobs in Chicago were created in the suburbs, where blacks make up 2 percent of the population.

The Reagan administration's response was neglect, but not since Hoover had such indifference been dressed up as an ideology. No efforts were made to reverse these trends, and programs that might have eased the impact of unemployment—such as employment training—were slashed or eliminated entirely. At the same time, Reagan and the conservative Republicans' deliberate political strategy of polarizing the electorate along racial lines increased the alienation and despair at the bottom. In the last years of the Reagan administration, demagogues like the Reverend Louis Farrakhan and the Reverend Al Sharpton fanned racial hatred and anti-Semitism, making reform unlikely and a reversion to violence more likely. These figures, feeding on hopelessness, were as authentic products of the Reagan era as the supply-siders.

The contrast with Nixon was dramatic. Nixon had also pursued a racially charged political strategy, but unlike Reagan, he understood that he was the President of all the people. Nixon's programs, such as the ambitious Family Assistance Plan that would have replaced welfare with a guaranteed annual income, would have substantially benefited blacks. Even on busing, a program that Nixon publicly and philosophically opposed, he instructed his administration to work behind the scenes to achieve, where possible, plans that were acceptable to blacks and whites. Affirmative action was among Nixon's legacies, one that became a symbol in the right's racial demagogy.

Reagan's deregulatory policies were literally a scandal—in agency after agency. His neglect here belied the conservative claims of frugal management. The price tag for the S&L imbroglio alone ran to more than $500 billion. Even where Reagan's policies were seen by business as directly aiding economic growth, short-term gains were set against long-term losses. No President since Hoover was more hostile to labor unions. In 1982, Reagan successfully ousted the federal air controllers' union after it went on strike, succeeding in gaining a public relations boost but resolving none of the problems that led to the strike and which only worsened. His appointees to the National Labor Relations Board and the Occupational Safety and Health Administration uniformly and reflexively favored business against labor. For instance, Reagan appointed a former management attorney to chair the NLRB, and during his tenure, over twice the percentage of complaints were decided in favor of management than had happened in the prior four decades of the board.

Reagan's attitude and appointments contributed to the precipitous decline of labor union membership—from 23.2 percent in 1980 to 16 percent in 1990—a decline directly correlated with a decline in real wages. From 1979 to 1989, the average weekly earnings of production workers declined by 1 percent. Combined with the drop in the dollar's value after 1985, this gave American manufacturers a significant cost advantage over their foreign competitors, but left American workers the poorer.

Reagan's free-market remedies failed to halt the decline of American industry. Some of this might have occurred in any case, but Reagan's opposition to government intervention and Secretary of the Treasury Donald Regan's insistence on propping up the value of the dollar accelerated the decline. As late as 1979, America enjoyed a trade surplus. In 1981, due in part to oil imports, it ran a $34.6 billion deficit; but by 1987, with the price of oil falling, the deficit had risen to a record $170.3 billion.

This trade deficit was primarily the consequence of the decline in American manufacturing. From 1980 to 1988—the years of "morning again in America"—the U.S. share of world exports in automobiles dropped 46 percent, computers 36 percent, microelectronics 26 percent, and machine tools 17 percent. In 1980, the United States controlled 60 percent of the world market in semiconductors; by 1988, it controlled 38 percent and the Japanese 50 percent.

Where the administration might have done something to halt decline, it balked. In 1982, when thirteen U.S. firms still controlled 56 percent of the world market in semiconductors— perhaps the crucial industry of the twenty-first century—the Commerce Department discovered that the Japanese were beginning to "dump" their computer chips below cost on the U.S. market. But administration officials, committed to upholding an abstract free market even when other countries violated it, blocked action until 1986. By 1988, only two of the thirteen American semiconductor firms remained.

In 1980, Reagan repeatedly blamed Carter for the plight of the economy, but his administration's rejection of programs begun by Carter—whether in worker retraining or industrial development—took its toll on American industry. As Ira Magaziner and Mark Patinkin wrote in *The Silent War*, one of the casualties of the Reagan administration's attitude toward government was the solar-power industry.

In 1978, the Carter administration, with broad industry support, started a program in the Department of Energy to develop a low-cost process for manufacturing photovoltaic cells. A homeowner tax deduction for solar panels was also included in that year's energy bill. By 1981, when the Reagan administration took office, the United States was well ahead of Europe and Japan in developing solar energy. Then the Reagan administration proposed an 80 percent cut in the Energy Department's solar budget. Congress finally agreed to a 50 percent cut. And the next year the administration eliminated Westinghouse's contract to develop solar cells. In 1983, the United States was still the world leader in producing solar cells—controlling 60 percent of the world market to Japan's 23 percent. By 1986, Japan, which was subsidizing private development, had 49 percent of the world market and the United States 27 percent.

Most of the decisions regarding trade and technology were made well out of the President's earshot. If the subject was not high taxes or the Soviet threat, Reagan usually lost interest. At one Cabinet meeting, called to discuss the eroding position of the country's high-technology industries, Reagan "appeared to doze off," wrote Commerce Department Counsel Clyde Prestowitz in his memoir *Trading Places*. Yet when the issue was clearly posed, Reagan's industrial patriotism was piqued. In 1984, the U.S. machine tool industry filed a petition for relief from foreign imports. The Commerce Department urged action, but for two years officials on the National Security Council and the Office of Management and Budget kept the issue off the President's desk. Finally in May 1986, after feuding became public, the matter was brought before Reagan. A White House official, thinking that he would cut Commerce off at the pass, made the first presentation. He began with a rhetorical question, "Can we depend on our allies for machine tools?" But before he could answer, "Yes," Reagan interrupted. "No," he said. "What is your next question?" Reagan agreed to place import restraints on Japan and Taiwan.

Most top administration officials were either doctrinaire proponents of free trade or uninterested in the whole subject. "Aircraft carriers and the Soviets are the big leagues. Trade and industrial economics are strictly bush leagues," recalled Prestowitz. None of the Reagan administration's economic policymakers who wrote memoirs—Budget Director David Stockman, Domestic Policy Adviser Martin Anderson, Secretary of the Treasury Donald Regan—discussed trade or technology issues in their books.

Indeed, the only times the administration took bold action were when the Pentagon argued that an industry was critical to waging the Cold War. In 1988, after four years of argument, the administration finally agreed to allow the Pentagon, through its Defense Advanced Research Projects Agency (DARPA), to fund Sematech, a facility in Austin set up to develop a manufacturing process for the next generation of computer chips. But by then it was almost certainly too late.

The administration's neglect of the country's industrial base led to a paradox that haunted Reagan. Under Reagan, as political scientist Chalmers Johnson remarked, the Soviet Union lost the Cold War, but Japan and Germany, not the United States, won it. While the United States was worrying about aircraft carriers and MX missiles, these countries were producing new generations of machine tools and computer chips. "After having spent $1 trillion for defense in the last ten years," Helen Bentley, a Maryland Republican congresswoman, said in 1990, "we find ourselves not stronger, but greatly weakened." But winning the Cold War didn't even require this wasteful expenditure. It was a price that didn't have to be paid.

From the beginning, Reagan's policy toward Communism and the Soviet Union was bedeviled by his contradictory instincts and the conflicting views of his chief foreign policy advisers. President Reagan shared Chambers's view that the Soviet Union was the "focus of evil" and that it sought world domination. At Reagan's first White House press conference, when a reporter asked whether détente with the Soviet Union—a policy begun under Nixon and continued with Carter—was still possible, Reagan emphatically answered no. The Soviet goal, he said, was "the promotion of world revolution and a one-world Socialist or Communist state." The Soviets, he warned in pseudo-biblical rhetoric, "reserve unto themselves the right to commit any crime, to lie, to cheat, in order to attain that."

Reagan's militant denunciation of the Soviet Union convinced many Americans and Western Europeans that he had no interest in reducing hostilities—provoking a massive anti-nuclear movement during his first term. At the same time, he frightened the Soviets into believing that nuclear war was imminent. As Soviet officials acknowledged later, the slightest miscue might have precipitated a catastrophe.

Yet Reagan continued to have faith that through personal intercession, he could achieve peace; he feared that if he didn't, Armageddon would be likely. In April 1981, Reagan sent a handwritten letter to Soviet General Secretary Leonid Brezhnev pledging his commitment to a "meaningful and constructive dialogue which will assist us in our joint obligation to find lasting peace." During his first term, Reagan also took small steps that, other things being equal, might have convinced the Soviets that he really wanted peace between the two countries. In April 1981, he removed the grain embargo against the Soviet Union. And he continued until 1986 (when he was manipulated by the anti-arms-control cabal in the Defense Department) to adhere to the provisions of SALT II.

But any chance that a clear message might get through was vitiated by the conflicts among Reagan's advisers. Secretary of State George Shultz, who replaced the temperamental Alexander Haig in 1982, led the forces within the administration favoring genuine negotiations with the Soviet Union. A veteran of the Nixon administration, Shultz recognized that a multipolar world was struggling to emerge from the confines of the Cold War. Ironically, Shultz was joined by Nitze, who in 1982 was appointed chief arms-control negotiator. Nitze had been a leading opponent of SALT II, but within the Reagan administration Nitze suddenly found himself a realist among Cold War evangelicals—as someone who could conceive of an agreement with the Soviet Union on mutually acceptable terms. The fact that Nitze became the administration dove showed how far American policy had strayed toward the apocalyptic anti-Communism of Burnham and Chambers.

Arrayed against Shultz and Nitze were Secretary of Defense Caspar Weinberger and his arms-control expert, Assistant Secretary Richard Perle, who were determined to block any possibility of agreement. Weinberger, surrounding himself with Churchilliana, believed that he was fighting World War II, only against the Soviet Union rather than Nazi Germany, and that any form of negotiation amounted to appeasement. On the wall behind his desk was a wartime quotation from Churchill: "Never give in, never give in, never, never, never, never; in nothing large or small, great or petty, never give in."

Weinberger and Perle were indirectly aided by CIA Director William Casey. Under Casey, the CIA dedicated itself to nourishing the wildest fears of Soviet aggression. Casey blocked reports that showed Soviet weakness—as late as 1986 the CIA was recording Soviet economic gains on the United States—while sending to the President ill-founded and highly biased reports demonstrating that the Soviet Union was engaged in a worldwide terrorist conspiracy, even masterminding the attempted assassination of the Pope in 1981.

Reagan had neither the will nor the knowledge to mediate between the conflicting parties. In 1982, Reagan agreed to a Perle proposal that both sides reduce their land-based forces by one-third, not realizing that such a proposal was completely unacceptable to the Soviet Union, which concentrated most of its strategic forces on land. Perle exploited Reagan's commitment to eliminating nuclear weapons to convince him to back the "zero option" proposal in Europe, a proposal that Perle advanced because he believed the Soviets would never accept it. In November 1983, after the United States deployed Pershing and cruise missiles in Western Europe, the Soviets broke off arms-control talks with the United States.

Reagan further muddied the waters of U.S.-Soviet relations

with his advocacy of the Strategic Defense Initiative, or "Star Wars." Reagan was attracted to the scheme precisely because he saw it as a hedge against Armageddon. His dream was to eliminate all nuclear weapons. Short of that, he wanted both countries to have impenetrable shields. Although Reagan later claimed in his memoirs that he never envisaged SDI as a foolproof umbrella, he consistently described it as such in his speeches and in private conversations. As late as 1986, he was describing SDI as a "shield that could protect us from nuclear missiles just as a roof protects a family from rain."

Reagan did not understand that what seemed purely defensive to him appeared to the Soviet Union as a means toward achieving an American nuclear first strike. Later, he would be upset because the Soviets would not accept his word that the United States would share SDI with the Soviet Union. Some of those responsible for SDI and Reagan's own advisers saw that the antimissile defense could potentially tilt the balance of the arms race in the United States' favor. One Stanford Research Institute report described an antimissile defense as guaranteeing "Pax Americana" for the next century. Others saw it as a gigantic pork barrel. Shultz, who was committed to détente, tried to make the best of SDI by conceiving of it as a useful bargaining chip in negotiations with the Soviets, but to Reagan it was the nonnegotiable centerpiece of his anti-Armageddon strategy.

Reagan's advocacy of SDI deepened the paralysis within the administration. While Shultz and Nitze tried to find a way around SDI, Weinberger and Perle arranged for a provocative and wholly ungrounded legal reinterpretation of the Anti-Ballistic Missile treaty, which banned testing of SDI components outside of the laboratory. Weinberger's reinterpretation —combined with Reagan's theology—threatened to destroy any prospect of arms-control negotiations with the Soviet Union. Only when Senator Sam Nunn, chairman of the Armed Services Committee, and Senator Joseph Biden, chairman of the Judiciary Committee, blocked the reinterpretation was the United States prevented from breaking with the treaty.

In his memoirs, Reagan credited pressure from SDI with achieving a "breakthrough" in U.S.-Soviet relations. This is less history than fantasy. The effect of SDI was at best minor and highly ambiguous. When Mikhail Gorbachev became General Secretary in 1985, he and his generation of leaders were already committed to economic reform; they already saw the reduction of Soviet military spending—totaling as much as a quarter of the national budget—as a prerequisite of reform. Their priority, as Gorbachev explained in an interview with *Time* in 1985, was to slow the arms race. SDI had a contradictory effect on the debate within the Soviet Union. On the one hand, it gave the reformers a further argument—that trying to keep up with the United States was both futile and self-destructive; on the other hand, it raised the level of paranoia among the Soviet hard-liners, making compromise and negotiation less likely.

Over the years, Reagan's insistence on the technologically infeasible program probably blocked the signing of a significant treaty reducing strategic arms. In 1986, the Soviets were willing to halve their strategic forces in exchange for postponing SDI testing for ten years, but Reagan demurred. Instead, the United States and the Soviet Union reached agreement only on eliminating intermediate-range missiles in Eastern and Western Europe—an agreement more significant for what it signified politically about U.S.–Soviet relations than for its substance. Finally, in 1988, Gorbachev, recognizing that SDI was a chimera, reached tentative agreement with Shultz on a START treaty, but by then it was too late. Conservatives, who had already fought the INF treaty, discouraged Reagan from pressing ahead with a new treaty in an election year.

If Reagan himself deserves credit for the breakthrough, it is on a different level. His willingness to meet with Gorbachev in 1985—and his amicable behavior during the Geneva summit —reduced Soviet fears that Reagan had raised with his rhetoric during the early 1980s. After the Geneva summit, Reagan also drew conclusions about Gorbachev's sincere intentions that were at odds with those of his fellow conservatives and that turned out to be correct. "I have to believe," he told his Cabinet, "that they share with us the desire to get something done, and to get things straightened out." He said of Gorbachev in an interview, "I think I'm some judge of acting, so I don't think he was acting. He, I believe, is just as sincere as we are in wanting answers." Had Reagan thought otherwise—had he allowed his ideological preconceptions to dictate his personal reaction—the Cold War might well have continued through the end of the century.

Two years later, in pushing the INF treaty, Reagan faced considerable opposition from conservatives in the Senate, including Dan Quayle, whom Bush would choose as his Vice President, and conservative columnists and policy experts, including Henry Kissinger and William F. Buckley, Jr. *National Review* headlined a special issue opposing the INF agreement: "Nuclear Suicide." But Reagan not only went ahead with signing the treaty, he revised his own conservative views of Soviet behavior. In December 1987, Reagan informed interviewers that the Soviet Union was no longer interested in "one world domination." Asked whether he still believed that the Soviet Union was the "evil empire," he explained that the United States and the Soviet Union now had "an entirely different relationship."

On one level, Reagan's insight into Soviet motives was mainly impressive because he, Ronald Reagan, had had it. It showed that, unlike other conservatives, he was not entirely wedded to visions from the past and could, if sufficiently pressed, recognize new realities. Judged against what other foreign policy experts knew, Reagan was simply acknowledging the obvious. Kennan, Fulbright, Lippmann, and other members of the realist school had understood since the late 1940s, if not before, that the Soviet Union was not on a messianic crusade for "one world domination." Kennedy had acknowledged as much in his American University speech in June

1963, and Nixon and Kissinger had made it a cornerstone of their foreign policy.

But Reagan saw in Gorbachev not merely a man with whom the "West could do business"—in British Prime Minister Margaret Thatcher's phrase—but also someone who was capable of ending the Cold War itself. It would take many liberals and conservatives, including Reagan's successor, George Bush, until the end of 1989, when the Berlin Wall fell, to recognize the enormous promise that Gorbachev held. To Reagan's credit, he saw it almost from the beginning and, in seeing it, encouraged its realization.

By the time he left office, Reagan also had begun to shut down the administration's attempt to "roll back" Communism in the Third World—dubbed the "Reagan Doctrine" by neoconservative columnist Charles Krauthammer. Like Reagan's nuclear doctrines, Reagan's counteroffensives in Nicaragua, Grenada, Angola, and Afghanistan had their roots in the militant conservatism of the 1950s. The Reagan Doctrine was the latest incarnation of James Burnham's strategy in *Containment or Liberation?*

This strategy had been updated by Jeane Kirkpatrick, who in an article in *Commentary* in 1979, "Dictatorships and Double Standards," had drawn a sharp distinction between the capitalist authoritarianism of Chile's Pinochet or Argentina's junta, which could evolve peacefully into democracy, and the Communist totalitarianism of the Soviet bloc, which could be altered only by violent revolution. Kirkpatrick's argument was intended to reconcile Wilsonian idealism with the conservatives' emphasis on toppling only Communist dictatorships. Reagan, impressed by Kirkpatrick's argument, appointed her his UN Ambassador, and she and CIA Director Casey became the chief proponents of a rollback strategy.

The problem with the strategy was that it had little basis in fact. Argentina's brutal junta, a favorite of Kirkpatrick's, could be ousted only after a war; Nicaragua's Sandinistas were deposed in an election. The distinction was also difficult to appreciate in practice. While the regimes targeted for overthrow by the administration were usually repressive, the liberators that the administration championed were equally, if not more, unsavory. It was hard to choose between the Nicaragua's Sandinistas and the CIA-created Contras, which recruited its leadership largely from former dictator Anastasio Somoza's National Guard, or between Angola's Marxist regime, which enjoyed amicable relations with American corporations and showed no sign of wanting to impose its will elsewhere, and the opposing UNITA forces, led by former Maoist Jonas Savimbi and funded by South Africa.

When Democrats in Congress balked at spending billions to fund Reagan's world counterrevolution, Casey and National Security Council aide Lieutenant Colonel Oliver North took matters into their own hands, seeking to establish a secret government within the government that would run and fund the counterrevolution. In November 1986, Casey and North's operation was exposed, leading to the Iran-Contra scandal and the downfall of those administration members associated with the Reagan Doctrine.

The scandal and his growing friendship with Gorbachev led Reagan to lose interest in his own doctrine. By the summer of 1987, Shultz had also recognized the futility of backing the Contras. In August 1987, Reagan and Shultz agreed to the plan proposed by House Speaker Jim Wright to seek a negotiated settlement of the war in Nicaragua. Reagan's conservative backers began to sport buttons, "Support the Contras, Impeach Reagan," while Reagan became increasingly disgusted with the Republicans in Congress who wanted him to continue funding the Contras. "These sons of bitches won't be happy until we have 25,000 troops in Managua, and I'm not going to do it," he told his last chief of staff, Kenneth Duberstein.

For conservatives, Reagan's embrace of Gorbachev and repudiation of the Contras cast a shadow of doubt over the decade. Reagan's victory in 1980 had created a boom for conservatives, who had never experienced national power. Indeed, as conservatives scaled the bureaucratic walls of Washington and as corporate contributions poured into conservative think tanks, it seemed that the conservative movement would attain the same kind of dominance over American politics that the liberal movement had achieved during the 1930s and the 1960s. But like other expectations generated by Reagan, it proved illusory.

The immediate beneficiaries of Reagan's victory were the think tanks and political organizations in Washington. The Heritage Foundation, begun in 1973 with a $250,000 grant from right-wing brewer Joseph Coors, moved in 1983 from a set of modest row houses to a $11 million edifice overlooking Capitol Hill. Heritage's staff of more than 100 published four or five position papers every week. The American Enterprise Institute (AEI), which had operated on a shoestring during the 1960s, boasted a $10 million budget by 1982.

Publications also flourished. The circulation of *National Review* and the conservative news weekly *Human Events* went over 100,000. Sun Myung Moon's Unification Church started a conservative daily in Washington, *The Washington Times*. On major college campuses, conservatives followed the lead of the *Dartmouth Review* and established their own newspapers. In each region, mini Heritage Foundations were established.

Conservative evangelicals, led by the Reverend Jerry Falwell and the Reverend Pat Robertson, also thrived, setting up political organizations like the Moral Majority and even taking over a major religious organization—the Southern Baptist Convention. The religious right appeared to provide conservative Republicans with the same kind of activist base that the labor movement had provided for Democrats. Political action committees like Terry Dolan's National Conservative Political Action Committee (NCPAC), which had helped Republicans win the Senate in 1980, threatened the Democrats with extinction in 1982.

But by the time Reagan left office, the conservative movement was in disarray. Facing a budgetary crisis, AEI had been forced to pare its programs. NCPAC was defunct. Richard Viguerie, the new right's direct-mail wizard, had been rescued from insolvency by Moon's Unification Church, while the church's *Washington Times* had been forced to close its foreign bureaus. No national leader stepped forward to take Reagan's place; the two presidential candidates who claimed to represent the movement—Kemp and Robertson—were bitterly feuding. And two of the main factions of conservatives—the neoconservatives and the traditionalists (dubbed the "paleoconservatives")—denounced each other in angry terms that they formerly reserved for liberals.

One reason for the conservative collapse was simply economic. After the expectations of a political realignment generated by Reagan's first landslide, conservative think tanks and political action committees got caught in a classic overproduction crisis. One group after another was set up, building projects were begun, new staffs hired, budgets expanded. When Republican conservatives failed to win the House of Representatives and lost the Senate in 1986, corporate donors began to lose interest; there were just not enough funds anymore.

Conservatives also suffered from the political uncertainty created by the end of the Cold War and the decline of the American economy. Since the early 1950s, opposition to the threat of Soviet Communism had united the different factions on the right—from the traditionalists primarily concerned with preserving an older America to the neoconservatives committed to a global anti-Communist crusade. But the Cold War's end deprived them of common purpose.

In Reagan's second term, the differences between the factions surfaced. The traditionalists, echoing the pre-World War II analysis of right-wing isolationists, wanted the United States to begin reducing the global commitments it had made in the course of the Cold War, while the neoconservatives wanted the United States to undertake a new mission to achieve "global democracy."

Even before Reagan left office, the quarrel had become very nasty. The traditionalists charged that the real motive of the neoconservatives, many of whom were New York Jews, was to preserve American support for Israel. In an October 1988 speech at the Heritage Foundation, Russell Kirk threw down the traditionalist gauntlet. "Not seldom it has seemed as if some eminent neoconservatives mistook Tel Aviv for the capital of the United States—a position they will have difficulty in maintaining as matters drift," he said. Midge Decter, the director of the Committee for the Free World, called Kirk's remark "a bloody piece of anti-Semitism."

The traditionalists charged that the neoconservatives were using their connections with the administration to secure jobs, while the neoconservatives accused the traditionalists of resurrecting what neoconservative Richard John Neuhaus called the "forbidden bigotries" of the old right.

With American industry in decline, conservative differences about foreign economic policy also surfaced. The new conservatives of the 1950s, ideologically committed to free-market principles, had joined liberal Democrats in favoring free-trade internationalism. But beginning in the 1970s, many of the small and medium-sized manufacturers who formed the financial backbone of the conservative movement began to be battered by imports. As the United States suffered chronic trade deficits, some of these conservatives, and the organizations they backed, favored a return to the protectionism of the old 1930s right wing.

One of the most important of these conservatives was Roger Milliken, the chairman of one of the country's most profitable textile firms, who had been a key financial supporter of *National Review* in the 1950s, Barry Goldwater's vice presidential bid in 1960, and Goldwater's presidential race in 1964. Later, Milliken helped fund the Heritage Foundation. In the 1980s, Milliken, threatened by cheap imports, stopped contributing to conservative organizations, including the Heritage Foundation, that remained wedded to free trade.

One of the oldest conservative organizations, the Business and Industrial Council, also changed course in the 1980s. Its president, Anthony Harrigan, began to worry about the trade deficit and the havoc he saw imports wreaking in many of his members' businesses. In *American Economic Pre-eminence*, Harrigan and William R. Hawkins dismissed free trade as "sophistry" and called for the United States to adopt what amounted to an industrial strategy of protectionism.

At the same time, many of the conservative think tanks, including Heritage, AEI, and the Center for Strategic and International Studies (CSIS), continued to espouse free trade, attacking even modest attempts to protect domestic industries from foreign price cutting or to survey foreign investment. The conservative think tanks sought funding from the same foreign companies and business associations that Harrigan's council and Milliken saw as the enemy. As foreign contributions poured in, the Business and Industrial Council and its supporters questioned the think tanks' patriotism and independence from foreign interests, while Heritage representatives accused Harrigan of being a "socialist."

Conservatives were returning to the factional disputes that paralyzed them during the 1930s and 1940s and had been suppressed by the Cold War and American prosperity. During his two terms, Reagan managed to hold the different sides loosely together in one coalition, but he failed to provide them with an overall vision that could carry them past his own term in office. What remained were disreputable campaign tactics, the main one being the exploitation of racial division. When he departed in January 1989, the disputes between the conservative camps became even more acerbic, and any semblance of a united movement was lost.

Reagan's departure from office, and the collapse of the conservative movement, did not immediately open the way for a new vision of America to emerge, but rather revealed the emptiness that lay just beneath the surface of American politics and that found vivid expression in the 1988 campaign. Reagan had pledged to fight the Cold War, but it had ended before he could raise his fist; he had promised to halt America's decline and to revive the American Century, but he failed abysmally. Reagan's new morning became the nation's long day's journey into night.

# 9

## *Lee Iacocca*

### The Car Salesman
### as Industrial Statesman

Now I always thought that Central America meant places like
Michigan, Ohio and Indiana (shows you how simpleminded I
am!). What about *our* Central America?"

—LEE IACOCCA, 1984

For a decade, Chrysler chairman Lee Iacocca blended the roles
of supersalesman and industrial statesman. Having won acclaim as America's premier corporate manager, he tried to
transfer the lessons he learned at Chrysler to the country as a
whole. He wanted to preserve the American Century, but not
through increasing the defense budget. He was obsessed with
preventing the decline, and disappearance, of American manufacturing. He wrote two books and gave numerous speeches
counseling cooperation among government, business, and labor to repel the Japanese challenge. He wanted government to
aid American heavy industry as a whole in the same way that
it had aided Chrysler in 1980. He wanted more money for
bridges, railroads, and schools and less for weapons. He advocated a "Marshall Plan for America." When opposition politicians were cowed by Reagan's landslide, Iacocca became the
prophet for a forgotten progressivism.

But as the Chrysler chairman was advising America how to
become strong again, his company began to falter. At the end
of the 1980s, Iacocca had to go on the road—not to save Amer-

ica, but to save Chrysler. With his company teetering on the edge of ruin, his role of salesman began to undermine his stature as a statesman: Iacocca's prescriptions for America were increasingly seen as self-serving anodynes for Chrysler. Iacocca's publicity campaign—aimed at inducing Americans to buy American cars—only reinforced suspicions that he was peddling inferior merchandise. Chrysler continued to decline, along with the reputation of its chairman.

Yet at the beginning of the decade, when Ronald Reagan was taking office and when Iacocca was first rescuing Chrysler and hawking his plan for saving American industry, he came as close as any businessman to understanding the maladies that had afflicted American industry and government. His showroom lectures on industrial decline told more about the state of America than the sophisticated bromides being peddled by think-tank economists. During those years, he joined a small group of capitalists—ranging from J. P. Morgan & Co.'s George Perkins to General Electric's Gerald Swope to Lazard Frères' Felix Rohatyn—who saw beyond the vaunted glories of laissez-faire capitalism.

Since World War II, nobody had succeeded in the U.S. auto business against greater odds and with more flair than Iacocca. An Italian Catholic among WASPs, a graduate of Lehigh rather than Yale, a salesman among financial wizards, he climbed to the top of his field before the age of forty. He did so by focusing his entire energies on getting ahead.

Iacocca was born in Allentown, Pennsylvania, a small steel town, in 1924. His parents were Italian immigrants, and his father rose from hot-dog stand owner to well-to-do restaurateur. Lee, the doted-upon only son, went to Lehigh in neighboring Bethlehem, where he initially studied mechanical engineering, but after finding that he was more interested in people than in machines, he switched to psychology and industrial engineering. Iacocca was recruited by Ford out of college, but decided to postpone going to Ford in order to take a graduate degree in industrial engineering at Princeton.

Iacocca was not particularly interested in higher learning. He thought having a master's degree after his name would help his career. As he wrote in his autobiography, "When I graduated from college, my attitude was: 'Don't bother me with philosophy. I want to make ten thousand a year by the time I'm 25, and then I want to be a millionaire.' " At Ford, he took the unusual step for an aspiring executive of going into sales rather than finance or engineering, but Iacocca knew where his own talents resided. In 1949, he became an area sales manager in Wilkes-Barre, Pennsylvania, and a disciple of supersalesman Charlie Beachem, whose motto was: "Make money, screw everything else." That year, the young Iacocca produced his first book, a manual entitled *Hiring and Training Truck Salesmen*.

By 1956, Iacocca had worked his way up to assistant sales manager for the Philadelphia region. Car sales were slumping because the public wasn't buying Ford president Robert McNamara's car-safety pitch. Iacocca came up with the first of his many famous gimmicks—selling the '56 Fords for $56 a month for 56 months. Iacocca's "56 for 56" sales pitch caught on and was used nationally, eventually helping Ford sell as many as 75,000 cars. An appreciative McNamara brought Iacocca to Dearborn, and three years later Iacocca became vice president and general manager of the Ford division.

Iacocca had a particular genius for marketing—for targeting a car's appeal to a particular group of customers. In 1964, he introduced the Mustang. Iacocca put a sports-car body on top of the platform and engine of Ford's bare-bones economy vehicle. The Mustang was functionally no different from the Falcon, but as Iacocca predicted, its styling carved out an entirely new youth market for automobiles—what two decades later would be called the "yuppie market." In its first year, the Mustang made a record $1 billion for Ford.

He was also a compelling salesman who could tout with utter conviction an innovation like the air bag that a week earlier he had derided as worthless. In his autobiography, he boasted how he had learned from Dale Carnegie's course to talk convincingly for two minutes on subjects he knew nothing about. "The point was to train you to think on your feet," Iacocca said, unaware of how such an anecdote reflected on his business practices.

Iacocca was a demanding boss, ready to discharge subordinates who didn't measure up to his standards. But his highly engaging personal style commanded loyalty among his managers, many of whom would later follow him to Chrysler. Unlike other executives at Ford and at GM, Iacocca was willing to brook disagreement and eccentricity. Some of the men he championed, like the prickly but creative Harold Sperlich, who helped design the Mustang, might have been weeded out in more conformist atmospheres, but at Ford, thanks to Iacocca, Sperlich could challenge the conventional wisdom.

Iacocca also had the distinct advantage of coming up through sales. Those managers like McNamara who had learned the business by poring over balance sheets were largely insulated from cars, car dealers, and their customers. Iacocca's focus was always on producing cars that sold. Given the choice between a bigger bottom line or an investment in a new model, Iacocca at Ford tended to support product over immediate profits. This put him at odds with the men he called "bean counters," but also made him the most successful auto executive of his day.

Iacocca's experience in sales—and his distinctly middle-class ethnic background—also made him less socially insulated from junior executives, car dealers, and even union leaders and shop-floor workers. At Ford, Iacocca maintained close relations between the hierarchy and the car dealers; at Chrysler, describing himself as a member of the "working rich," Iacocca would become friendly with the head of the United Auto Workers (UAW). When he visited Chrysler factories, he acted like a presidential candidate, shaking hands, exchanging comments, rather than as the typical remote executive.

Iacocca's success at Ford, however, led to a bitter struggle for power with its autocratic chairman, Henry Ford II. Iacocca himself was partly to blame. When the Mustang came out, he maneuvered his photo onto the cover of both *Time* and *Newsweek*, eclipsing the company's head in the public's mind. Iacocca's passion for publicity constantly rankled Ford. In the 1970s, Iacocca's North American branch didn't do very well, while Ford's international sales under Philip Caldwell (who eventually succeeded Iacocca) enjoyed skyrocketing success. But out of spite and jealousy, Henry Ford also made Iacocca's job difficult, if not impossible. The willful chairman vetoed Iacocca and Sperlich's plan for a minivan and for a front-wheel-drive fuel-efficient compact car—two projects that might have boosted the company during the stagnant 1970s. In 1976, Ford forced Iacocca to fire Sperlich, who immediately hired on at Chrysler. On July 13, 1978, after Iacocca unsuccessfully tried to rally the Ford board of directors, Henry Ford finally fired him.

Three months after having been let go, Iacocca became the president of Chrysler. Iacocca found a company on the rocks. The same day he arrived at his office, Chrysler announced that it had lost $160 million in the third quarter of 1978—its largest loss ever. The company's losses stemmed partly from bad luck and unfortunate circumstances. As the smallest of the Big Three automakers, it was the least able to weather the deep recession of 1974–75, the onset of costly new environmental and safety regulations, and the threat to large cars posed by the rising price of gasoline and by cheap Japanese imports. But the company also contributed to its own troubles by botching union negotiations, allowing its network of dealers to deteriorate, and pouring money into big cars at the very moment the Arab oil boycott was forcing up gas prices.

As interest rates and gasoline prices once again began to climb in 1979, Chrysler looked as though it might have to declare bankruptcy. Iacocca and Chrysler's chairman, John Riccardo, who later that year would resign in favor of Iacocca, went to the Carter administration for help. Iacocca had one ace up his sleeve. At the end of 1977, a year before Iacocca signed on, Sperlich had talked Riccardo into building the four-wheel-drive compact that Ford had spurned. The K-car —the name for the car chassis, or platform, on which different models would be constructed—was expected to come on-line in late 1980, creating a new line of compact cars, and Iacocca and Sperlich were counting on it to rescue the company. The problem was to get through 1979 and 1980 without going under; and for that Iacocca sought a loan guarantee from the government that would allow Chrysler to borrow more money.

Prior to joining Chrysler, Iacocca himself had been a typical free-market Republican and an avid backer of Richard Nixon. In November 1971, he had visited Nixon to plead with him to rescind a federal order making air bags mandatory on cars. "You can really see that safety has killed all of our business," Iacocca, who would later father the disastrous Pinto, complained. And as he saw Chrysler slipping, he joined Riccardo in blaming Democratic-sponsored government regulations for all the company's woes. But as he began lobbying the White House and Capitol Hill for a loan guarantee, Iacocca discovered that Democrats skeptical about the free market's inherent virtue and efficiency were far more interested in helping him than were Republicans.

In hearings before the House and Senate banking committees, Iacocca did not disguise how strange he felt pleading for government intervention. "I have been a free-enterpriser all my life," Iacocca told the Senate committee. "I come here with great reluctance. I am between a rock and a hard place. I cannot save the company without some kind of guarantee from the federal government." Iacocca argued that a loan guarantee was "a far better investment than a $10 billion government loss in reduced revenues and increased unemployment benefits."

Iacocca's opponents included many of his former allies. The Business Roundtable, a lobby organized by large corporations, put out a statement opposing loan guarantees. "Whatever the hardships of failure may be for the particular companies and individuals, the broad social and economic interests of the nation are best served by allowing this system to operate as freely and as fully as possible," it said. Iacocca, indignant, withdrew Chrysler from the Roundtable. Several Wall Street bankers, including Peter Peterson of Lehman Brothers and Walter Wriston of Citicorp, testified against Chrysler. "There is no avoiding the fact that it is an attempt by the government to move economic resources to places where they would not otherwise go," explained Citicorp's Wriston, whose reckless lending to Third World governments would later precipitate the Third World debt crisis. "Such distortions inevitably lead to less, not more, productivity—and therefore to fewer jobs, less return on investment, and fewer bona fide lending opportunities for banks and everyone else."

Ralph Nader—a left-wing trustbuster in the Jeffersonian tradition—also joined the chorus against the bailout, charging that Chrysler's woes were entirely its own doing. "Chrysler's problems flow from a two-decade pattern of mismanagement which includes an overextension of the company worldwide, the production of too many of the wrong kind of vehicles at the wrong time and the production of too few of their better-selling vehicles at the right time," Nader told the Senate banking committee.

Nader, Wriston, and the Roundtable had a point: Chrysler had contributed to its own problems, and bailing out Chrysler would distort the normal workings of the free market. But what they failed to acknowledge was that in 1979, with American manufacturing reeling from foreign competition, the normal workings of the market would not necessarily result in the greatest prosperity for Americans. In just a decade, Japanese imports had gone from 13 to 25 percent of the American market, and the Japanese were beginning to compete in midsize as well as compact cars. Jobs would be lost in the United States, as imports made up the difference from Chrysler's loss; and the United States would be a lesser player in the world market. This might not matter to an investment banker with global clients, but it did matter to American manufacturers and workers and to their political representatives.

Congress was far more persuaded by studies showing that, counting not only Chrysler workers but workers dependent on Chrysler's business, almost 500,000 jobs could be lost in the near term. It passed a bill guaranteeing $1.2 billion in loans to the company and setting up a Loan Guarantee Board composed of the Secretary of the Treasury, the chairman of the Federal Reserve Board, and the Comptroller of the Currency to ensure that Chrysler used its funding wisely. Iacocca had to report Chrysler's earnings and investment decisions to the board monthly, and the board later forced him to pare salaries, renegotiate the union contract, and sell off luxuries like the company jet. The government had bailed out private companies before, but never on this scale and never with this kind of public supervision.

Iacocca resented the government's oversight, but under the glare of public attention, he was at his best; in the three years when Chrysler was trying to survive, he set a model for American corporate management in the late twentieth century—one that he himself would later ignore. Iacocca created a level of cooperation between the company and the UAW that was unprecedented in American manufacturing. Iacocca invited UAW president Douglas Fraser, whose lobbying had been critical to Chrysler's success in Washington, to become a member of the company's board of directors. In exchange for wage concessions, Iacocca reduced his own salary to a dollar and initiated a profit-sharing agreement with the union. The company and the union established a system of worker-management cooperation on the shop floor, and regular monthly meetings were set up between top company executives and UAW leaders. The union had a formal say in both the highest- and the lowest-level decisions at Chrysler.

Most of these measures were common in Europe, and they had been advocated by American progressives, including Herbert Croly, since the 1920s, but they had never been tried on this scale. American managers and union officials had assumed ongoing class conflict rather than cooperation. But Iacocca broke ranks with his fellow managers, edging Chrysler toward a model of labor-management relations based on the assumption that through cooperation, productivity would increase rather than lag and the company would prosper rather than collapse.

Under the watchful eye of the Loan Guarantee Board, Iacocca also made investment decisions that would benefit Chrysler well into the 1980s. He sold off peripheral businesses and plowed the few funds he had available into new models for the 1980s. In 1980, Iacocca spent $500 million to begin building the minivan—the small buslike car for large families on trips—that he and Sperlich had failed to build at Ford. "The hell with what people say," Iacocca told Sperlich. "Somehow we'll find a way to do it. For God's sake, let's not forget we're here to do cars."

Peterson, Wriston, and the Business Roundtable predicted doom for Chrysler, but Iacocca and the company defied its critics. In the first quarter of 1982, in the midst of a deep recession, Chrysler, buoyed by sales of its K-car, registered its first profits of the decade. In 1983, it had a profit of $925 million, the largest in the company's history, and in July of that year, it paid back the $1.2 billion in loans seven years ahead of schedule. Where the company had lost $1.1 billion in 1979, it netted $2.4 billion in 1984. Chrysler's share of the North American car market went from 7.9 percent in 1980 to 9.7 in 1983 and then 10.8 in 1985. By 1985 Chrysler was selling 250,000 minivans a year at a profit of $4,000 per vehicle.

Chrysler's turnaround was aided by investment tax credits that the Reagan administration promoted in 1981 and by Japan's agreeing under administration pressure to limit its auto exports to the United States. But these measures paled in importance next to Sperlich's foresight in pressing for the K-car and Iacocca's success in managing the company until it could reap the rewards of the new models.

The publicity surrounding Chrysler's turnaround made Iacocca a glamorous partygoer and a coveted after-dinner speaker and talk-show guest. His autobiography, projected by Bantam to sell 500,000 copies, sold nearly six million and stayed atop best-seller lists for a year. (Both Iacocca's autobiography and a subsequent book of advice and anecdote, *Talking Straight*, were faithfully assembled by ghostwriters from Iacocca's dictated utterances.) Reagan appointed him to oversee the restoration of the Statue of Liberty, a special honor for a son of Italian immigrants who had come through Ellis Island. An August 1985 poll had him beating George Bush 47 to 41 percent in the 1988 presidential race, and a "Draft Iacocca for President" movement was set up in Washington.

Iacocca used the platform created by his fame to spread a political and economic message drawn from his experience in rescuing Chrysler. What he said directly contradicted not only his own past positions as a free-market Republican but also those of the Reagan administration and its conservative supporters. In his inaugural address, Reagan had proclaimed that for America's flagging economy, government was not the solution, but the problem. Taking the opposite tack, Iacocca argued that government was the only solution to industrial decline. "If we're going to endure these times without crashing into a tree, government has to play a bigger role," Iacocca wrote in *Talking Straight*. "We've got to have more planning (oh, that dirty word) and controls to right our course."

Iacocca had believed that the free market, if left to itself, would allocate resources in a way that would achieve the greatest national prosperity, but now he had his doubts. "The plain truth is that the marketplace isn't always efficient," he wrote in his autobiography. Iacocca was highly critical of the merger wave of the 1980s and of the proclivity of investors to place their faith in short-term profits. Once an apostle of profits, he now talked in Veblenesque fashion of the importance of quality. Iacocca contrasted his own ethic with that of the money manager. "I'm looking to build that better mousetrap and to create more jobs. He can't spend a second thinking about those things because dollar signs are all that interest him."

During the 1982 recession, Democrats like Richard Gephardt, the late Gillis Long, and Tim Wirth began to advocate what they called "industrial policy," and Iacocca became one of its principal proponents. He wanted government to establish a "Critical Industries Commission" in which representatives from business, government, and labor could work out a "Marshall Plan" for saving American industry through subsidies and trade protection. Iacocca's own bias was reflected in his defining of the objectives of the commission—aiding "sunset" industries like steel and auto rather than "sunrise" high-technology industries. Iacocca also backed massive spending for America's decaying infrastructure of roads, sewers, and bridges, to be financed through an oil-import fee.*

Iacocca argued persuasively that losing high-paying industrial jobs would depress America's standard of living by transferring higher-value-added production overseas. "Take away America's $10-to-$15-an-hour industrial jobs and you under-

---

* In *Public Investment and Private Sector Growth*, published by the Economic Policy Institute in 1990, economist David Alan Aschauer attempted to show that the slowdown in spending on infrastructure was a major cause of the poor industrial performance in the 1970s and 1980s. In the 1980s under Reagan, public investment in bridges, roads, sewers, electric power, and mass transit was half the percentage of GNP that it was in the 1970s under Carter and Nixon and one-fourth the rate of the 1950s and 1960s.

cut the whole economy. Oops—there goes the middle class!"
And Chrysler, as Iacocca would often point out, was the nation's largest private employer of blacks and represented the
backbone of what had been a viable black working class.

At the same time, Iacocca rejected the Reagan administration's attempt to revive the Cold War. In 1982, in the midst of
the Reagan military buildup—prompted by unfounded fears of
Soviet superiority—Iacocca called for the adminstration to cut
5 percent out of the military budget for three years running
and to invest in bridges, sewers, transportation, and education.
"Without a strong, vital industrial infrastructure, we're a
nation bristling with missiles that surround a land of empty
factories, unemployed workers, and decaying cities," Iacocca
wrote in *Newsweek*. Iacocca dismissed Reagan's anti-Communist program as a paranoid fantasy, describing the President as
"a major league ideologue [who] thinks in terms of freedom
fighters in Nicaragua and evil empires and Communists lurking
behind trees."

Iacocca mocked the proposal of the Reagan-appointed Kissinger Commission to spend $8 billion on the "economic de-
velopment of Central America." "Now I always thought that
Central America meant places like Michigan, Ohio and Indiana
(shows you how simpleminded I am!). What about *our* Central
America?"

Iacocca assumed that the Cold War was all but over and that
the American Century was drawing to a close, but he was not
content to allow the United States to lose its economic supremacy. For the goal of world military power, Iacocca substituted world economic power, and for the Soviet military
threat, Iacocca substituted the threat of Japan's economic
power. He described America's "current conflict" with Japan
as "a trade war" in which the United States was losing. "We're
up against a formidable competitor, and all things being equal,
we'd be lucky to stay even with them," Iacocca wrote. "But
all things are not equal. The field where this game is being
played is not level. Instead, it's strongly tilted in favor of Japan.

As a result, we're playing with one hand tied behind our back. No wonder we're losing the war!"

Iacocca had a point. For two decades, Japan had used predatory trade tactics, keeping out foreign goods, while subsidizing its own exports, to defeat American manufacturers. In the aftermath of World War II, the United States, concerned about Japan's becoming a viable counterweight to Soviet power in the Far East, overlooked and even sometimes encouraged Japanese protectionism, but Japan was still following these practices in the 1980s, while proclaiming its adherence to free trade. Iacocca wanted the United States to fight back by demanding that Japan reduce its growing trade surplus with the United States. He was for "fair trade," not free trade, he wrote. "Fair trade involves some selective—and temporary—restraints against the one country in the world that is running such a lopsided negative trade balance with us."

In selling automobiles in the United States, Japan enjoyed special advantages that went beyond its production of quality cars. Japanese firms thoroughly dominated their home market—in 1991, for instance, U.S. firms accounted for one percent of auto sales in Japan, while Japanese firms accounted for 31 percent of sales in the United States. This meant that Japanese firms could reap large profits at home while tolerating lower profit margins or even losses abroad in order to win a larger share of the market. Japanese firms also belonged to massive *keiretsus,* or conglomerates, that supplied them with cheap capital and parts and allowed them to juggle their costs in order to best their competitors.

In addition, those Japanese firms that set up plants in America enjoyed certain intangible benefits over the older American firms. Most of them set up shop in rural, white, non-union areas and recruited a young work force. They not only paid their workers less, but didn't have to pay pensions to retirees. By 1990 the Big Three were paying one retiree pension for every worker currently employed. If the United States continued to allow the Japanese to compete without restrictions in the American market, it was likely that within a decade not only Chrysler but the entire American automotive industry would be decimated, and as many as a million workers would lose their jobs.

This was a warning of industrial doom that by the late eighties began to be heeded by politicians from both parties, but particularly by Democrats from industrial states. In the 1988 election, Congressman Richard Gephardt based his campaign for President on the demand for fair trade, but after winning the Iowa primary, he ran out of money in the South.

But there were serious problems with Iacocca's message. In criticizing Japan's trading practices, Iacocca began to endow the Japanese with the same kind of all-encompassing evil powers that the anti-Communists of the 1950s had attributed to the Soviets. Where he had earlier blamed money managers, Reaganites, and even some fellow industrialists for America's afflictions, Iacocca now used the Japanese as an excuse for every ill that befell Chrysler or the national economy. When Iacocca had to shut down a Chrysler factory in Kenosha in 1988, he blamed the shutdown on Japanese unfair trade practices. And when Chrysler began to experience losses again in 1989, Iacocca put the entire blame on Japanese factories in America. "We didn't anticipate that the transplants would cut us off at the knees," he explained.

Unfortunately, Chrysler's own problems were partly Iacocca's doing. While the Chrysler chairman was advising the Reagan and Bush administrations on how to restore the national economy, and while he was telling would-be managers how to achieve success, Iacocca was neglecting his own company. Flushed with his own fame and glory, Chrysler's chairman got caught up in the transient and destructive enthusiasms of other businessmen-celebrities. He fell prey to the Reagan-era ethos of possessive individualism, in which a CEO's prowess was measured by his power brokering. He forgot his own injunctions against money managers and merger makers. He became more interested in making deals than in making cars.

If Iacocca had followed his own advice, he would have used the record profits the company earned from 1984 to 1988 to finance new mid-size and full-size models for the late 1980s, when the K-cars would be obsolete. Instead, Iacocca made virtually every mistake he had warned against. He failed to put money into new cars and frittered away profits and vigor on acquiring companies that were peripheral to Chrysler's mission.

These acquisitions betrayed a certain vanity as well as calculation. In 1980 Iacocca had been particularly upset when the government loan board forced him to sell off the company's Gulfstream corporate jet; now he could say he owned the whole Gulfstream company. Iacocca blithely summed up his "strategy" in *Talking Straight*. While working on the Statue of Liberty, he wrote, "I killed some time by buying American Motors, Lamborghini, and a piece of Maserati. I even bought an airplane company."

The deals that didn't go through were even more revealing. In 1985, Iacocca and Allied Signal CEO Ed Hennessy tried to buy Hughes Aircraft, which GM eventually purchased for $6.2 billion. Undeterred, Iacocca and Hennessy tried to involve investment banker Felix Rohatyn in a plan to buy GM. "The plan for Chrysler and Allied Signal to buy GM was almost delusional," says Dan Luria, principal scientist at the Industrial Technology Institute, a Michigan think tank. "Iacocca got completely caught up in the CEO as deal maker."

The deals took resources and attention away from Chrysler's main avenue to survival and success: building a new line of mid-size and full-size cars to compete in the most lucrative segment of the auto market. At the beginning of 1988, the first signs of Iacocca's inattention to his product emerged: figures showed that Chrysler's car sales for 1987 had dropped a whopping 22.8 percent. And they would continue to decline over the next three years. In 1990, Chrysler lost $2 billion in auto sales.

As Chrysler began to slip in the late 1980s, a chastened Iacocca tried to stage a repeat of the company's earlier comeback. In November 1988, he launched an ambitious $15 billion plan to bring out a slew of new models in the early 1990s. To raise the money to keep going, Iacocca began selling off the companies he had bought during the mid-1980s, closing plants, and cutting Chrysler's white-collar work force. He also began a new advertising campaign that appealed directly to commercial patriotism. The combination of print and broadcast spots were patterned on the "Made in America" campaign that helped his company survive during the 1980s. Tagged "Advantage: Chrysler," they rested on a comparison between Japanese and American cars.

The campaign assumed that if customers would only look, they would discover that Chrysler cars were now better than Japanese cars. But the problem was that few Americans outside of Chrysler's management were ready to believe that. Most major surveys, including those by *Consumer Reports* and the California-based J. D. Power & Associates, rated Chryslers behind the leading Japanese autos. In early 1991, *Consumer Reports* put the final nail in Chrysler's advertising campaign, warning that the new transmissions that Chrysler was putting in its cars and new minivan were faulty.

Iacocca's campaign was also tainted by a certain hypocrisy. Chrysler still owned about 13 percent of Mitsubishi, and the two companies operated a joint plant in Normal, Illinois. Since 1971, Chrysler dealers had been marketing the Mitsubishi-made Colt cars and were selling Chryslers with Mitsubishi-made six-cylinder engines, including the Normal-built Eagle Talon, the only 1990 model to win raves from car magazines.

As he tried to win customers for Chrysler, buying time before new investments could bear fruit, Iacocca continued to advocate industrial policy, but he now focused entirely on protecting American car makers from the threat posed by competition from Japanese companies. In his books, Iacocca had insisted he was not a "protectionist," but in a February 1991 *New York Times* Op-Ed piece, he proudly embraced the label:

Those who say that protectionists have their heads in the sand have it exactly backward. The real ostriches are those who believe that we can survive economically by simply ignoring those who target our market while protecting their own.

The same month, Iacocca led a delegation of Big Three automakers to the White House to demand that President Bush put a cap not only on Japan's imports but on its market share in the United States. Such a proposal went beyond anything that Iacocca had advocated before and would have been tantamount to guaranteeing American companies a fixed share of the American market, but it accorded with the strategy that the European Economic Community used to protect its car makers from destruction. What was missing was any instrument to assure the public, which would subsidize such a plan, that American car makers would not squander their profits in worthless acquisitions. Yet, in the circumstances, it would not have mattered what kind of proposal the automakers made. At that point, the Bush administration would have rejected any proposal for government assistance.

When he was not blaming the Japanese, Iacocca was now blaming American workers rather than managers. In an interview in the April 1991 *Fortune*, Iacocca attributed the success of Japanese car makers in America to their building plants in rural rather than Northern urban areas where they didn't have to hire drug addicts. "Should I go to Iowa to build a plant and screen the workers to make sure they're young and they haven't been on drugs? Do that kind of screening in Detroit and you won't have anybody working for you," Iacocca explained. Such a statement was not only cruel but foolish, alienating Chrysler's workers in Detroit, many of whom had waited patiently for the company to reopen the Jefferson Avenue plant it had closed for retooling in 1990.

Iacocca was descending into the unsavory depths. Yet he remained one of the few American corporate executives who had a broader view of American industry's perils. If he demonized the Japanese and blamed his own workers, and if he ignored his own incompetence and that of other managers, he nevertheless pointed to a very real danger: the difficulties of American manufacturing firms in auto, steel, and other key industries in competing with the firms that enjoyed the close cooperation and support of their government and of networks of banks and suppliers. Other executives were too preoccupied with their own businesses to wage a national political struggle, or they were more afraid that by encouraging any government intervention, they would spell their own doom. The Reagan and Bush administrations were simply oblivious to the problem. As Iacocca plumbed the depths, they continued to skim the surface of American economic life, suggesting that anyone who looked deeper was somehow unpatriotic.

# 10

# George Bush and the
# Next American Century

If anyone tells you America's best days are behind her, they are
looking the wrong way.

—GEORGE BUSH, January 16, 1991

On December 7, 1988, one month after George Bush was
elected President of the United States, Soviet President Mikhail
Gorbachev came to New York to address the General Assembly
of the United Nations. His speech clearly signaled the end of
the Cold War. He announced large unilateral reductions in
Russian armed forces and declared his intention to withdraw
many of his troops from Warsaw Pact countries. In addition,
the Soviet President called for a new concept of international
relations to replace the Cold War division between East and
West. The "scientific and technological revolution," Gorbachev
said, transformed national problems into "global problems"
and made impossible the "preservation of any kind of closed
societies. Today, further world progress is only possible through
a search for universal human consensus as we move forward
to a new world order."

As Bush took office in the wake of Gorbachev's speech, he
had an opportunity to transform American foreign and domestic policy that for four decades had been held hostage to
the Cold War. Bush could continue what Nixon and Kissinger

had begun haltingly to do—reforming the way that America conducts itself in the world. But more important, he had a chance to succeed where they had failed, by forging a new conception of America's purpose in the world that flowed from Americans' understanding of their domestic well-being.

During his first term, Bush did achieve notable successes in foreign policy—securing peace in Nicaragua and Angola and ousting Iraqi dictator Saddam Hussein from Kuwait. But behind these successes lurked failure. While capable of responding to gross acts of international piracy, Bush had difficulty coming to terms with the revolution in the Soviet Union, the collapse of the Cold War and of the Western alliance, and the shift of international priorities from geopolitics to geoeconomics that Nixon had foreseen in 1971.

With the threat of Communism gone, Bush was also utterly unable to articulate a new sense of America's purpose. In 1988, emulating Reagan, he ran on the hollow promise of retaining the American Century. As the 1992 election neared, he began calling for a "next American Century," reducing Luce's call to arms to a campaign slogan. Bush not merely failed to create a credible link between Americans' pursuit of domestic happiness and their global responsibilities; he seemed indifferent to the average American's well-being. He allowed the nation's economy to decline and the social divisions between rich and poor, white and black to widen. After Bush's first term, Americans were poorer, meaner, and even less sure than before of what their role in the world was.

Bush came to office with a more impressive résumé than any chief executive since Nixon. After serving as a Houston congressman from 1966 to 1970, he had been UN Ambassador, chairman of the Republican National Committee during Watergate, the chief of the American Liaison Office in Beijing (before full diplomatic recognition was granted), and the director of the Central Intelligence Agency—all during the heyday of Nixon and Kissinger's foreign policy. After running unsuccessfully for President in 1980, he served for eight years as Reagan's Vice President, participating in major presidential decisions. Yet, in spite of these qualifications, Bush lacked certain qualities that were important to a President at the end of the American Century.

If Reagan eloquently conveyed an anachronistic concept of America, Bush had difficulty conveying *any* concept whatsoever. It was not that Bush lacked intelligence or articulateness; rather, he spent too much time enmeshed in the details of life—papers to sign, decisions to make—without ever pausing to reflect on what they meant. He was unreflective to a fault. The Edward Everett Hale epigraph that he chose for his ghost-written autobiography was unintentionally revealing:

Look up and not down; *look out and not in*; look forward and not back; and lend a hand [my emphasis].

Bush had convictions, but they were either strongly personal—his gee-whiz optimism, for instance—or so clichéd that they seemed insincere. Even though he had served under Nixon and Kissinger and had been influenced by their methods, he had never tried to reconceptualize America's role in the world. Instead, he had absorbed their lessons unconsciously—the way a boy learns to ride a bicycle. Thus, when he came into office, he could not adapt their realism to the 1990s.

Bush also lacked the background to refashion America's domestic priorities. Like other members of the post-World War II policy elite, Bush thought of foreign policy as the higher calling and domestic policy as an extension of electoral politics. As President, he became engaged in domestic concerns only to the extent that they appeared to threaten his political majority. And when he become engaged, he had only the most superficial grasp of the causes of American economic decline. A former independent oilman and the son of a Wall Street investment banker, he was thoroughly committed to the laissez-faire conservatism of Sumner, Coolidge, and Reagan. As an official in the Nixon administration, he was forced to alter his Cold War assumptions; but he had never had to reassess his sentimental attachment to the magic of the free market. Projecting his own success onto America, he imagined that America's economic ills could be cured simply by hard work and the invisible hand.

In dealing with domestic concerns, Bush also did not possess any sense of urgency. As someone who had tried to span the different worlds of upper-class Connecticut and nouveau-riche Texas, Bush had unusual difficulty identifying with average Americans. As President, he seemed as distant from a laid-off Chrysler worker in St. Louis as from a Kurd on the Turkish–Iraqi border. Although he became completely familiar to Americans, they still wondered what he really cared about and stood for.

Bush, born in 1924, was raised in Greenwich, Connecticut, a bedroom community for wealthy Wall Streeters like his father. Prescott Bush was the managing partner of Brown Brothers, Harriman, one of the foremost investment banks of its day, and Bush's mother, Dorothy, was a prominent sportswoman. George Bush's father had grown up during Theodore Roosevelt's presidency, and like many upper-class men of his day, had been influenced by the Rough Rider's example. Like Roosevelt, he sought to transcend the image of the effete white-gloved patrician and to achieve success independently of his family. Immediately after graduating from Yale in 1917, Prescott Bush enlisted in the Army and served briefly in France. After returning home, he went to work for a hardware company in St. Louis, rather than joining his father's successful manufacturing firm in Ohio. He was hired in 1930 by Brown

Brothers, Harriman as an expert in reviving failing companies and rose quickly to the top of the firm.

Like Roosevelt, Prescott Bush also aspired to public service, and in 1950, when he was fifty-five, he quit investment banking to run for the Senate. He narrowly lost, but then won in 1952. He was a typical Yankee Republican, conservative on business matters, but respectful of the Constitution and endowed with a spirit of *noblesse oblige* on social issues. His voting record was similar to that of Republicans Kenneth Keating of New York and George Aiken of Vermont. In 1954, he voted for McCarthy's censure, and in 1961—before retiring the next year because of ill health—he sponsored civil rights bills that would have forbidden discrimination in employment and guaranteed voting rights.

The Bushes sent George to Phillips Andover, an exclusive boarding school in Massachusetts that prepared its students for Yale and Harvard and more broadly for leadership positions in society. Like his father, George Bush was determined to transcend the image of his class. After graduating in 1942, Bush immediately joined the Navy to become a flier. Shot down over the Pacific, he earned a Distinguished Flying Cross. He entered Yale in 1945, where he followed his father's precedent—captaining the baseball team and being "tapped" for Skull and Bones, Yale's most prestigious secret society. In addition, Bush made Phi Beta Kappa and, upon graduating, was prime material for a Rhodes scholarship if he didn't want to join his uncle Herbert Walker's investment-banking business. (Brown Brothers, Harriman frowned on fathers hiring sons.) Instead, Bush insisted on traveling his own way.

Bush sought the challenge of succeeding in unfamiliar terrain. He drove the Studebaker his parents had given him for graduation out to Texas, where he went into the oil business. Bush did not have to make his way from the ground up as Nixon and Reagan had. His first job—as a drill-bit salesman—was for a firm owned by one of his father's friends, and when he started his own business, it was with capital from his uncle. He never endured poverty or the anxiety of being without a job. But he nevertheless experienced the sensation of making it on his own.

Like his father, George Bush was not primarily interested in getting rich. Instead, he was driven by a fierce competitive instinct that abated after he achieved success. In 1953, Bush and Hugh and Bill Liedtke became partners in an oil company they called Zapata Petroleum—Bush contributing capital through his uncle's connections. By the late 1950s, the partners had hit enough oil wells to become millionaires. But Bush then lost interest. Hugh Liedtke went on to become the billionaire owner of Pennzoil, while Bush became involved in Republican politics in Houston, selling his part of the company in 1965 to devote himself full-time to winning office.

Bush transferred the same desire to win and succeed to politics. Like his father, he was a Republican, but Texas's Republican politics were not like Connecticut's. Republicans in Texas bore no trace of the party of Lincoln; they had emerged in the 1950s as the conservative alternative to the Democratic Party, particularly on civil rights. In Houston, where Bush joined the party, the local organization was divided between conservatives and ultra-conservative members of the John Birch Society, who believed that Communists were in control of the American government. As he would do time and again, Bush made his mark by conciliating the two wings of the party, winning election in 1962 as county chairman against a Birch Society member, but then inviting Birch members to fill party offices.

Neither at the beginning nor at the end of Bush's political career did he display abiding convictions on domestic issues. He entered politics to win and to serve rather than to accomplish certain purposes or to represent a distinct constituency or cause. His fundamental trait was his optimism, which had been nurtured as a child and reinforced by his own successes in the military, college, and business.

When circumstances required, Bush adjusted his convictions. This was particularly true on civil rights. In 1964, running for the U.S. Senate against liberal incumbent Ralph Yarborough, Bush vigorously opposed the 1964 Civil Rights Act and spoke favorably of George Wallace's segregationist presidential candidacy. In 1966, running for Congress, he opposed an open housing bill, but two years later he joined nine House moderate Republicans in voting for it. In 1970, he backed the Nixon administration's Philadelphia plan for establishing racial quotas on federal contracting jobs, but two decades later was leading the fight against a Democratic civil rights bill because it encouraged—far more subtly, if at all, than Nixon's plan—racial quotas.

Bush underwent a similar political conversion on abortion. As a Houston congressman, he sponsored bills to give federal money for family planning. He was chairman of a task force on family planning that in the summer of 1970 issued a report implicitly favoring the liberalization of abortion laws. In the 1980 presidential primaries, he opposed a Constitutional amendment banning abortion. But when he became Reagan's presidential running mate that July, he dutifully agreed to change his position and thereafter became an adamant foe of abortion.

If Bush had underlying convictions, they were probably closer to those of his father than to those of the conservative Republicans he publicly identified with during the early 1960s and again in the 1980s. In Congress and as a Nixon official, his closest friends and advisers were Republican moderates like New York Representative (and later Senator) Charles Goodell, Pennsylvania Senator Hugh Scott, Supreme Court Justice Potter Stewart, and Wisconsin House member Bill Steiger. But Bush did not have the same attitude of *noblesse oblige* that his father and other upper-class Republicans had. He never became known as a champion of the less fortunate. Instead, he sometimes displayed the callous individualism characteristic of the Sunbelt entrepreneur.

In 1970, Nixon convinced Bush to give up his House seat to run again against Yarborough. With the country moving right, Bush seemed a shoo-in, but Yarborough was upset in the primary by conservative Democrat Lloyd Bentsen. "If Bentsen is going to try to go to my right, he's gonna step off the edge of the Earth," Bush declared. But Bentsen succeeded in muting Bush's tendentious appeal to the far right, while capturing the traditional Democratic vote. Nixon had promised Bush an administration post, and that December, at Bush's request, he appointed him the new UN Ambassador.

Bush was at the UN when Nixon reversed American policy toward China. Initially skeptical, Bush became an enthusiastic convert to the Nixon–Kissinger approach when the Chinese UN representatives turned out to be more hostile to the Soviets than to the Americans. Like Nixon and Kissinger, Bush began to conceive of the Cold War in terms of a balance of power rather than a conflict of ideologies. In 1974, Bush even turned down Gerald Ford's offer of plum ambassadorships to either Great Britain or France to take over the American liaison office in Beijing—a post that took him far from Washington, but placed him at the center of Kissinger's new geopolitics.

During the early 1970s, Bush also became an active member of the foreign policy establishment. In 1971, he joined the Council on Foreign Relations and in 1975 he was one of the founding members of David Rockefeller's Trilateral Commission. He came to see himself as the anointed successor to the Cold War elite of Acheson, Harriman, Nitze, and the Bundys. At one Council on Foreign Relations meeting in 1975, a peeved Bush, growing impatient at a discussion of Vietnam led by

McGeorge and William Bundy, exclaimed on behalf of a new generation, "You Bundys have had your chance."*

In 1978, Bush decided to claim the succession by running for President. But his campaign was not based on his convictions on foreign or domestic policy. Through his experience in Texas and in the Nixon administration, Bush also acquired a narrow—sometimes cynical, sometimes naïve—view of politics. Like Nixon, he came to see winning as paramount and was willing to alter his views accordingly. But he didn't revel in political calculation the way that Nixon did. For Bush, the ideal election was one devoid of issues, like a high school contest for student council president.

In his race for the Republican nomination, Bush tried to avoid any political identification. When one reporter asked him before the January Iowa caucus, "How would you define yourself ideologically? Moderate or conservative?" Bush replied, "I don't want to be perceived as either." He ran on his competence ("George Bush, a President you won't have to train"), the comparison of his physical vigor with Reagan's (he jogged every morning for the benefit of the press), and his optimism (captured in the vacuous slogan, "Up for the Eighties"). After winning the Iowa caucus, he stressed that he would win because of his "Big Mo," a phrase he borrowed from football commentator Don Meredith. It was as if politics were simply a game.

But then Bush was destroyed in New Hampshire by Reagan's ideological onslaught on taxes and abortion and by brigades of conservative activists armed with pamphlets warning that Bush was an Eastern establishment liberal. From then on, he identified himself strictly as a conservative. By the end of the campaign, when Senator Orrin Hatch was given a pile of unidentified campaign speeches to read, he chose Bush's as the most conservative of the lot. Bush hadn't become a conser-

* In 1979, justifiably fearing attack from the right in the presidential primary, Bush dropped his membership in the Council and the Trilateral Commission. But Bush maintained the connection with the foreign policy elite. In 1981, he helped arrange a Trilateral Commission meeting in Washington and was its featured speaker.

vative true believer, but he now believed that he had to appear to be one.

In the 1988 presidential election, Bush cynically modeled his campaign on Reagan's 1980 effort. Just as Reagan had gone after Carter for imputing a "malaise" to Americans, Bush accused his congenitally optimistic opponent, Michael Dukakis, of the sin of pessimism. For Bush, an optimistic belief in the American Century was a prerequisite of patriotism. Charging his opponent with believing that "the American Century has . . . drawn to a close," Bush declared, "We're on the optimistic side; we're on the American side." Bush also exploited racial divisions by highlighting a Dukakis program that furloughed a black rapist. And in the face of crippling deficits, he threw fiscal caution to the winds by pledging not to raise taxes—a promise that he was forced to break two years later. While Bush won in a landslide, it was an inauspicious beginning to his presidency.

During his first term, Bush, imagining himself to be following in Nixon's footsteps, sought to make his mark in foreign policy. Where Reagan had emphasized domestic economic policy at the expense of foreign policy during his first years, Bush emphasized foreign policy almost to the exclusion of domestic policy. He took every opportunity to go abroad. He met in Washington with the leaders of tiny countries, while refusing to confer with senators or his own Cabinet members about domestic issues. In September 1991, for instance, when the United States was still suffering from an economic downturn, Bush sat down with leaders of twenty-one countries, including Liechtenstein and Micronesia, but couldn't meet with sixteen Republican House members who wanted to discuss family leave for American workers. According to a *Wall Street Journal* report, he held only three meetings that month with individual

Cabinet secretaries who had domestic responsibilities, and two of these meetings were aboard *Air Force One* en route to political events.

Bush reveled in the daily challenge of statesmanship. He even admitted during his first year that he yearned for a war in which he could test himself, lamenting to ABC reporter Diane Sawyer that he hadn't yet "been tested by fire." But Bush was not equally interested in or adept at reconceptualizing America's foreign policy goals. He drew heavily on what he had learned from Nixon and Kissinger. He solicited their advice, and he saw his foreign policy as a continuation of what they had accomplished. Most important, he chose as his National Security Adviser Brent Scowcroft, who had served under Kissinger in the Nixon and Ford administrations and had afterward joined Kissinger's consulting firm, Kissinger Associates, as its vice chairman. Scowcroft became the most influential foreign policy maker in the administration, more than Bush's friend James Baker, whom the President named to be Secretary of State.

Scowcroft, a retired air force general, was one of a first generation of post-World War II defense intellectuals. He received a Ph.D. in international relations and had become a convert to foreign policy realism before he joined the Nixon administration in 1971, but he had nevertheless fallen under Kissinger's spell. In the 1980s, he co-authored articles with Kissinger and defended him against his critics. In the Bush administration, he played the same role intellectually that Kissinger had played in the Ford administration.

But Bush and Scowcroft suffered the curse of imitators. While Nixon and Kissinger's realism had provided a means of comprehending the world of the 1970s, this same realism—translated by Bush and Scowcroft—did not provide a useful guide to the new world of the 1990s.

Nixon and Kissinger's realism had been particularly suited to breaking through the fog of emotion in which Cold War evangelism had shrouded U.S.-Soviet and U.S.-China relations. In their diplomacy, Nixon and Kissinger ignored nations' internal practices and their ideologies. They assumed that the conflicts among nations were rooted in tradition and geography rather than in transient ideologies or forms of government. They saw the possibility of conducting fruitful negotiations with Communist states and of allying with one against another—possibilities that had eluded their fellow conservatives. But their realism also had potential weaknesses.

In ignoring nations' internal policies, they assumed that changes in a nation's government and ideology did not necessarily affect its foreign relations. From the standpoint of American national interest, they argued, it didn't necessarily matter whether another country were ruled by an elected parliament, a king, or a dictator. As a result, realists like Kissinger and Nixon often found themselves offending Americans who believed that the nation's foreign policy should encourage democracy and condemn dictatorship. But more important, because they ignored nations' internal policies, realists like Kissinger and Nixon had difficulty understanding revolutionary periods when a nation's domestic upheavals did alter its foreign policy.* Thus, Nixon and Kissinger's realism worked well in charting America's relations with Brezhnev's Soviet Union, but broke down when applied to Gorbachev's Soviet Union and to the post-Cold War Western alliance.

As soon as Gorbachev came into power, Nixon and Kissinger found themselves at a loss. While Reagan, to his credit, quickly sensed that the Soviet leader meant to end the Cold War, both Nixon and Kissinger expressed deep skepticism about his intentions. Kissinger described Gorbachev's climactic December 1988 UN address as "public relations pressure," and Nixon in

* Kissinger was perfectly aware of the problem. In *A World Restored*, Kissinger distinguished between the diplomacy appropriate to a "revolutionary" and to a "legitimate" order, but once in office, he failed to act on the distinction.

his book *In the Arena* warned that "Gorbachev's principal reform has been to concentrate more power in his own hands than any Soviet leader since Stalin." Both men were highly critical of the INF treaty and of the START treaty that Reagan and Shultz had virtually completed when they left office. They saw Gorbachev as a more refined version of Brezhnev and, while not urging confrontation, called for the same incremental negotiations that they had undertaken in the early 1970s. They didn't seek the Cold War's end—it eluded their imaginations—but rather a "New Yalta" that would place a demilitarized, independent Eastern Europe between NATO and the Soviet Union.

In his first year, Bush and Scowcroft adopted Nixon and Kissinger's strategy in U.S. relations with both the Soviet Union and China.* Bush and administration officials tried to curb what they saw as the "euphoria" surrounding Gorbachev and the START talks. Scowcroft announced in his first television interview that "the Cold War is not over" and accused Gorbachev of trying to drive a wedge between the United States and Europe. Even though Bush knew otherwise, he warned that the Soviets under Gorbachev were continuing to augment their strategic arsenal. On Scowcroft's advice, Bush suspended the START negotiations in order to undertake a "strategic review." The decision was another echo of the Nixon years. "It was a reaction to the gushy attitude of the Reagan administration at the very end," explained NSC official Peter Rodman, who had also worked under Kissinger in the Nixon and Ford administrations. "We wanted to dampen the euphoria about Gorbachev. Nixon had done the same thing when he came into office when he wanted to slow down the arms control bandwagon and not be rushed into it by political expectations."

---

* Baker's impulse was to be far more positive toward the Soviet Union and the START treaty. Baker was a lawyer and a power broker who craved results. But he also wanted to make his mark on foreign policy and was reluctant to be seen as simply completing what his predecessor George Shultz had begun. Therefore, Baker went along with Bush and Scowcroft's strategy, while registering his dissent from the skeptical and even antagonistic statements about Gorbachev and the Soviet Union coming out of the National Security Council.

As a result of their review, Bush and Scowcroft decided to give priority to negotiations to reduce conventional arms in Europe. They argued that if the United States and the Soviets signed a strategic arms treaty before reducing conventional forces, the United States would be placed at a disadvantage because of its inferior conventional forces. This was a specious argument—under the terms of START, the United States would enjoy a strategic advantage, with 9,000 long-range nuclear weapons still pointed at the Soviet Union—but Bush and Scowcroft were playing the same game of perceptions that the United States and the Soviet Union had played since Nitze's NSC-68. They were not willing to recognize what Reagan had seen clearly: that arms negotiations were now a means not to stabilize but to end the Cold War. Theirs was a realism that could not comprehend changing reality.

The START treaty was eventually signed—three years after the administration took office. By then, billions had been wasted on new weapons systems, and the United States had lost the chance to press ahead with even deeper reductions. When the Soviet Union dissolved, the Senate had still not ratified the treaty, and the United States had no agreement that would apply to the strategic weapons that were in republics outside of Russia.

In the summer of 1989, Bush also applied Kissinger and Nixon's strategy to U.S. relations with China. After the Chinese leaders massacred protesters at Tiananmen Square that June, Bush responded to popular outrage, publicly condemning their actions and promising a cutoff of military sales and high-level diplomatic contacts. But at the same time he secretly took Nixon and Kissinger's advice to maintain contacts in order to retain China's allegiance against the Soviet Union.* Scowcroft

* In a private eighteen-page letter to Bush after the Tiananmen massacre, Nixon argued that the United States should maintain a "cooperative relationship" with China's leaders to prevent the Soviet Union from forming an alliance with China against the United States. "Gorbachev is not a closet democrat, a philanthropist, or a fool," Nixon wrote. "His handshake will be warm, but based on his past record we can assume he will have a card or two up his sleeve."

and Deputy Secretary of State Lawrence Eagleburger (another Kissinger Associates alumnus) were sent twice to China in the six months after Tiananmen Square to assure the Chinese leaders of American support.

Bush went considerably beyond those actions that would have been required to maintain diplomacy and trade with another country. Instead, he acted as if the United States still needed China's support against the Soviet threat. The United States continued arms sales to China, and Bush even vetoed a bill preventing the deportation of Chinese students in the United States who had demonstrated against the regime and who faced imprisonment upon their return home.

Bush and his top advisers were acting as if they still had to maintain the triangular relationship. As Scowcroft explained it, the policy was based on an exact analogy between 1971 and 1989. In 1971, the United States had opened relations with China in spite of the Cultural Revolution; in 1989, the Bush administration was maintaining cordial relations in spite of Tiananmen Square. "It was the same logic," he said.

At the end of Bush's first year, he did change his view of Gorbachev. After Gorbachev acquiesced in the Berlin Wall's fall, Bush and Scowcroft finally realized that the Soviet leader was not trying to sow discord in the Western alliance but was genuinely committed to ending the Cold War. But now they swung from one extreme to another—from skepticism to faith, from calculated indifference to a fond embrace. In the name of a new realism, they identified Gorbachev as the instrument of a new world order in which the United States and the Soviet Union would cooperate to end age-old conflicts and vendettas. They leaped from détente to the post-Cold War world that Nixon had dimly anticipated in his Kansas City speech. But

Bush's view of Gorbachev was no more realistic now than it had been before.

By the time Bush embraced Gorbachev, the Soviet leader had become embattled within his own country, and the Soviet Union itself was beginning to fall apart. Gorbachev was challenged not only by old-line Stalinist generals but also by independence movements in the Soviet republics and by democratic reformers like Boris Yeltsin. Now Bush and Scowcroft, identifying Gorbachev with stability, spurned the independence movements and Yeltsin. They based American policy entirely on Gorbachev's continued rule of a centralized Soviet Union. The absurdity of this policy became apparent in August 1991. Two weeks before the Soviet coup, Bush, visiting the Ukraine, endorsed Gorbachev in a speech and warned the Ukrainians that the United States would not support a "suicidal nationalism." Four months later, the Ukraine was an independent nation, Gorbachev was gone, and American policy was in a shambles.

The administration's failure to anticipate the breakup of the Soviet Union—like its failure to take advantage of the completed START negotiations in 1989—probably did no lasting damage to America's position in the world. It was a case of missed opportunities rather than of fatal errors. But it was symptomatic of the administration's deeper problem in foreign policy. Incapable of comprehending the present, the administration was unable to shape the post-Cold War future. Not just in the Soviet Union, but in almost every area of diplomacy, Bush fought yesterday's battles. He clung, for instance, to NATO with the same tenacity with which he had held on to Gorbachev, chiding French and Germans, who established their own defense force, for doing what the United States had long recommended. He refused to develop a new conception of the Western alliance that would allow the United States to stem the chaos engulfing Eastern Europe and the republics of the former Soviet Union. Prodded by Scowcroft, he endorsed fantastically expensive weapons systems—among them, the $25 billion Midgetman mobile missile—that no longer had any relevance to deterrence or world order. Bush's realism continually lagged behind reality.

The administration's greatest success came in the Persian Gulf. It not only repelled the Iraqi invasion, setting an important global precedent; it also created the conditions for ending a decade-long hostage crisis and for initiating talks between the Israelis and the Palestinians. But in the Gulf, too, Bush's policy suffered from the way he applied Nixon and Kissinger's realism.

In Bush's first eighteen months, he attempted to play balance-of-power politics, tilting toward Iraq to balance the power of Iran and Syria. The administration assumed that Saddam Hussein was merely another oil-state despot who could be won over by aid and encouragement. In spite of repeated warnings and seven decades of conflict over the Iraq-Kuwaiti border, Bush was totally unprepared for Saddam's brutal conquest of Kuwait in August 1990, but with some prodding from Margaret Thatcher, he decided to "draw a line in the sand." The Iraqi dictator's invasion forced Bush to recognize that he was a genuine menace to the region who might use his new wealth, combined with a growing nuclear and chemical potential, to wreak havoc in Saudi Arabia and eventually Israel. Demanding that Iraq withdraw, Bush and Baker took advantage of the Cold War's end to win Soviet and United Nations approval of sanctions against Hussein.

Bush also anticipated that force would eventually have to be used to oust Saddam Hussein from Iraq, but he defined American objectives in realistic terms, resisting arguments that he should seek Saddam Hussein's removal from Iraq as well as from Kuwait. Bush accepted the arguments of Scowcroft and Kissinger that it would be not only militarily infeasible but strategically unsound to use American forces to overthrow the Iraqi dictator. The United States would become hopelessly mired in Middle Eastern politics in the same way that it had gotten bogged down in Lebanon. The administration also rejected any plan to create a democracy in Kuwait. The goal was to repel the invasion and restore stability.

But in the heat of battle Bush abandoned his own strategy. Through clandestine broadcasts and in his own speeches, Bush called on Saddam Hussein's opponents to overthrow him, implying that the United States would sustain their effort. But after driving the Iraqis out of Kuwait, the U.S. forces pulled up rather than seeking to destroy the Iraqi dictator's ability to quash rebellion; and Saddam Hussein's army crushed the Shi'ites and Kurds that the United States had incited against him. Thousands were killed, and the United States became the unofficial guardian of 800,000 Kurdish refugees on the border of Turkey and Iraq.

In Kuwait, too, Bush failed to use the victory over Saddam Hussein to nudge the emirate toward political reform, which would have been consistent with a realistic goal of promoting stability. Following Nixon and Kissinger, Bush adopted a realism that assigned no role to democratic reform.

Bush's conduct of the war also suffered from another flaw that had plagued Nixon and Kissinger's diplomacy. Bush was unable to provide a compelling public justification for his own policies in the Persian Gulf. Unable to draw the connection between his post-Cold War foreign policies and American well-being, Bush fell back upon the evangelical assumptions of Cold War and even pre-Cold War American foreign policy.

In his first major addresses on the Iraqi invasion in August and September 1990, Bush drew an inappropriate analogy between Saddam's threat to the Persian Gulf and Hitler's threat to Europe in the 1930s, while comparing his own role to that of Winston Churchill and Franklin Roosevelt. "Appeasement does not work," Bush warned the nation in a televised address on August 8, 1990. "As was the case in the 1930s, we see in

Saddam Hussein an aggressive dictator threatening his neighbors."

Bush consistently appealed to Americans' evangelical rather
than realistic understanding of their situation. He insisted that
Saddam was "more evil" than Hitler and that the Gulf crisis
was "the greatest moral issue since World War II." And he
asserted that "among the nations of the world, only the United
States has the moral standing and the means to back it up."
Ignoring America's economic decline, Bush portrayed the war
against Saddam as a way to create a "next American Century."
"If anyone tells you America's best days are behind her, they
are looking the wrong way," Bush declared in his January 16,
1991, State of the Union address. "The potential of the American people knows no limits . . . We are the nation that can
shape the future."

When Bush was not playing Franklin Roosevelt or Winston
Churchill, he was imitating Woodrow Wilson. Borrowing a
phrase used by Wilson in 1919 but also by Gorbachev in October 1988, Bush promised that out of the war would emerge
a "new world order." "The crisis in the Persian Gulf . . . offers
a rare opportunity to move toward . . . a new world order
. . . in which the nations of the world, East and West, North
and South, can prosper and live in harmony," Bush declared
in his September 11, 1990, address to a joint session of Congress. In his State of the Union address, he described a "new
world order where diverse nations are drawn together in common cause to achieve the universal aspirations of mankind—
peace and security, freedom and rule of law."

But pressed to define more clearly what he meant—how,
for instance, the brutal Syrian regime's participation represented a new coalition on behalf of "freedom and rule of
law"—Bush and his advisers demurred. Scowcroft, who coined
the term without any reference to its past, described it later
merely as a "catchphrase." In a *Los Angeles Times* column, Kissinger, fearing the onset of woolly idealism, observed that the
nations brought together to fight Iraq—ranging from Syria to

Denmark, Saudi Arabia to China—did not represent a common commitment to a new "community of nations," but rather a temporary and tenuous alliance created by the most unusual circumstances. "United States policy makers must recognize that the new world order cannot be built to American specifications. America cannot force feed a global sense of community where none exists," Kissinger concluded.

In the wake of the American triumph, Bush framed the lessons of the American victory as a reaffirmation of the American Century. Speaking on May 29 at the Air Force Academy graduation, Bush summed up the lessons of the victory. "More recently, many here and abroad wondered whether America still possessed the strength and the will to bear the burden of world leadership. My fellow Americans, we do and we will. Through strength of example and commitment we lead," Bush said. Then he reaffirmed America's evangelical mission in words that echoed John Winthrop. "We do not dictate the courses nations follow, but neither can we overlook the fact that our examples reshape the world. We can't right all wrongs, but neither can any nation lead as we can."

Bush's grandiose conception of America reflected a lingering nostalgia rather than a dawning awareness of America's position in the world. Like a strong narcotic, it had a temporary soothing effect, but after it wore off, the patient felt even worse than before. Indeed, Bush's comparison of Saddam to Hitler led Americans to denigrate Bush's accomplishment in the Gulf—to see Iraqi's dictator's survival as evidence that the American effort failed. And as the nation's intractable economic and social problems resurfaced, Bush's evocation of a "next American Century" spurred a new disillusionment with American foreign policy. Bush's rhetorical internationalism, like Wilson's, even ended up inspiring a surge of old-time isolationism.

If Bush's geopolitical strategy suffered from obsolete notions, his international economic strategy suffered from the lack of any notions at all. Bush seemed unaware of or indifferent to international economics. Committed to the rhetoric of Luce's American Century, he refused to acknowledge that the United States had suffered an economic decline. He ignored the heart of Nixon's realism: the understanding that the bipolar Cold War conflict was giving way not to a unipolar world defined by American military strength but to a multipolar world shaped by American economic weakness. In such a world, international economics would take precedence over classical geopolitics. Instead, Bush relegated questions about trade and foreign investment to the same level as domestic politics.

When Bush did take action in international economics, he was guided by anachronistic or inappropriate models. Bush was held captive by the post-World War II orthodoxy about free trade. According to this view, the United States would automatically benefit from a free-trade regime, even if other countries did not fully adhere to it. Such a view reflected the unique position of the United States after World War II, when it accounted for 50 percent of the world's GNP, but was inappropriate to a period when the United States faced sharp competition from other nations' government-subsidized exports and from firms that enjoyed captive home markets. To survive in this increasingly competitive world, the United States had to protect its own industries from decimation. But Bush and his administration were still fighting the battles of 1947.

The administration's policy toward Japan epitomized Bush's unwillingness to recognize that economics had displaced military power as the fulcrum of international power. Bush balked at forcing Japan to work out a more equitable trading relationship with the United States—responding only when forced to do so by congressional pressure. At the same time, unwilling to abandon America's military responsibilities, Bush did nothing to encourage Japan to assume its rightful place in international politics. He shied away from sponsoring Japan's permanent membership on the UN Security Council. Instead, the United States spent as much as $60 billion in 1990 on the American military in Asia, indirectly subsidizing Japan and the other Asian economies while widening its own budget deficit.

In January 1992, facing declining popularity due to the recession, Bush changed a planned trip to Japan from a diplomatic visit to the country's new Prime Minister to a trade mission. He recruited eighteen corporate executives, including Lee Iacocca and the heads of Ford and General Motors, to accompany him, and when in Japan he pressed for trade concessions from Japanese automakers. The concessions were irrelevant to the fate of the American automobile industry, which was bound up with its ability to compete with the Japanese in the United States rather than in Japan. Instead of demonstrating a new seriousness, the trip showed the extent to which Bush was willing to treat international economics as a political sideshow. Wrote political scientist and Japan expert Chalmers Johnson afterward: "It was little more than an attempt to manipulate symbols the Administration thinks will make voters salivate . . . and to provide the appearance of an economic policy where there is none."

The administration's one major initiative in international economics was to expand the North American Free Trade Area (NAFTA) to include Mexico. But Bush's plan, while justified in principle, was marred by his dogmatic commitment to free trade and by a facile analogy between NAFTA and the European Economic Community (EEC). The EEC was based on rough equality among its members, but Bush was prepared to open American borders with a nation whose per capita annual income is still only $2,000. Rather than countering Europe and Asia's trading blocs, the administration's link with Mexico could instead provide Asian and West European countries with a low-wage platform from which to export goods to the United States duty-free, driving more American companies out of business. The Washington-based Economic Strategy Institute estimated that Bush's plan, unless augmented by stringent controls, could cost the United States by 1999 as much as 900,000 jobs and create an additional $30 billion trade deficit.

In November 1991, however, after Democratic Senator Harris Wofford used his opposition to the free-trade agreement to defeat his Republican opponent, Bush's Attorney General Richard Thornburgh, Bush decided to postpone further negotiations on the pact until after the 1992 elections. The decision demonstrated again that Bush was not serious about international economics.

Americans' disenchantment with Bush's foreign policy was reinforced by his failure to stem the decline of the American economy. During his first term, the descent that began in the late 1960s continued. The United States continued to fall behind Japan, its most important rival, in high technology. In 1990, the four top holders of American patents were Japanese companies. That year, the United States ran a $22 billion trade deficit with Japan in telecommunications and computer equipment. In making industrial robots, the machine tool of the future, the United States lagged several miles behind Japan and several city blocks behind Germany. By 1990, foreigners had captured 74.5 percent of the American market in robotics. American workers were steadily sinking lower in the international division of labor.

Japanese firms also used the recession to gain greater control of the American market and of American manufacturing. While American firms, battering by declining profits, wooed foreign capital, Japanese firms, operating out of a captive home market, sacrificed profits in U.S. sales for gaining market share. Japanese automakers increased their capacity while each of the big three—Chrysler, General Motors, and Ford—cut back. Japanese firms bought into the U.S. entertainment industry—second only to aerospace in its export earnings—purchasing both

Columbia Pictures and MCA. The Japanese also bought up American producers of critical semiconductor equipment—including one, Semi-gas, that had played an important role in Sematech's efforts.

Rigidly optimistic, and committed to a laissez-faire faith in markets, Bush refused to act to stem the decline of American industry. Bush's predecessor, Ronald Reagan, believing that America's defense future depended on the vitality of its industry, had granted congressional and industry requests to fund high-technology industries, including Sematech. But Bush attempted to kill those projects approved during the Reagan administration; he refused to intervene to protect firms like Semi-gas from foreign purchase; and he rejected new proposals for subsidizing industrial research and commercial technology. One victim was the Defense Advanced Research Projects Agency (DARPA), the small Pentagon agency that had played a critical role in subsidizing the growth of the computer industry.

During the Reagan administration, DARPA had overseen the funding of Sematech, and under director Craig Fields was planning to fund research into high-definition television and other commercial high-technology ventures. But Bush and his top economic advisers—Budget Director Richard Darman, Chief of Staff John Sununu, and Chairman of the Council of Economic Advisers Michael Boskin—rejected on ideological grounds a government role in promoting commercial technology. In April 1990, citing Fields's loan of $4 million to a small but highly creative Silicon Valley firm that faced a takeover by the Japanese, the White House forced the director out of his job. It took $20 million of the paltry $30 million that Fields had allocated to high-definition television and disbursed it to Panama for post-invasion aid. And it pressured Sematech to reorient its researches to technology that could be used by the military rather than the civilian sector.

Arguing that it was inappropriate for government to interfere with private investment, the administration also attempted to curb other efforts to stimulate American industry. In 1991, it proposed to cut by 70 percent the government grant to the National Center for Manufacturing Sciences, a consortium established to research new machine-tool technology. It interceded with members of the National Advisory Committee on Semiconductors to prevent the publication of a report favoring government intervention.

The administration also neglected or ignored other areas in which government could play a constructive role in stimulating industry. Public investment in infrastructure, including roads, bridges, sewers, mass transit, and electric power, had played a significant role in America's postwar economic growth. But Bush continued Reagan's practice of curtailing these expenditures. Public investment in infrastructure, which was 1.9 percent of GNP from 1956 to 1970, fell to 0.9 percent during the Reagan years and to 0.8 percent in 1990 under Bush.

Energy conservation had also become important for holding down America's trade deficit and for reducing industrial costs. Nixon's and Carter's energy plans had dramatically reduced energy consumption—consumption per dollar of GNP had declined 26 percent from 1972 to 1986. Reagan dismantled Carter's conservation measures, and as a result, energy consumption began to rise during the last two years of his term. Bush, reflecting the narrow priorities of the oil industry, followed Reagan's example. His National Energy Strategy, which he unveiled during the war with Iraq, simply continued Reagan's emphasis on providing greater profits for oil companies in order to increase domestic supply. It had no significant measures for conservation, from oil import fees to a gasoline tax. Writing in *The New Republic*, Gregg Easterbrook described Bush's program as "so undistinguished that it makes past efforts like Richard Nixon's Project Independence seem positively inspired."

In his election campaign, Bush pledged to become an "education President," but he allowed his education policy to be dictated by narrow political concerns. In his first year, Bush held a promising "national education summit" at which the nation's governors set goals for educational reform. In April 1990, Bush introduced his own program, "America 2000," but instead of emphasizing those reforms that were widely acceptable, he touted the politically explosive issue of vouchers. A voucher program was different from public school choice, which many educators backed and which several states and school districts had already adopted. Choice allowed parents to choose which public school their child attended, creating pressure for diversity and excellence within the public school system, but vouchers would be disbursed directly to parents and could be used to fund private at the expense of public education. Their most likely effect would be to starve the public schools, relegating them to the same status as the welfare system and leaving the less well-to-do with even less savory options than before.

But the Bush administration liked vouchers for their political appeal. The immediate beneficiaries of vouchers would be two important electoral constituents—fundamentalist Christians who established private academies after Southern schools were integrated and school prayer was ruled unconstitutional and middle-class Catholics who sent their children to parochial schools.

During Bush's first term, the divisions in American society continued to grow, exacerbated by a recession that began in 1990 and then, like a bad cold, refused to go away. But Bush, like Reagan, rejected the progressive commitment to using government as an instrument for creating social equality. He vetoed legislation raising the minimum wage and extending unemployment benefits. At the behest of business, he even vetoed an innocuous bill that provided workers four months of *unpaid* paternal leave. He appointed antilabor representatives to the National Labor Relations Board. And he promoted a reduction in the capital gains tax. Over 80 percent of the benefits from this tax cut would have gone to the top one percent of Americans, those making over $100,000 a year.

To soften his image and demonstrate his concern for the less fortunate, Bush flaunted his tax returns, showing his generous contributions to charity, including the United Negro College Fund. To alleviate poverty and anomie, he recommended that better-off Americans join voluntary charitable organizations. In his 1991 State of the Union address, Bush called on "every American to prepare for the next American Century" by undertaking charitable activity:

> The problems before us may be different, but the key to solving them remains the same. It is the individual who steps forward . . . We all have something to give. So if you know how to read, find someone who can't. If you've got a hammer, find a nail. If you're not hungry, not lonely, not in trouble—seek out someone who is.

Such prescriptions even predated the business conservatives of the 1920s. They recalled the injunctions of nineteenth-century ministers like Henry Ward Beecher to their upper-class flock.

Bush's hauteur, his neglect of the domestic economy, and his emphasis on high-wire geopolitics while American industry continued to lose ground led to a sharp counterreaction. Bush's blithe optimism gave birth to a brooding pessimism. By the end of 1991, Americans were as pessimistic about their future as they had been in the late 1970s. An October poll by the Council on Competitiveness, a nonprofit business group, found that 75 percent of Americans thought that "the nation's ability to compete is stagnant or declining." Seventy-three percent thought that the "most difficult period for America is still ahead."

Bush's shallow internationalism also gave birth to a resurgence of the traditional isolationism of Bryan, Borah, and America

First. Hardly a week went by in Congress without new bills being introduced to curb foreign aid. In the same Council on Competitiveness poll, 68 percent thought that "the U.S. is providing too much help for foreign countries and not doing enough to put America first." Bush's Democratic critics were calling for cutting off foreign aid and withdrawing from America's commitments in Europe and Asia without putting forth an alternative conception of how the United States should participate in world politics. And within the Republican Party itself Bush faced an openly isolationist challenge from paleoconservative columnist Patrick Buchanan, formerly a Nixon speechwriter and Reagan's Director of Communications.

Buchanan advocated a return to the principles of America First, the isolationist organization that in 1941 fought American participation in the war against Hitler. In fall 1991, Buchanan and *Washington Times* columnist Sam Francis planned to revive the old organization, but then Buchanan decided instead to challenge Bush for the presidency. "The incivility and brutality of our cities, the fading away of the Reagan Boom, the rise of ethnic hatred, are concentrating the minds of Americans on their own society. What doth it profit a nation if it gain the whole world, and lose its own soul?" Buchanan declared in a manifesto published in *The Washington Post*.

Buchanan set himself to run not only against the Bush administration but against the foreign-policy elite in Washington. He wrote:

At the American Enterprise Institute, Brookings and Heritage Foundation seminars, phrases like America First may yet get a big howl—as the boys decide the fate of the Punjab—but in a nation that hasn't seen real growth since Old Dutch rode off to Rancho Cielo, questions are being asked: What are we getting for $15 billion in foreign aid? Why, 46 years after WWII, are we defending Germany and Japan while they steal our markets? Why must we

# *Epilogue*

## The Beginning and the End
## of the American Century

... for we all of us, grave or light, get our thoughts entangled
in metaphors, and act fatally on the strength of them.

—GEORGE ELIOT, *Middlemarch*

Both at the beginning and at the end of this century, Americans
have faced challenges to their conception of themselves. During
the period from the 1890s through World War I, America
ceased to be a primarily rural, agricultural nation populated by
yeoman farmers, and became an urban, industrial nation dominated by large corporations and a wage-earning working class;
at the same time, America and Germany began to displace
Britain as the workshop of the world, and the United States
found itself thrust into the growing conflict over the redivision
of the world market. Industrialization undermined Americans'
Jeffersonian vision of themselves, while America's emergence
as a world power threatened the nation's historic isolationism.

Similarly, in the period from the late 1960s through the
1980s, America ceased to enjoy the absolute economic superiority it had gained after World War II. The march of prosperity
that began in 1940 came to a halt. Class divisions that had
narrowed began to widen. At the same time, America's adversary for four decades—the Soviet Union—finally collapsed
under the weight of its own internal problems. As the Cold

War wound down, America's alliances became obsolete, and its guiding assumptions about its place in the world became irrelevant.

Americans at the turn of the century responded vigorously to their challenge. The aptly named progressive era was a time of great intellectual and political upheaval. Americans plunged fearlessly into the unknown, using the experimental method of the sciences to guide their way. These years produced, among others, the philosophers William James and John Dewey, social critics Herbert Croly, Brooks Adams, and Thorstein Veblen, new political movements, including the populists, socialists, and Wobblies, a national ruling class committed to domestic reform and internationalism, and two outstanding Presidents, Theodore Roosevelt and Woodrow Wilson.

But what of recent decades? Where are the philosophers and critics, the vibrant new political and social movements? Where is the spirit of experimentation? And where are the new political leaders?

George Bush claimed that he was carrying out the legacy of the earlier era. At the beginning of his presidency, George Bush announced he felt a special affinity for Theodore Roosevelt, whom he described as a "take-charge kind of person." Bush replaced Calvin Coolidge's portrait in the Cabinet room with Roosevelt's. "I'm an Oyster Bay kind of guy," he told a visitor to the White House. "Maybe I'll turn out to be a Teddy Roosevelt." In May 1990, he invited historian David McCullough, who had written a book on Roosevelt's youth, to the White House to lecture on Roosevelt's life.

Bush and Roosevelt did have similar backgrounds. As Bush told *The Washington Post* in April 1989, Roosevelt "came out of the same elitist background that I do." Like George Bush's parents, Theodore Roosevelt's could trace their lineage back to the early settlers. His father was a wealthy importer in New York who in 1877 was appointed Collector of Customs of the Port of New York. Theodore Roosevelt was educated by private tutors before entering Harvard in 1876. After graduation, Roosevelt entered New York politics. "My whole career in politics," he explained later, "is due to the simple fact that when I came out of Harvard I was firmly resolved to belong to the governing class, not the governed."

Both Roosevelt and Bush tested themselves by moving West and by going to war. In 1884, Roosevelt, disconsolate over the death of his first wife, left for the Dakota Badlands, where he spent two years as a rancher and cowboy. And then, in 1898, he resigned as McKinley's Assistant Secretary of the Navy to lead a company of Rough Riders in the Spanish-American War. But here the resemblance ends. In their character, interests, philosophies, and practice as Presidents, the two men could not have been more dissimilar.

Roosevelt was a man of reflection as well as action. By the time he became President, he had written a major history of the West, the four-volume *Winning of the West*, and a study of naval warfare, *The Naval War of 1812*. He was as responsible as Captain Alfred Thayer Mahan and Brooks Adams for re-conceptualizing America's role as a world power. Bush, by contrast, had considerable intelligence, but little power of reflection. He neither read nor studied, and what he brought to the office were fragments of theories, opinions, and sentiments gleaned from several decades of public service.

Roosevelt, a patrician, felt that in order to exercise leadership he had to learn how to be comfortable with the average citizen. He disdained the men of his class who had "the slightest fear of the people on the other side." Roosevelt typically set out consciously to learn about other Americans. Before becoming President, he served in the New York Assembly and as New York City's police commissioner and as governor of New York. He recruited his Rough Riders from the cowboys he had met in the Badlands.

Bush, by contrast, was not comfortable with men and women who did not share his own background. Even in Texas, he socialized with other Ivy League graduates who had come to Midland to prove their mettle and get rich. And unlike Roosevelt, he was defensive about his own background. "They say I'm a patrician. I don't even know what the word means. I'll have to look it up," the Yale graduate told the press in 1980.

When Roosevelt took office, he realized—perhaps better than anyone of his generation—that the nation stood at a crossroads. He was fascinated by international politics, but he believed that he had to give equal if not more weight to overcoming the divisions in wealth and power created by industrialization and the growth of monopolies. In 1899, he wrote his friend British diplomat Cecil Arthur Spring-Rice:

> My own feeling is that we shall have to pay far more attention to the tremendous problems of capital and labor than to any question of expansion for the next 50 years, and this although I am an expansionist.

When Roosevelt received the Nobel Peace Prize in 1910 for resolving the Russo-Japanese War, he donated the prize money to a foundation "to forward the cause of industrial peace." He did so, he explained in his Nobel speech, because

> in our complex industrial civilization of today the peace of righteousness and justice, the only kind of peace worth having, is at least as necessary in the industrial world as it is among nations. There is at least as much need to curb the cruel greed and arrogance of part of the world of capital, to curb the cruel greed and arrogance of part of the world of labor, as to check a cruel and unhealthy militarism in international relations.

As President and then as leader of the Progressive Party, Roosevelt acted according to these precepts, championing social reform, such as federal workers' compensation and the eight-hour working day, advocating a graduated income tax and an inheritance tax on large fortunes. He established a Cabinet-level Department of Commerce, which included a Bureau of Corporations to make sure that private companies respected the public interest. While he shared many of the prejudices of his time and class, he was unusually attuned to the plight of the outcast. He offended many white Southerners by inviting Booker T. Washington to visit the White House. He criticized Californians for the "wicked nonsense" of their anti-Oriental laws.

On each of these counts, Bush was entirely different. He disdained domestic affairs. He felt no commitment to creating equality or to using government's power to aid the less fortunate. He was willing to foment racial division for political ends. And he was a laissez-faire conservative rather than a progressive. He represented precisely the view of government and society that Roosevelt and the progressives rejected.

The difference between Roosevelt and Bush is, unfortunately, the difference between the beginning and the end of the American Century. At the beginning of this century, Americans grasped, if imperfectly, the novelty of their situation and attempted to come to terms with it, participating in social movements and electing individuals of superior understanding to the presidency. In the last decades of the century, Americans fell prey to nostalgia and to a callous individualism that ignored nation and community. They nourished illusions about the power of the market and about America's standing in the world.

Americans cannot emulate the genius of the progressive era any more than Bush can mimic Theodore Roosevelt. The challenges posed by America's decline—and by an economically interdependent world in which America's military power is increasingly irrelevant—are fundamentally different from those faced by Roosevelt and Wilson. But if we want to halt our nation's descent, we, like the Americans of the progressive era, will have to recognize the difference between style and substance and between reality and illusion.

# Bibliography

I have relied primarily on the writings of the people themselves and, where possible, interviews and private papers. But I also want to mention certain books and articles that were important to my understanding.

### Prologue

On America's evangelical background, see Perry Miller, *Errand into the Wilderness*, Harvard, Cambridge, 1956, and David W. Noble, *The Progressive Mind*, Rand McNally, Chicago, 1970. Also useful on this subject are Loren Baritz, *City on a Hill*, John Wiley, New York, 1964, Ernest Lee Tuveson, *Redeemer Nation: The Idea of America's Millennial role*, University of Chicago, Chicago, 1968, and Charles L. Sanford, *The Quest for Paradise: Europe and the American Moral Imagination*, University of Illinois, Urbana, 1961. On America's laissez-faire tradition, the classic work is Louis Hartz, *The Liberal Tradition in America*, Harcourt, Brace, New York, 1955. For the progressive tradition, I relied on Martin J. Sklar, *The Corporate Reconstruction of American Capitalism 1890–1916*, Cambridge University, New York, 1988. See also William Appleman Williams, *The Contours of American History*, World, Cleveland, 1961.

### Chapter 1

Croly's most important writings are *The Promise of American Life*, Macmillan, New York, 1909, and *Progressive Democracy*, Macmillan, New York, 1914. His articles in *The New Republic* have never been collected in book form. Perhaps the most interesting is "The Eclipse of Progressivism," October 27, 1920. For Herbert Croly's life, the best sources are David W. Levy, *Herbert Croly of the New Republic*, Princeton University, Princeton, 1985, and Charles Forcey, *The Crossroads of Liberalism*, Oxford, New York, 1961. For the historical background, I used Sklar, op. cit., George Mowry, *The Era of Theodore Roosevelt*, Harper, New York, 1958, N. Gordon Levin, *Woodrow Wilson and World Politics*, Oxford, New York, 1968, Carl P. Parrini, *Heir to Empire*, Pittsburgh University, Pittsburgh, 1969, David Seideman, *The New Republic: A Voice of Modern Liberalism*, Praeger, New York, 1986, and Daniel P. Moynihan, *On the Law of Nations*, Harvard, Cambridge, 1990.

## Chapter 2

In his last years in office, Henry Wallace had aides help him with his books and speeches, but he was a brilliant man, quite capable of writing his own. One impressive pamphlet, *America Must Choose*, was largely taken from a speech that Wallace gave extemporaneously. Wallace's most important works are *Agricultural Prices*, Wallace Publishing Co., Des Moines, 1920, *America Must Choose*, World Affairs Pamphlets, No. 3, 1934, Foreign Policy Association, New York, and World Peace Foundation, Boston, *Statesmanship and Religion*, Round Table Press, New York, 1934, *New Frontiers*, New York, 1934, *Whose Constitution?*, Reynal & Hitchcock, New York, 1936, *Technology, Corporations, and the General Welfare*, University of North Carolina, Chapel Hill, 1937, and *The Century of the Common Man*, Reynal & Hitchcock, Cornwall, 1943. For Wallace's gullibility, *Soviet Asia Mission*, Reynal & Hitchcock, Cornwall, 1946, is a must. For Wallace after leaving the Truman administration, his *New Republic* articles are invaluable.

For Henry Wallace's life and thought, see Henry Wallace, *The Price of Vision: The Diary of Henry A. Wallace, 1942–1946*, edited and with an introduction by John Morton Blum, Houghton Mifflin, Boston, 1973, Edward L. and Frederick H. Schapsmeier, *Henry A. Wallace of Iowa: The Agrarian Years, 1910–1940*, Iowa State University, Ames, 1968, and Torbjorn Sirevag, *The Eclipse of the New Deal and the Fall of Vice-President Wallace*, Garland, New York and London, 1985. The best work on Wallace's foreign policy is J. Samuel Walker, *Henry A. Wallace and American Foreign Policy*, Greenwood, Westport, 1976. On Wallace as Secretary of Agriculture, see Theda Skocpol and Kenneth Finegold, "State Capacity and Economic Intervention in the Early New Deal," *Political Science Quarterly*, Summer 1982, Vol. 97, No. 2., Richard S. Kirkendall, *Social Scientists and Farm Politics in the Age of Roosevelt*, Columbia, New York, 1966, and Grant McConnell, *The Decline of Agrarian Democracy*, Atheneum, New York, 1969. Henry R. Luce's article is reprinted in *The American Century*, Farrar & Rinehart, New York, 1941. For Luce's life, see W. A. Swanberg, *Luce and His Empire*, Scribner's, New York, 1972. For Wallace and the Truman White House, see Clark Clifford, with Richard Holbrooke, *Counsel to the President*, Random House, New York, 1991, Curtis McDougall, *Gideon's Army*, Vols. 1 and 2, Marzani and Marzani, New York, 1965, and Norman Markowitz, *The Rise and Fall of the People's Century*, Free Press, New York, 1973.

For Roosevelt's foreign policy, the most useful book I've read is Warren F. Kimball, *The Juggler: Franklin Roosevelt as Wartime Statesman*, Princeton University, Princeton, 1991. Unlike Wilson or Theodore Roosevelt, Franklin Roosevelt made few general philosophical statements on public policy that were not intended to win over a particular constituency. The closest Roosevelt came to spelling out his ideas on a postwar world order and on Wallace and Wilson was in interviews that he gave to *Saturday Evening Post* editor Forrest Davis, published in Forrest Davis, "Roosevelt's World Blueprint," *Saturday*

*Evening Post*, April 10, 1943, and Forrest Davis, "What Really Happened at Teheran," *Saturday Evening Post*, May 13, 1944. Davis's articles, based on these interviews, were reviewed by the White House for accuracy prior to their publication.

### Chapter 3

Lippmann's early views can be seen in *A Preface to Politics*, Mitchell Kennerly, New York, 1913, and *Drift and Mastery*, Mitchell Kennerly, New York, 1914. Lippmann's turn toward elitism in the 1920s is evident in *Public Opinion*, Harcourt, Brace, New York, 1922, and *The Phantom Public*, Macmillan, New York, 1925. His view of the New Deal and his later version of progressivism is evident in *The Method of Freedom*, Macmillan, New York, 1934 (more pro-New Deal), and *The Good Society*, Little, Brown, Boston, 1937. His realism in foreign policy can be found in *U.S. Foreign Policy: Shield of the Republic*, Little, Brown, Boston, 1943, *U.S. War Aims*, Little, Brown, Boston, 1944, and *The Cold War*, Little, Brown, Boston, 1947.

For Walter Lippmann's life, an incomparable source is Ronald Steel, *Walter Lippmann and the American Century*, Vintage, New York, 1981. Also useful are Forcey, op. cit., and Marquis Childs and James Reston, eds., *Walter Lippmann and His Times*, Harcourt, Brace, New York, 1959.

For George Kennan's life, his *Memoirs 1925–1950*, Little, Brown, Boston, 1967, is classic, but Kennan tends to sand off the rough edges of his pre-1948 views of the Soviet Union in the light of his post-1948 views. In Kennan's 1950 lectures, *American Diplomacy*, University of Chicago, Chicago, 1951, he summed up his realism. Also useful on Kennan's life are Walter L. Hixson, *George F. Kennan: Cold War Iconoclast*, Columbia, New York, 1989, and David Mayers, *George Kennan and the Dilemmas of American Foreign Policy*, Oxford, New York, 1988. In *Strategies of Containment*, Oxford, New York, 1982, John Lewis Gaddis describes Kennan's strategy.

Good sources on Nitze's life include David Callahan, *Dangerous Capabilities: Paul Nitze and the Cold War*, HarperCollins, New York, 1990, and Strobe Talbott, *The Master of the Game: Paul Nitze and the Nuclear Peace*, Knopf, New York, 1988. Nitze's memoirs, *From Hiroshima to Glasnost: At the Center of Decision*, Grove Weidenfeld, New York, 1989, are not particularly revealing. For the debate on NSC-68, see Gaddis, op. cit., Steven L. Rearden, *The Evolution of American Strategic Doctrine: Paul Nitze and the Soviet Challenge*, Westview, Boulder, 1984, Paul Y. Hammond, "NSC-68: Prologue to Rearmament," in Warner R. Schilling, Paul Y. Hammond, and Glenn H. Snyder, *Strategy, Politics, and Defense Budgets*, Columbia, New York, 1962. Also useful are John Lewis Gaddis and Paul Nitze, "The Development of NSC-68," *International Security*, Spring 1980, and Gregg Herken, "The Great Foreign Policy Fight," *American Heritage*, April–May 1986.

Useful for background on the period are *The Wise Men* by Walter Isaacson and Evan Thomas, Simon and Schuster, New York, 1986, *Shattered Peace* by

Daniel Yergin, Houghton Mifflin, Boston, 1977, *The Truman Doctrine and the Origins of McCarthyism* by Richard Freeland, Schocken, New York, 1974, Melvyn Leffler, *Preponderance of Power*, Stanford, Palo Alto, 1991. Recent scholarship on the origins of the Cold War includes Peter Stavrakis, *Moscow and Greek Communism, 1944–1949*, Cornell, Ithaca, 1989, Alec Nove, *Stalinism and After*, Allen & Unwin, London, 1981, Robert H. McNeal, *Stalin: Man and Ruler*, New York University, New York, 1988, Dmitri Volkogonov, *Stalin: Triumph and Tragedy*, Grove Weidenfeld, New York, 1991, Charles Gati, *Hungary and the Soviet Bloc*, Duke University, Durham, 1986. Besides Kennan's, the outstanding memoir of the period is Dean Acheson, *Present at the Creation*, Norton, New York, 1969. State Department documents can be found in the annual volumes *Foreign Relations of the United States*.

### Chapter 4

The most convincing and comprehensive account of the Chambers-Hiss imbroglio is Allan Weinstein, *Perjury*, Knopf, New York, 1978. Details about Chambers's career on *National Review* are in John B. Judis, *William F. Buckley: Patron Saint of the Conservatives*, Simon and Schuster, New York, 1988. Chambers's main work is *Witness*, Random House, New York, 1952. But see also *Ghosts on the Roof*, edited and with an introduction by Terry Teachout, Regnery, Washington, 1990, *Odyssey of a Friend: Whittaker Chambers' Letters to William F. Buckley, Jr., 1954–1961*, edited by William F. Buckley, Jr., and *Cold Friday*, edited by Duncan Norton-Taylor, New York, 1964. Interviews: William F. Buckley, Jr., William Rusher, Ralph de Toledano, Jim McFadden, Anthony Dolan.

### Chapter 5

Burnham's important transitional works are *The Managerial Revolution*, John Day, New York, 1941, and *The Machiavellians*, John Day, New York, 1943. See also "Lenin's Heir," *Partisan Review*, Winter 1945, and Dwight Macdonald's response, "Beat Me, Daddy," *Partisan Review*, Spring 1945. His foreign policy classics are *The Struggle for the World*, John Day, New York, 1947, *The Coming Defeat of Communism*, John Day, New York, 1949, and *Containment or Liberation?*, John Day, New York, 1952. An interesting and neglected later work is *Congress and the American Tradition*, Regnery, Chicago, 1959. Less interesting but a classic of the right is *The Suicide of the West*, Arlington, New York, 1964. Burnham's essays during the dispute over Khrushchev's speech and the invasion of Hungary appeared in *National Review*.

The best book on Burnham's life and thought is John P. Diggins, *Up from Communism*, Harper & Row, New York, 1975. Useful on Burnham's thought and influence are Samuel T. Francis, *The Political Thought of James Burnham*, University Press of America, Lanham, Md., 1984, George Nash, *The Conservative Intellectual Movement in America*, Basic Books, New York, 1976, and Judis, op. cit. George Orwell's essay "James Burnham and the Managerial

Revolution," *Collected Essays*, Vol. 4, Harcourt, Brace, New York, 1968, is very illuminating. Interviews: William F. Buckley, Jr., James Burnham, Jr., E. Howard Hunt, Ralph de Toledano, Gerhart Niemeyer, James McFadden, Priscilla Buckley, William Rusher.

## Chapter 6

Fulbright, like Henry Wallace, was perfectly capable of writing his books, but for later works such as *The Crippled Giant*, he relied increasingly on his aide Seth Tillman, an able historian in his own right. Fulbright's view of democracy can be seen in "The Elite and the Electorate," J. William Fulbright, 1963, Center for the Study of Democratic Institutions. His foreign policy writings include *Prospects for the West*, Random House, New York, 1963, *Old Myths and New Realities*, Random House, New York, 1964, *The Arrogance of Power*, Random House, New York, 1966, and *The Crippled Giant*, Random House, New York, 1972.

For Fulbright's life, I used *The Price of Empire*, J. William Fulbright with Seth P. Tillman, Pantheon, New York, 1989, Haynes Johnson and Bernard Gwertzman, *Fulbright the Dissenter*, Doubleday, New York, 1968, Eugene Brown, *J. William Fulbright: Advice and Dissent*, University of Iowa, Iowa City, 1985, and William C. Berman, *William Fulbright and the Vietnam War*, Kent State University, 1988.

Goldwater's views can be found in *Conscience of a Conservative*, Victor Publishing, Shepherdsville, Ky., 1960, and *Why Not Victory?*, McGraw-Hill, New York, 1962. He published two virtually identical autobiographies, *With No Apologies*, William Morrow and Company, New York, 1979, and *Goldwater*, with Jack Casserly, Doubleday, New York, 1988. I also consulted Dean Smith, *The Goldwaters of Arizona*, Arizona, Flagstaff, 1986.

On the Vietnam background, see *The Pentagon Papers*, Bantam, New York, 1971, and Stanley Karnow, *Vietnam*, Viking, New York, 1983. Interviews: William Fulbright, Seth Tillman, Dean Burch, Lee Edwards, William F. Buckley, Jr., Clifton White, Denison Kitchel.

## Chapter 7

Nixon's two-volume *Memoirs*, Warner, New York, 1978, contains some useful information. *Six Crises*, Doubleday, New York, 1962, is his most revealing book. *In the Arena*, Simon and Schuster, New York, 1990, is disappointing. For Nixon's early life, I found Roger Morris, *Richard Milhous Nixon: The Rise of an American Politician*, Henry Holt, New York, 1990, the most useful. For Nixon's life, I consulted Stephen Ambrose, *Nixon*, Vol. 1: *The Education of a Politician, 1913–1962*, Simon and Schuster, New York, 1987, *Nixon*, Vol. 2: *The Triumph of a Politician, 1962–1972*, Simon and Schuster, New York, 1989, and Herbert S. Parmet, *Richard Nixon and His America*, Little Brown, Boston, 1990. For Nixon's thinking on Vietnam, I found Herbert S. Parmet, "History, Historians and Richard Nixon," *Thesis*, Spring 1991, useful.

Kissinger's most important works are *A World Restored*, Houghton Mifflin, Boston, 1957, *Nuclear Weapons and Foreign Policy*, Harper, New York, 1957, *American Foreign Policy: Three Essays*, Norton, New York, 1969, and the two-volume memoirs, *White House Years*, Little, Brown, Boston, 1979, and *Years of Upheaval*, Little, Brown, Boston, 1982.

The best book on Kissinger's intellectual development is Stephen R. Graubard, *Kissinger: Portrait of a Mind*, Norton, New York, 1974. For Kissinger in action, I made use of Roger Morris, *Uncertain Greatness*, Harper & Row, New York, 1977, and Marvin Kalb and Bernard Kalb, *Kissinger*, Little, Brown, Boston, 1974, and Seymour Hersh, *The Price of Power*, Summit, New York, 1983. The best book on the strategic debate is Raymond Garthoff, *Détente and Confrontation: American-Soviet Relations from Nixon to Reagan*, Brookings Institution, Washington, 1985. On the "Nixon shocks," see Robert C. Angel, *Explaining Economic Failure: Japan in the 1969–1972 International Monetary Crisis*, Columbia, New York, 1991, and William Safire, *Before the Fall*, Doubleday, New York, 1975. On the Kansas City speech, see James Chace, "The Five Power World of Richard Nixon," *New York Times Magazine*, February 22, 1972. Interviews: Henry Kissinger, Roger Morris, Richard Nixon (memorandum), Ray Price, William F. Buckley, Jr.

### Chapter 8

For Reagan's life, I used his two autobiographies, *Where's the Rest of Me?*, Hawthorn, New York, 1965, and *An American Life*, Simon and Schuster, New York, 1990. But more interesting are Lou Cannon's three books about Reagan—*Ronnie and Jessie*, Doubleday, New York, 1969, *Reagan*, Putnam's, New York, 1982, and *President Reagan: The Role of a Lifetime*, Simon and Schuster, New York, 1991. Also useful are Bill Boyarsky, *Ronald Reagan: His Life & Rise to the Presidency*, Random House, New York, 1981, and Garry Wills, *Reagan's America*, Doubleday, New York, 1981. On the strategic debate in 1980, I used Jerry W. Sanders, *Peddlers of Crisis*, South End, Boston, 1983, and Norman Podhoretz, *The Present Danger*, Simon and Schuster, New York, 1980. For the background on the Soviet Union, I relied on Robert Kaiser, *Why Gorbachev Happened*, Simon and Schuster, New York, 1991. On William Casey's use of intelligence, see the Senate Select Committee on Intelligence's report on the nomination of Robert Gates, Exec. Rept. 102-19. For Reagan's economic policies, the best sources are Clyde Prestowitz, *Trading Places*, Basic Books, New York, 1988, and David Stockman, *The Triumph of Politics*, Harper & Row, New York, 1986. See also Ira Magaziner and Mark Patinkin, *The Silent War*, Random House, New York, 1989, Aaron Bernstein, "Busting Unions Can Backfire on the Bottom Line," *Business Week*, March 18, 1991, and Lawrence Mishel and David M. Frankel, *The State of Working America*, Economic Policy Institute, Washington, D.C., 1991. Interviews: Clyde Prestowitz, Paul Nitze, Vladimir Pechatnov, Anthony Dolan, John Ritch, Patrick Buchanan.

### Chapter 9

Iacocca's two books, *Iacocca*, Bantam, New York, 1984, and *Talking Straight*, Bantam, New York, 1988, contain useful information. For background on Iacocca, I used Peter Collier and David Horowitz, *The Fords*, Summit Books, New York, 1987, Robert B. Reich and John D. Donahue, *New Deals: The Chrysler Revival and the American System*, Times Books, New York, 1985, Peter Wyden, *The Unknown Iacocca*, William Morrow, New York, 1987, and David Halberstam, *The Reckoning*, William Morrow, New York, 1986. Interviews: Lee Iacocca, Thomas Dennome, James Harbour, Daniel Luria, Maryann Keller, Donald Stillman, Douglas Fraser, Marc Stepp, David Cole, Bud Liebler.

### Chapter 10

For George Bush's life, I used his autobiography, *Looking Forward*, Doubleday, New York, 1987, Barry Bearek, "Team Player Bush," *Los Angeles Times*, November 22, 1987, Richard Ben Cramer, "George Bush: How He Got Here," *Esquire*, June 1991, and Jefferson Morley, "Bush and the Blacks," *New York Review of Books*, January 16, 1992. On Gorbachev's and Bush's concept of a new world order, I learned from Stanley R. Sloan, "The US Role in a New World Order," Congressional Research Service, March 28, 1991. On the 1988 election, see Sidney Blumenthal, *Pledging Allegiance*, HarperCollins, New York, 1990. On Bush's foreign policy, I benefited from Don Oberdorfer, *The Turn*, Poseidon, New York, 1991, Bob Woodward, *The Commanders*, Simon and Schuster, New York, 1991, Kevin Buckley, *Panama*, Simon and Schuster, New York, 1991, and John Dinges, *Our Man in Panama*, Random House, 1990. On Bush's economic policy, I made use of Gregg Easterbrook, "Waste of Energy," *The New Republic*, March 18, 1991, Clyde V. Prestowitz and Robert B. Cohen, *The New North American Order*, Economic Strategy Institute, Washington, 1991. James Fallows, "The Romance with Mexico," *New York Review of Books*, November 7, 1991, Jonathon Weber, "America's Search for a Competitive Edge," *Los Angeles Times*, October 25, 1991, William F. Broad, "Pentagon Wizards," *New York Times*, October 22, 1991, William A. Cox, "Productivity, Competitiveness and U.S. Living Standards," Congressional Research Service, October 8, 1991, and Leslie Helm, "Power on the Pacific Rim," *Los Angeles Times*, May 21, 1991. For Buchanan's position, see Patrick Buchanan, "Come Home, America," *Washington Post*, September 8, 1991. Chalmers Johnson commented on Bush's Japan trip in "Japan's Lesson," *New York Times*, January 22, 1992. Interviews: James Pinkerton, Newt Gingrich, Peter Rodman, John Deutch, Michael Farren, Stanley Sloan, R. James Woolsey, Richard Haas, Ed Hewett, Brent Scowcroft, James Chace.

### Epilogue

On George Bush and Theodore Roosevelt, see Sidney Blumenthal, "Bull Moose," *The New Republic*, January 7, 1991. On Roosevelt, see Roosevelt's

*Autobiography*, Macmillan, New York, 1914, and *The New Nationalism*, Prentice-Hall, Englewood Cliffs, 1961. Also important are George Mowry, *The Era of Theodore Roosevelt*, Harper & Row, New York, 1958, John Milton Cooper, *The Warrior and the Priest*, Harvard, Cambridge, 1983; and Edmund Morris, *The Rise of Theodore Roosevelt*, Random House, New York, 1979; Christopher Lasch, ''The Moral and Intellectual Rehabilitation of the Ruling Class,'' *The World of Nations*, Knopf, New York, 1973.

# Acknowledgments

In writing this book, I was fortunate to have a wise and understanding editor, Linda Healey. She gave me the encouragement and counsel I needed to turn an inchoate idea into a book with a beginning and end. My agent, Kathy Robbins, made this book possible, as well as providing helpful advice and support. Jack Lynch copyedited the manuscript. And Jonathan Galassi and Phyllida Burlingame ably shepherded it through the last stages of publication.

I got considerable help from my friends. Sidney Blumenthal and James Gilbert suffered through the entire manuscript and provided invaluable criticisms and suggestions. I got helpful advice on individual chapters from William Burr, Torrie Dickinson, Max Holland, Walter Isaacson, Michael Kazin, David Moberg, Robert Schaeffer, Sam Tanenhaus, and Seth Tillman. I received assistance with initial attempts at profiling some of my subjects from Hendrick Hertzberg, Dorothy Wickenden, and Leon Wieseltier of *The New Republic*, Sheryl Larsen of *In These Times*, Jackie Blumenthal of the Wallace Centenary Project, and Evan Smith of *Business Month*.

Several people helped me obtain relevant documents and other materials. Thea Koehler of the U.S. Senate Library was unfailingly helpful. John Taylor of the Nixon Library in Yorba Linda sent me materials about Nixon's Kansas City speech, including a photocopy of his original outline, and arranged for the former President to respond to my inquiries about the speech. Lawrence Mishel of the Economic Policy Institute was a precious source of statistics and economic analysis. Richard Barnet let me see a speech he had given comparing Lippmann's and Kennan's positions on the Cold War. Jefferson Morley shared his researches on George Bush's political record in the 1960s. William Burr furnished me with useful materials on the origins of the Cold War. And John Canham-Clyne sent me materials on the CIA in the Reagan years. My wife, Susan Pearson, and my daughters, Hilary and Eleanor, provided me with hope and diversion.

# Index